The Citizen Planner:

A HISTORY OF THE
NEW JERSEY FEDERATION
OF PLANNING OFFICIALS

The Citizen Planner:

A HISTORY OF THE
NEW JERSEY FEDERATION
OF PLANNING OFFICIALS

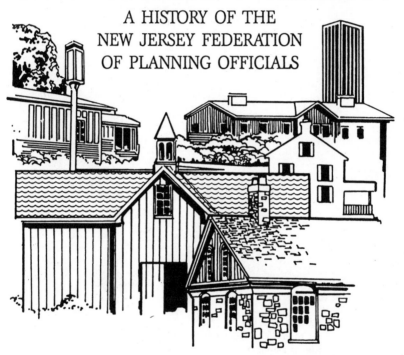

Judith Apter Klinghoffer

CENTER
FOR URBAN
POLICY RESEARCH

Published in the United States of America
by the Center for Urban Policy Research
Building 4051—Kilmer Campus
New Brunswick, New Jersey 08903

Library of Congress Cataloging-in-Publication Data

Klinghoffer, Judith Apter.
   The citizen planner : a history of the New Jersey Federation of
Planning Officials / by Judith Apter Klinghoffer.
      p. cm.
   ISBN 0-88285-130-6
   1. New Jersey Federation of Planning Officials—History.
2. Regional planning—New Jersey—History.   3. City planning—New
Jersey—History.   I. Title.
HT393.N5K57 1989   89-31622
307.1'2'060749—dc 19   CIP

To Rachel and Abraham
who were always there

Contents

Foreword		xi
Acknowledgments		xv
1	The Search for Order	1
2	In the Beginning	8
3	The War Years—From Boom to Bust?	27
4	Which Way to Turn?	48
5	Life Amidst the Clover	82
6	"The Times They Are A-Changing"	119
7	The New Guard	152
8	Facing the Future	185
Appendix 1: Planning Activities		193
Appendix 2: Publication Activities		197
Appendix 3: Income and Expense Reports		209
Appendix 4: Conference Activities		213
Appendix 5: Constitution		217
Appendix 6: Presidents		225
Appendix 7: Federation Membership		229
Index		233

About the Author

Judith Apter Klinghoffer is an experienced educator and free-lance historian. She pursued undergraduate and graduate studies in history, philosophy, and education at Hebrew University in Jerusalem and has a graduate degree in American and public history from Rutgers University. She is the coauthor of *Israel and the Soviet Union: Alienation or Reconciliation?*

Ms. Klinghoffer is currently preparing, on behalf of the United States Department of Justice, Bureau of Justice Statistics, a comprehensive account of the evolution of the collection and analysis of criminal justice statistics by the federal government.

ERRATUM
The fifth word of the second line in the first
paragraph on Page xi should be self-appointed
instead of appointed.

Foreword

This is the fifty-year story of a unique organization spawned by a handful of dedicated citizens appointed to carry out the mandates of a land-use law through unpaid service on planning and zoning boards of adjustment. The founders of the New Jersey Federation of Planning Officials (the Federation) saw the need at this seminal stage of planning to equip themselves as lay planners with necessary know-how, cooperate with fellow board members throughout the state, and work toward such improvements in the planning process as societal changes and goals of development would inevitably require.

The founders' version and initial dedication provided a dynamic pattern for education and communication between papers, agencies of the state, Rutgers University, and the New Jersey State League of Municipalities. Impressed with the commitment of lay planners to the goals of the Federation, professional planners and attorneys highly skilled in land-use law volunteered their pro bono services, an invaluable contribution of expertise.

Challenges, successes, compromises, and some failures along the way characterize the Federation history as it responded to the needs and goals of its members. Whatever the results, volunteer lay planners cannot be faulted for lack of energy and time expended.

A dollar index may appropriately measure this effort. There are 567 communities in New Jersey. A conservative estimate of time spent by members of planning and zoning boards of adjustment at regularly scheduled meetings and on-site inspections exceeded 600,000 hours in 1987. Assuming an average salary of only $20,000 a year, say $11 an hour, these lay planners donated more than $6.5 million to their communities. This estimate does not take into account out-of-pocket expenses, travel time to educational meetings, seminars, and participation as panelists or service on standing or ad hoc committees. To this $6.5 million equivalent should be added the services of topflight attorneys and professional planners. Our professional supporters donate many hundreds of hours each year authoring technical bulletins, contributing articles to our periodicals, and participating as speakers and panelists at area educational meetings. Professionals serve on the board of directors of the Federation, joining hands with lay members on committees and organizing the Annual State Planning Conference. Additionally, professionals provide legal guidance for Federation projects directed to adapting legislation to the changing needs of the times. The reader merely needs to apply the fees earned by top professionals to estimate the dollar value of this benefit to the Federation.

One more thought to burnish the self-defined, but richly deserved, halo of planners. (The reader is invited to write whatever history deemed necessary to cover planners displaying horns and tails.) While we live and work necessarily in a political system, the board of directors of the Federation operates within an ethic eschewing partisan politics. We believe the majority of the lay planners try to address resolutions of the public good versus private property rights on a similar, nonpartisan basis.

Thousands upon thousands of citizens have been active in planning since 1938, the founding year of the Federation. The facts, events, and people identified with this history are the result of extensive research by its author, Judith Apter Klinghoffer. While some movers and shakers at the local, county, or state level may not be named, the historic committee charged to produce a history is confident that the author strove for objectivity.

Further, the Federation sincerely thanks the Center for Urban Policy Research, Rutgers University, and its acting director, Dr. Robert W. Burchell, for publishing this history. Dr. Burchell has contributed many technical articles used by the Federation in its educational mailings to members, and now his role in favorably evaluating the manuscript as highly readable and with a message worthy of an audience beyond the borders of New Jersey makes the effort of all involved worthwhile. We are most appreciative.

No history of this length could recognize the contributions of every participant over a fifty-year span. We hope, however, that Harry Hosking, the first president of the Federation, contemplating the half-century roster of citizen planners, named or unnamed, would be reasonably pleased with the continued flourishing of the spirit and goals embodied in his poem.

The Historic Committee
B. Budd Chavooshian
Harry A. Maslow
Evan R. Spalt, Chairman

NOT FOR SELF

It was once amidst a' dreaming,
    That a vision came to me
Of the greatness of the future,
    Of the things that are to be.

Now, a.hazy recollection,
    Then, a wondrous thing to see;
What sort of land was this,
    Where I found myself to be?

In the shadows there were things
    I never saw before,
Of a nature and a greatness
    Beyond where we can soar.

There were creatures, men and women,
    Just like us, and yet,
A gulf there was between us,
    A goal we've not yet met.

There were signs of satisfaction
    In a quiet peaceful way;
There dwelt a loving people
    In a "people loving" way.

There was naught of rush and bustle
    Or of cunning look or fear;
There was common understanding
    Of the things we hold so dear.

I beheld a farflung city
    On a scale so wide and grand,
That the measure of its greatness
    Is not seen upon our land.

There was health and recreation,
    There were highways fine and wide,
And a thought for each one's neighbor
    Could be seen on every side.

It was a new style way of living
    Beyond that which we know,
But the seed of it was planted
    In our time, long ago.

The seed looks not like flower,
    Yet to flower it will grow,
So the fruits of our endeavor
    Will yet begin to glow.

FOREWORD

To us there is the challenge
  To plant the seed aright.
We will never see the harvest
  Nor feel its great delight.

It's for us to work together
  With our hearts upon the goal;

There's a joy in doing something,
  A reflection in the soul.

Steadfast in our purpose,
  We go forward only when
We plan and build the future,
  Not for self but for all men.

by Harry Hosking

Acknowledgments

First and foremost, I would like to thank the New Jersey Federation of Planning Officials for presenting me with the opportunity to discover the world of planning, which I found most absorbing. The organization also has to be commended for granting me unlimited and unconditional access to its files and members, as well as providing me with moral and financial support. I am especially grateful to the members of the Federation's historic committee, for their hard work and unwavering commitment to this project.

Numerous past and present Federation members were kind enough to grant me interviews during my research while others read and commented on the manuscript at various stages of its preparation. I am indebted to them for their contributions and would like to single out the input of Budd Chavooshian, Evan Spalt, William Cox, Fred Stickel III, Dick Ginman, Jene Schneider, and Tom Hyde.

My special thanks also go to the New Jersey Historical Commission for agreeing to underwrite some of my research expenses and to Professor Rodney Carlisle of Rutgers University for his faith and encouragement, as well as his willingness to serve as a link between the organization and me during my residency in London.

Finally, this study would have never been completed without the gracious assent of my husband, Arthur, to be saddled with the copy editing of the original manuscript and the consent of my daughter, Joella, to learn more than she ever wanted to know about planning, New Jersey, and the Federation.

1

The Search for Order

The history of planned cities is as old as civilization itself. Even a cursory examination of prehistoric Indus Valley cities will uncover the carefully planned nature of those ancient urban centers. However, while such traditional city planning was a static one and occurred before a city was built, the modern planning movement's goal was the reform and redirection of existing urban centers.

During the middle of the nineteenth century, scientific progress made possible the building of integrated systems of water and drainage in areas of high-population density, and this brought an end to periodic outbreaks of epidemics. The installation of lighting fixtures (first gas and then electricity) and the emergence of a police force made city streets safer and more accommodating. The increased health and security, along with the traditional attractions of urban life, caused elites in the English-speaking world to shift their primary residence from the country to the city. These new city dwellers, who brought with them their traditional appreciation of the beauties of nature, joined forces with the emerging professional classes, especially architects, in an attempt to build the "city beautiful." Large central parks and wide avenues remain their legacy.

At the turn of the century, the influx of the poverty-ridden immigrants soon created a serious hazard to the health and safety of the city and its inhabitants. The "city practical" movement was born, led by social scientists, who set out to alleviate the dehumanizing condi-

1

tions in such areas; engineers, who tried to map the physical layout of cities; and lawyers, who began to develop the legal basis for state control of urban development. Various codes regulating the materials, height, and population density of urban dwellings were beginning to be enacted by city governments.

Once a precedent was established and the right of government to interfere with a private citizen's use of his own property was acknowledged, city fathers began to use this prerogative in order to protect their "city beautiful" by restricting the spread of tenements into adjoining areas. This was done by the adoption of zoning laws. Zoning was based on the belief that the state has the right to limit the use of one individual's private property to secure the value of another individual's private property. To make such a proposition more palatable, zoning was presented as a way to separate incompatible uses in order to promote public welfare.

At first, the justices remained loyal to the proposition that a man's property is his castle and were reluctant to validate zoning regulations. In New Jersey, the courts even refused to recognize the constitutionality of the state's 1924 Zoning Enabling Act. Only after the United States Supreme Court found that zoning was constitutional and New Jersey passed a constitutional amendment empowering the legislature to permit municipalities to adopt zoning ordinances did the Garden State's courts throw in the towel. Still, the courts' constant references to terms such as "public welfare" and avoidance of "arbitrariness" forced zoners into the arms of planners. Planners would provide the rationalization for zoning, and zoning would become a tool of planning.

Meanwhile, another set of young reformers began to discuss the need to direct the future development of whole regions along pre-planned lines based on careful studies of the present and reasonable projections about the future. They devised the plan for the rebuilding of Chicago after the great fire and then moved to New York and founded the Regional Plan Association (RPA). During the twenties, these men devised their plans and tried to sell them to a growing number of adherents within the state and national establishments.

Planning was an integral component of the progressive movement's "search for order" through professionalization and bureaucratization. In 1923, New York established the first state planning agency and Los Angeles the first county planning commission; others then began to follow suit. When Franklin D. Roosevelt assumed the presidency, he brought with him to Washington one of the fathers of the movement, Harold L. Ickes, who was put in charge of the National Planning Board. The federal government was beginning to direct large sums of money into states and localities and, to ensure that it would be spent rationally, it insisted that state and regional planning boards be established "to make plans within the framework of the national program."[1] New Jersey dutifully appointed its own state board in 1934, and the New Jersey Federation of Official Planning Boards (the Federation) was established four years later, in 1938. (See discussion regarding evolution of the organization's present name in Chapter 5.)

Despite all the political, economic, and social changes that took place during the following fifty years, the New Jersey Federation remained faithful to the ideology of that unique period in American history. It is an ideology that rejects both traditional "laissez-faire" and "statist" policies, opting instead for "a middle way" that historians call "corporate liberalism." Ellis W. Hawley defines this term in the following manner:

> A corporate system is one whose basic units consist of officially recognized, non-competitive, role-ordered occupational or functional groupings. It is also one with coordinating machinery designed to integrate these units into an interdependent whole and one where the state properly functions as coordinator, assistant, and midwife rather than director or regulator. In such a system there are deep interpenetrations between state and society, and enjoying a special status is an enlightened social elite capable of perceiving social needs and imperatives and assisting social groups to meet them through enlightened concerts of interests.[2]

The Federation's creation, organization, goals, and methods of operation can serve as an ideal illustration of the way such a system functions. The State Planning Board assisted in the creation of the Federation. State planners helped, participated in, and used the organization, including serving on the Federation's board of directors; directors also served on various state commissions. The two bodies held joint conferences, advertized each other's activities, helped each other politically and financially, and, most importantly, developed an excellent understanding of each other's needs and priorities.

Richard Ginman, the last director of the Division of State and Regional Planning, remarked: "The Federation provided a convenient forum for telling our story. I never felt that it was a hostile audience. I do not say that the Federation people never asked pointed questions, but I never had the feeling that it was one of those things where it is us against the world. I guess it was just that we were always involved with them, we were familiar faces, we were there as much sometimes listening to something somebody else had to say as we were there now saying something on our own, so that I found that format was very useful. We exploited it, but not in the sense that we tried to control or maneuver it."[3]

The relationship thus described appears to be a classic example of the "vision of a state that would organize a concert of recognized interests and then function as a part of that concert's planning and coordinating apparatus."[4] However, it is important also to emphasize that once a governmental body is assigned the role of midwife and nurse to a particular group of private interests, it develops a strong dependence on the group's support in order to secure its own survival within the state system. This dependence might create difficulties for the governmental agency during periods of breakdown in the state or national consensus.

The same interdependency, though tempered by organizational integrity, is apparent in the Federation's relationship with the other organizations that functioned as members of the recognized concert of interest. They included the New Jersey State League of Municipalities (the League) and its affiliates, the various academic institutions (especially Rutgers University), professional organizations (most importantly the American Planning Association), and regional leadership bodies (such as RPA). These disparate organizations developed a high degree of cooperation based on long-term familiarity, friendship, and trust, as well as the recognition of the unique interests, priorities, and acknowledged expertise of each institution.

These organizations were not always expected to see eye-to-eye on all issues, but once a deal was struck, they were supposed to maintain their loyalty to the coalition even in face of great internal opposition. The story of the licensing of professional planners is an excellent case in point, as are all the major land-use laws in New Jersey.

The successful functioning of such systems is greatly dependent on "the special status enjoyed by an enlightened social elite." This cluster of individuals not only perceives and articulates society's needs but also actively participates in the day-to-day operations of a number of separate organizations simultaneously and over a long period of time. This participation enables these individuals to spot the issues on which consensus can be built and select the time most appropriate for the formation of the coalition necessary to translate that consensus into legislative action.

Fred G. Stickel III is an outstanding member of this elite. He is the League's counsel, the Federation's associate counsel, and the former president of the Institute of Municipal Attorneys. Stickel played a major role in the formation of both the 1953 and the 1975 planning enabling legislation, participated in numerous state-appointed commissions, and is considered one of the major authorities on municipal law in New Jersey. B. Budd Chavooshian is yet another example of institutional interpenetration. After long years as the head of the state planning unit, he moved to an academic position as a professor of planning at Rutgers University while all the time retaining his Federation directorship and playing a key role in various governmental commissions.

The governmental commissions are one of the most important instruments used by the state to forge a consensus of "enlightened opinions," as well as to make increased control of the private sector more palatable (as in the case of the Pinelands Commission). These are appointed bodies but, in addition to acknowledged experts, the head of state would be sure to appoint representatives of the various organizations that have recognized interests in the matters to be addressed by the commission. As a result of the quality of the Federation's leadership, the organization usually ended up with several of its members serving on the planning-related commissions, though only one was an official representative of the Federation.

Actually, the quality of the Federation directors is not surprising considering the evidence concerning the composition of planning boards nationally gathered by the American Planning Association and the membership in New Jersey, which was gathered and evaluated by Harvey Moskowitz, professional planner. Both surveys clearly demonstrate the elitist nature of planning board membership:

> Appointing authorities have consistently drawn from the better educated, professionally trained and long term residents of their communities to serve on planning boards. Almost by definition these groups earn more money, are overwhelmingly homeowners, and logically following, are predominantly married, most with dependent children at home. For better or worse, this group has largely determined the physical landscape of the state, and while there has been some criticism of the result, there can be no question that they have modeled New Jersey's physical structure on their own background, goals and aspirations.[5]

Missing from this description, according to Harry A. Maslow, a former Federation president, is his own characterization of planners as "fiercely independent" and "no shrinking violets." All these qualities are essential to the practitioners of the planning ideology. After all, the essence of this perspective is the creation of a method whereby groups of unelected, public-minded citizens would be given the right not only to define "public good" but also to use powerful tools with which to limit private and public actions they deemed detrimental to that "public good." The concept smacks of paternalism and was initially criticized by its opponents as un-American. This was one of the reasons that the proponents of this ideology were motivated to form an organization that would bring together like-minded individuals and would act as a support unit for its members, as well as a disseminator and propagator of the planning ideology. It is the story of this organization that is the subject of this study.

Notes

1. Alan W. Steiss, "Three Decades of State Planning," *Jersey Plans*, vol. XI, no. 3 (1960):9.

2. Ellis W. Hawley, "The Discovery and Study of 'Corporate Liberalism'," *Business History Review,* vol. LII, no. 3 (Autumn 1978):312.

3. Interview with Dick Ginman, May 21, 1986.

4. Hawley, *op. cit.,* p. 316.

5. Harvey S. Moskowitz, "Who Plans: A Look at New Jersey Planning Board Members," *The Federation Planner* (April 1984):3.

2

In the Beginning

The New Jersey Federation of Official Planning Boards (the Federation) was founded in the West Orange town hall on November 30, 1938. In attendance were representatives from the planning bodies of all levels of government: federal, state, county, and municipal. The stated purpose of the new organization was "to arrange a systematic planning campaign for the future of the state."[1] Following some speeches emphasizing the need for such a new organization, the delegates proceeded to form the Federation and to adopt the constitution and bylaws previously prepared by the organizational committee.

Full membership was to be extended only to official planning boards in New Jersey, that is, "any planning board in the state which has been appointed by a duly constituted governing body."[2] The Federation was to have its first annual meeting in the spring of 1939, at which time it was to elect a board of directors, officers, and regional directors (see chart). The Federation was to be financed by annual membership dues ranging from $5 to $25, depending on the size of the township.

A seven-member interim executive committee was given the task of running the Federation's affairs and laying the groundwork for its first annual conference. Harry E. Hosking was elected chairman of the executive committee, and he in turn appointed Benjamin M. Taub, Ernest P. Biro, and Frederick T. Rubidge as chairmen of the

NEW JERSEY FEDERATION OF OFFICIAL PLANNING BOARDS
ORGANIZATION CHART

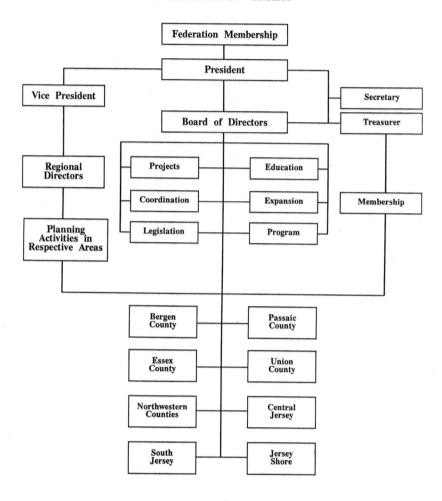

conference, legislative, and planning problems committees, respectively.[3]

The Federation newsletter, *The New Jersey Planner*, made its debut on February 23, 1939. It gave tentative dates and panel locations for the first annual conference, to be sponsored jointly with the State Planning Board, and it invited contributions and suggestions from interested parties. It also promised to sponsor a movement to bring about a state constitutional amendment enabling municipalities to zone land,[4] and it offered its services as an information clearinghouse for the broader aspects of planning, such as the interpretation of planning laws or appropriate administrative procedures.

In preparation for the conference, the directors attended various municipal and county planning board meetings to urge the boards to become Federation members and to participate in its future activities. The executive committee also investigated the possibility of future affiliation with the New Jersey State League of Municipalities (the League). A resolutions committee was formed, exhibits were prepared (including some from the New York Regional Planning Board and the Federal Housing Administration), and a conference program was formulated.

The first Federation conference and annual meeting was held in the Robert Treat Hotel in Newark on Saturday, April 22, 1939. By that time, the interim executive committee had accomplished its goal: It succeeded in turning over to the elected officers of the Federation "a live, going organization—a real factor in the planning movement in New Jersey."[5] However, there was very little difference between the temporary and the permanent leadership of the new organization.

The *New Jersey Municipalities*[6] summarized the conference this way: "The first Annual Conference of the New Jersey Federation of Official Planning Boards . . . accomplished that for which its promoters had hoped. It brought together representatives of official and unofficial planning boards, zoning commissions, civic bodies interested in planning, and a generous sprinkling of individual advocates of planning. It permitted a better understanding of municipal, county, regional, and state problems and the need of a permanent state-wide organization to assure co-operative effort in the interest of all the people of the State."[7]

The speed and efficiency displayed by the organizers reflected the caliber of the people involved. There was John Sloane (the son-in-law of Thomas Edison), banker and public citizen, vice chairman of the State Planning Board and later a director of the National Committee on Housing, and an original organizer of the Tri-State Anti-Pollution Commission. There were young, ambitious lawyers such as Biro and Taub (later a deputy attorney general of the State of New Jersey), who were deeply involved in developing the legal basis of planning. They were joined by engineers interested in mapping the physical layout of the community, such as Harold Osborne, chief engineer of AT&T and future president of ASPO (American Society of Planning Officials) and RPA (Regional Plan Association); Major George Farny, highway engineer and president of the New Jersey Park and Recreation Association; and Glenn Reeves, port development engineer for the New York Port Authority. Also present were architects turned town planners, such as John Kelly and Marcel Villanueva, along with full-time planning consultants, such as Eduard Jacobson, the consultant director of the City of Newark Planning Project, and Russell VanNest Black, consultant director of the New Jersey State Planning Board and future president of AIP (American Institute of Planning). Such architects and consultants would soon carry the banner for the professionalization and institutionalization of planning as a staff function of government.

The founders of the Federation were "true believers" in the ideology of planning. They were convinced that the adoption of planning tools by an ever-widening circle of governments would result in more efficient management of all localities and thus make a significant contribution to the public good. Furthermore, like all pioneers, they were prepared to spend an inordinate amount of their time and money to enhance their cause. The Federation's first president, Hosking, expressed the group's feeling when he claimed that "there must be a rebirth of the desire to do what is right for all, for no reason but that it is right."[8] This is not to imply that the founders were unaware of the practical benefits that activity in such an organization produced. Obviously, important contacts were made, influential people were met, and careers were enhanced, but the stature of many of the leaders seems to have diminished the importance of such considerations.

EARLY FEDERATION LEADERS

Harry E. Hosking

Marcel Villanueva

Benjamin M. Taub

Russell VanNest Black

Besides individual local planning activists, who felt the need to have an organization that would provide them with a beneficial support group, the Federation enjoyed the enthusiastic support of the State Planning Board, the League, and the RPA, a relationship that has lasted until today. The director of the State Planning Board, in whose offices the preliminary meetings for the formation of the organization had taken place, not only called the creation of the Federation "a milestone in the progress of planning in this state," but he also promised his board's "cooperation to the fullest extent of its ability."[9] This commitment was immediately translated into a willingness to share the credit for the State Planning Board's annual conference with the Federation; into editing, printing, distributing, and cosponsoring the Federation's newsletter; handling the publicity for the organization's actions; and even developing a tradition according to which board members would sit on the Federation's board of directors.

The League accepted the Federation as its affiliate, invited the Federation to participate in its annual conferences (without any cost to the Federation), and reported on the activities of the organization in its own publication, *New Jersey Municipalities*. This journal also published articles written by the Federation's directors. As for the RPA, its directors were always prepared to speak before the Federation's gatherings, and some of them became directors of the Federation as well.

Why this sudden interest in planning, and why was the creation of a federation of local planning boards seen by the planning community as such an important milestone in the development of planning in New Jersey?

The answer is simple. Planning activists realized that if planning at any level—federal, state, or regional—was to survive and prosper in a decentralized democracy like the United States, it would have to develop a grass-roots constituency. The creation of the Federation was deemed an appropriate way to develop just such a constituency. Localities also offered an important outlet for the concrete implementation of planning ideas, as well as future employment opportunities for budding planning professionals.

The planning movement was a progressive response to the failures of unhindered capitalism and rapid industrialization. It proposed to rationalize governmental operations through the application of business methods to the public sector. This necessitated the use of governmental police power to limit the rights of private ownership. This practice was attuned to the international tendency, with American planners greatly influenced by their British counterparts. The horrors of the depression certainly seemed to offer fertile soil for the implementation of progressive techniques by the New Dealers. However, as the totalitarian governments became the most enthusiastic and systematic proponents of central planning and international tensions sharpened ideological conflict, American planners found themselves increasingly on the defensive.

In a special address, celebrating the twenty-fifth anniversary of the Federation, Hosking reminisced: "Planning was not easy in those early days. We were suspect! A planner was a Nazi, a Fascist, a communist, a busybody or just a plain nut. In one community a local dowager, peering through her glasses, said, 'so, you are the young whippersnapper who is going to tell us what to do with property in our family for generations.'"[10] Planning smacked of governmental control and, as such, seemed contrary to the American spirit of liberty.

To planners, the winds of war also renewed memories of the aftermath of World War I. Villanueva, the Federation's first secretary and second president, emphasized: "Today, when the neutrality law is about to be repealed and the expansion of industries is anticipated, it is particularly significant that municipalities should adopt measures for control. Mushroom growth, which occurred during the World War, should not be repeated. At least zoning laws should be adopted."[11]

The urgency felt by planners was not necessarily shared by most politicians. The preponderance of planning boards was created in order to satisfy federal requirements that tied federal funding of state and local recovery projects to a review of the proposed spending by an appropriate planning body. This was one of the ways the New Deal used its leverage to promote progressive ideals. As public works began to lose their momentum, many state planning boards were abolished, and county boards lost their vitality. It became evident that without popular support, planning activity would grind to a halt.

The State Planning Board was then receiving 80% of its funds from the federal government while most of its work consisted of studies on behalf of, or for the benefit of, local government. The board realized that cuts in federal appropriations would have to be made up by the state. Since a growing number of states were dismantling planning boards, a federation of local planning boards could become an important ally in the state board's own fight for survival.[12]

Furthermore, while planning was losing the support of state and federal governments, it was making consistent progress on the local level. By June 1938, the state had fifty-seven official planning boards and one hundred ninety-six zoned municipalities, an increase of nineteen planning boards and sixteen zoning ordinances during the past two years, plus four newly created county boards.[13]

Unfortunately, the proliferation of local planning boards presented its own problems of coordination. During the first Federation conference, J. M. Faust of the National Recreation Association explained:

> There is a great need, in our present state of social organization, for a common-denominator group which may bring together the problems of the social engineer, of the health engineer, and those interested in recreational activities of people and other phases of human welfare into an integrated coordinated whole. One of the most hopeful and significant developments of the time is the ever widening realization of this need for planning in municipality, county and state. However, it must be borne in mind that the same danger of cross-purposes and lack of integration may arise unless planning boards themselves band together in an agency such as the New Jersey Federation of Official Planning Boards. This cooperation should be carried on in the closest consonance with the State Planning Board and with regional boards, where such exist.[14]

There was also the problem of the funding of the local planning boards, as only seven of these boards had sufficient operational funds. Hosking vividly described the working conditions of the newly appointed lay planners: "Funds to carry on the work? Says the planner to the town council, 'could we have $1.80 to buy a few stamps?' 'Shh! the Taxpayers might hear you—Nazi master plan, you know.' An exaggeration? For exactness, yes; for the feelings sometimes, no."[15]

Such a proliferation of local planning boards, lacking both funds and expertise, could have been proven disastrous to the future of planning. The new boards would probably have been unable to achieve any valuable results, and the claim of critics that planning was just another expensive bureaucracy would have been substantiated. A statewide federation was therefore needed to educate and coordinate local planning, advertise successful planning board actions, create popular approval of planning, and lobby on behalf of adequate funds for all planning boards.

Politics was yet another major stumbling block before the beleaguered planner. Taub, the Federation's treasurer and third president, told his colleagues how a planning commission citizens' advisory committee, which was appointed by the mayor to pay off political debts, ended up calling for the abolition of the planning commission. Taub repeatedly explained:

> When planning becomes official, it inevitably becomes political, and its importance as an instrument of public service depends primarily upon the attitudes of changing administrations, which may or may not reflect an informed public opinion. In order for the Federation of planning boards to operate successfully, it must have every official municipal and county planning board cooperate. In this way, the Federation can successfully operate and create public opinion strong enough to raise the issue of planning above political consideration.[16]

The League had two additional reasons for supporting the Federation. The League realized that such an organization could also empower municipalities by ensuring that not only would the power to plan remain largely in their own hands but the municipalities would be given adequate tools to carry out their new function. The Federation's first legislative committee chairman described one of the vital local planning issues of the day in the Federation's first newsletter:

> Among the many problems to be taken up, our New Jersey Zoning and Enabling Act seems to command our first atten-

tion. . . . Our State Constitution omits the right to give to the governing bodies of municipalities the right to zone land. In spite of the countless number of efforts made by the municipalities to pass . . . zoning ordinances with land zoning provisions, the courts have steadfastly held that no such power exists. It will be necessary, therefore, first of all to sponsor a movement to bring about a constitutional amendment and then have the subsequent legislatures ratify the same.[17]

The planning activists' shared assumption was that local planning board members, whether they were political appointees, troublemakers, or conscientious public citizens, already had a natural affinity for planning. Board members could not fail to realize that their power and prestige would grow by belonging to such an organization. The lay planners, by getting appointed to the planning board, had already proven a certain amount of leadership ability and therefore could become effective molders of public opinion. It was the Federation's task to organize, educate, and energize its membership, then it had to send these members back into their respective communities to spread the gospel and prove the Federation's and their own value by some significant action. It was also just as crucial to convince localities of the value of appointing a planning board, which in turn would join the Federation. The larger the Federation was to grow, the greater would be its potential influence on the legislature, not only in legal matters but also in budgetary ones.

How does a new Federation go about attempting to fill such a tall order? During its first few years, the organization emphasized promotion more than coordination, education, legislation, or lobbying. Of course, many activities had more than one function.

In those troubled times, Hosking believed that the first order of business was to discredit the view that planning was totalitarian and un-American. Planning, he claimed, was as American as apple pie since the Mayflower Compact was the first American planning document. Furthermore, he claimed that planning was no longer a luxury but a necessity: "Europe has found how to make totalitarian states effective. We must do likewise for democracy."[18] Planning could not only make government effective, but it could also invigorate and protect the American tradition of participatory democracy. Hosking called on the planning board to become "the coordinating method through which citizens may practically have a voice in what is to be done."[19] He urged local planning boards to enlist the help of various citizens' advisory groups in a relentless effort to enhance the community quality of life so that "we would once more be assured that we are back on a true democratic course and we would no longer fear the conditions we now see in countries abroad which seem to be having their beginning here."[20]

Others emphasized the more prosaic, practical benefits of planning. Zoning, as a tool of planning, protects property values and lowers taxes, that is, planners can save much more money than they cost. A study conducted by the State Planning Board discovered that premature platting of land was the cause of great financial hardship to municipalities. The land was subdivided, the plats remained unsold and became delinquent, but the municipalities still owed taxes to the county and state. In addition, the avoidable expense in additional services to this land would cost localities in New Jersey $125 million, with the taxpayer picking up the bill.[21] Planners can also figure the cost to the municipality of the services needed by each housing unit and determine the minimum tax return necessary for a housing unit to pay for the services it receives from the township. Thus, in the minutes of the directors meeting of July 1939, one finds the following: "Among appropriate subjects for the coming conference the following were advanced: 1. How planning will reduce taxes. 2. What planning can do for you."

Conferences were important since they served the promotional, integrative, and educational functions of the organization. In its first years of operation, the Federation established a tradition of two conferences a year, one held in the spring (together with the State Planning Board) and the other in the fall. In addition, it would occasionally sponsor or cosponsor smaller conferences dedicated to a particularly "hot" topic. The issues dealt with included highway and recreational needs of the state, local planning problems, small houses, urban rehabilitation, Radburn's cluster housing, and a special conference dealing solely with garden apartments (the latter were just making their debut in the state). In addition to the New Jersey planning specialists included as speakers, an effort was made to expose the audience to federal officials, as well as planning experts from other states.

The Federation Planner was a more problematic, but no less significant, tool of the Federation. Gaining as wide a readership as possible was deemed so important that copies were sent to all planning boards, whether members of the organization or not (members received additional copies). Besides advertising the Federation's activities, the newsletter carried items concerning planning developments around the country; topical essays on pertinent subjects, such as large-scale housing, flood control, and zoning legislation; examinations of court cases; and local planning news. At times, the newsletter also urged its readership to actively support or oppose specific pieces of legislation or appropriation.

This newsletter ran into difficulties since the Federation lacked the necessary funds for such an operation and was incapable of publishing it on its own. The dues of the small membership (it reached thirty-three in 1941) were not sufficient to enable the organization either to rent an office or pay a staff. Fortunately, the directors were prepared to write articles and even to edit the paper. However, they still needed help with the printing and distribution of the publication. The State Planning Board did take upon itself to provide the necessary assistance, but it proved unreliable due to its unstable personnel and fluctuating budgets. Thus, *The New Jersey Planner*, which was supposed to graduate in 1940 from being "issued now and then" to being issued monthly, in reality averaged only four irregular publications a year. This problem was solved only when Taub took upon himself the editing of the newsletter and the organizing of a lobbying effort on behalf of sufficient appropriation for the State Planning Board.

Financial difficulties also hampered an early attempt to edit, publish, and distribute the proceedings of the conferences. These publications had to be terminated after a year due to the expense of hiring stenographers. Even the doubling of the minimum dues from $5 to $10 did little to solve the problem. Eventually, *The New Jersey Planner* started publishing the more important papers presented in the conference. Such papers included addresses before the Federation in Newark, N.J., on December 4, 1941, by Jacob Crane (the federal assistant defense housing coordinator) on "Long Term Redevelopment of Cities" and Russell VanNest Black on "Urban Redevelopment: Principles and Procedures."

Federation views and activities were also reported in the New Jersey local newspapers, such as the *Passaic Herald News, Paterson Morning Call, Newark Star Ledger,* and the *Newark Evening News,* especially if they involved "local color." Even more helpful was the *New Jersey Municipalities,* which not only carried announcements of the Federation's conferences but also published articles written by the Federation directors.

A great publicity coup was achieved when, following a successful lobbying effort, Governor A. Harry Moore designated the week of the Federation's first anniversary (and second annual conference) as "Planning Week in New Jersey." At the governor's invitation, Hosking, as president, drew up a list of suggested activities around the state. Great emphasis was given to familiarizing high school students with the basic tenets of planning. Various Federation members addressed local adult and student groups, and essay contests achieved varying degrees of success depending on local interest and cooperation (Passaic County alone had sixteen hundred entries).

The Federation's local activities were not limited to official planning weeks as directors sold their wares in meetings of civic group and party organizations, as well as town halls. They were particularly interested in organizing regional or county meetings where individual local problems could be addressed and municipal and county collaboration could be enhanced. This was the specialty of the regional directors, and a measure of success was recorded in Passaic, Bergen, Union, and Morris counties. Such activities, the leadership believed, served both the Federation's coordinative effort and its promotional one. New Jersey had a strong home-rule tradition, and the localities were fiercely independent. It was not easy to foster cooperation between municipalities or between municipality, county, and state agencies. Just providing a forum for constructive discussion of mutual problems was deemed beneficial.

Beyond talk lay action. The directors believed that a specific improvement achieved by an individual planning board was worth ten conferences, but action brought them into conflict with politicians, vested interests, and accentuated the paucity of funds.

A uniquely intimate look at the problems faced by the activist is revealed by the verbatim minutes of a special board meeting recorded on July 8, 1940. Here are some excerpts:

Sloane: We aren't getting enough done in the various towns. I suggested that we take County Maps and ask each Board Member to mark out in colored pencil the thing that will help. Then try to get the respective towns busy on these things. Indicate also those which are most important—roads, parks, parkways, flood control, airports, sewers, etc. The State Planning Board could classify them as to whether they are state, county, or municipal. It will give us publicity. If we had enough money to offer a prize, get it into the high schools.

Pond: I think it might be carried on down to your county and local boards. In that way, it would be a local matter.

Farny: I have gone thru all that. Nothing came of it. You must have the preliminary work gradually building it up. Unless you prepare the field for it you can't do anything.

Sloane: Ask each of the Boards to write down what they are interested in, and work on one county.

Farny: Let us try our efforts on one community first.

Hosking: Why not one in each county?

Villanueva: Essex County is full of local recommendation. Each municipality has its own and the others are not interested. In Orange, we suggested extending High Street to Montclair. We thought it was a county affair. The county has no funds. We don't know whether anything like that can be done. It always involves money and the towns are not always able financially to pay for these things. I think we are bound to be disappointed again and again. I think what Mr. Sloane has said is good. It is only by hammering and coming back at things that we will get people interested in these things.

Sloane: A simple thing like the City of Newark turning over South Orange Avenue and Bloomfield Avenue to the State—we can't get these things done. The county won't allow it.

Hosking: We rub elbows with the politicians. We have convinced them that if they "play ball" with the Planning Board, they get somewhere and we do, too. Our Planning Board membership was not what it should be. It had a nice sounding title, but not much was done. We set out to get rid of our "dead wood."

Sloane: That is a difficult task.

Hosking: We did it in Livingston. You have got to do it yourself. We gave everybody a definite job to do. We pushed them for things. The laggards became embarrassed and resigned. We brought in a younger group. Most of them junior executives in business.

Sloane: You get further with the younger element. In West Orange, we have one which is very old.

Villanueva: I think Livingston and Montclair have done more than anyone else along that direction. They do a lot of good work.

Biro: Have you some concrete suggestions to give us? I think Irvington is typical. The minute the planning board becomes too active, the town fathers think we are trying to steal the show. They are appointed by the commissioners. They throw cold water on everything. We have no citizen committee.

Villanueva: I can tell you what not to do first. . . .

The ASPO presented the Federation with yet another challenge. It wished to organize a New Jersey chapter of the national organization. The directors, though preferring to maintain their independence, did acknowledge the advantages that affiliation with such a broader organization could offer, especially in the area of publication. They simultaneously were wary of the duplication of effort, as well as of the possible loss of membership that would result from the existence of two competing statewide federations. Interestingly enough, the president of ASPO, Harold Osborne, was a founder and director of the Federation, but the numerous committees that were appointed at various times during the Federation's first three years all reached the same conclusion: A national affiliation, attractive as it may be, would have to result in much higher membership dues, which many planning boards could not afford. Thus, membership would fall, and a large membership was mandatory for the accomplishment of the Federation's goals.

The ASPO challenge became the direct cause of the Federation's first serious attempt to test its leverage with the state legislature. In January 1940, the State Planning Board hired a new staff member, whose duties specifically included aiding the organization in "whatever ways could prove most helpful."[22] This staff member became the editor of *The New Jersey Planner*. Six months later, the publication was again suspended due to the lack of appropriation by the State Planning Board. This suspension coincided with the ASPO's attempts to organize a New Jersey chapter. The Federation's leadership felt vulnerable since it thought that the organization owed its membership more for their money than two conferences a year. After failed attempts by the Federation to renew the publication of the newsletter independently, the State Planning Board relented, though editing remained a Federation function. Simultaneously, and perhaps not coincidentally, the Federation mounted a successful lobbying campaign that included telegrams and personal appeals to members of the state legislature. The aim was to assure adequate appropriations for the State Planning Board. The June 1941 issue of *The New Jersey Planner* reported:

THE NEW JERSEY STATE PLANNING BOARD

It will be very gratifying to these Planners interested in the work of the New Jersey State Planning Board, particularly those who used their efforts on behalf of the Board, to learn that the Legislature Appropriations Committee included the State board in the Main Appropriation Bill which passed April 30, 1941.

The amount of the appropriation granted is $16,870 for the fiscal year 1941–42. In addition, the Legislature on the same day passed a Supplemental Appropriation Bill in the amount of $7500 to continue the work of the Board for the balance of this fiscal year. Both of these bills have received the signature of Governor [Thomas] Edison.

It seemed that the Federation successfully displayed its influence at the local level as well. Samuel Rabkin, chairman of the Federation's membership committee, claimed: "Federation membership will augment the standing of your board in your community. Many activities can be bolstered by the fact that the Federation's approval is upon them. The Federation has often lent its weight towards securing favorable reaction on specific problems facing some individual board."[23]

Rabkin further insisted that "planning in New Jersey is much more widely recognized in official circles since the advent of the Federation."[24] There had been a steady increase in the number of new planning boards, the size of their appropriation, and in the number of zoned municipalities. Nevertheless, it was impossible to isolate the organization's influence upon these developments from related factors, particularly as its leadership greatly overlapped with that of other planning and civic organizations (such as the RPA, ASPO, American Institute of Architects [AIA], and the local Chamber of Commerce or the local Bar Association) and with other state and federal agencies (such as the Works Progress Administration, the State Planning Board, and the state recreation and highway departments). Still, the Federation conferences were well attended, and membership was increasing. Unfortunately, the relatively small pool of potential members limited its growth and fund-raising potential, rendering it dependent on state support.

Another problem that had plagued the Federation since its inception was that while supposedly a statewide organization, in reality its membership and leadership were heavily weighted toward the northeastern part of the state. This was inevitable since not only was the northeast the center of planning activity but, as of 1938, there were no planning boards in existence south of New Brunswick and Long Branch. The Federation did include a "southern area," with Dr. William Carpenter of Princeton serving as its regional director. Interestingly enough, no awareness of this problem is to be found in the Federation's minutes, which leads one to conclude that no systematic campaign was mounted to address this disparity. It was discussed, however, by Black in his 1938 article in the *New Jersey Municipalities*.

The Federation's record on legislative matters was just as unimpressive. The organization did pass resolutions at its first conference calling for a constitutional amendment authorizing municipalities to zone the use of land; authorizing county planning boards to approve or disapprove of plats in municipalities lacking legal planning boards; and endorsing a bill providing for the acquisition and development of freeways in the highway system. However, no further Federation action was recorded on behalf of these goals.

Inevitably, as the winds of war blew ever more strongly, the Federation, together with the rest of the state and the country, became heavily engrossed in the war effort. New initiatives of any kind therefore had to await more peaceful times.

Notes

1. "Municipal and County Boards in Federation," *Passaic Herald News*, November 12, 1938.
2. "What Is an Official Planning Board?" *The New Jersey Planner* (April 1939):4.
3. "Leonard Ward Helps to Organize State Plan Boards," *Paterson Call*, December 1, 1938.
4. Ernest P. Biro, "Report of Chairman of Legislative Committee," *The New Jersey Planner* (February 1939):3.
5. Harry Hosking, "Gentlemen," *The New Jersey Planner* (February 1939):1.
6. A publication of the New Jersey State League of Municipalities.
7. "N.J. Federation of Official Planning Boards," *New Jersey Municipalities* (May 1939):15.
8. Harry Hosking, "Modern Town Meeting," *New Jersey Municipalities* (June 1940):1.
9. Charles P. Messick, "Gentlemen," *The New Jersey Planner* (February 1939):2.
10. Federation's Minutes, November 21, 1963, p. 2.
11. Marcel Villanueva, "Planning Today for Our Communities of Tomorrow," *New Jersey Municipalities* (November 1939):15.
12. Alan W. Steiss, "Three Decades of State Planning," *Jersey Plans*, vol. XI, no. 3 (1960):9.
13. Russell VanNest Black, "New Jersey Moves Ahead with Local Planning and Zoning," *New Jersey Municipalities* (June 1938):14.
14. "N.J. Federation of Official Planning Boards," *op. cit.*, p. 15.
15. Federation's Minutes, July 8, 1940, p. 7.
16. Benjamin M. Taub, "What Is Planning and Its Necessity to a Community," *The New Jersey Planner* (June 1941):1.
17. Biro, *op. cit.*, p. 3.
18. Harry Hosking, "A Real Planning Problem—American Way," *New Jersey Municipalities* (October 1940):22.

19. Harry Hosking, "Modern Town Meeting," *op. cit.*, p. 22.

20. *Ibid.*, p. 23.

21. Black, *op. cit.*, p. 14.

22. "Federation Will Get More Aid from State Planning Board," *The New Jersey Planner* (January 1940):1.

23. Samuel Rabkin, "Are You Affiliated with the Federation?" *The New Jersey Planner* (September 1941):1.

24. *Ibid.*, p. 2.

3

The War Years—
From Boom to Bust?

The forties presented the Federation with a series of challenges and opportunities. The infant organization confronted the problems produced by the war era with great energy and flexibility, determined to take advantage of the unique circumstances that the emergency created. However, when World War II ended, the Federation's boom turned into bust, and the very survival of the organization seemed in doubt. What had happened?

Some say that generals always fight the last war; this might also be said of planners. World War I brought the country unprecedented and uncontrolled growth generated by war-related industries. The peace was followed by a depression caused by the difficulties of switching from a war economy to a peacetime one. Planners expected the scenario to repeat itself but believed that careful short-term and long-term planning would be capable of ameliorating the harshness of the adjustment period.

During the late thirties, planners had watched with growing anxiety the inevitable approach of the war but were reluctant to address the issue directly. Marcel Villanueva explained:

> As realists, and only because we receive very little recognition from the public and officials at large, all our energies have been directed towards the most obvious deficiencies. . . . For

instance slums and traffic snarls are things that everybody can
understand, but should we have talked of the "Military Value"
of planning two years ago we would have appeared alarmists
instead of practical idealists.

The public, until now, disliked and scoffed at the idea that we
would ever be in a military emergency. So, in all frankness,
what we will try to do now could have been under way long
before this, very obviously.[1]

So planners endeavored to encourage the appointment of planning
boards, the passage of zoning ordinances, the gathering of information, the growth of intermunicipal and county cooperation, and the
education of the public concerning the basic tenets of rational community development. In short, planners wished to put in place the
mechanisms of control that would facilitate taking the appropriate
action when the emergency needs would become much more widely
recognized.

The German blitzkrieg awakened the Americans to their own vul-
nerability to attack. "Home Guards" were established in various
localities, intent on defending vital facilities in their communities.
During the summer of 1940, the following discussion was recorded
at the Federation's special directors' meeting:

> *Farny:* I thought we were going to discuss industrial-
> preparedness, and Home Guard. That is on the top page. I
> have been asked to cooperate with several committees in
> regard to these. . . . We are working with the Legion in Morris
> county.
>
> *Sloane:* Who?
>
> *Farny:* Independent citizens—who have been in one way or
> another connected with some civic association.
>
> *Taub:* The statute should be amended. I think we have an
> effective legislative committee. We probably may be able to
> have the law amended.
>
> *Farny:* A citizens committee—to do something. Organize into
> a troop. We have to protect certain things. It's a question of
> good will.

Taub: If I tried to do anything in Passaic, they'd say "You stick to planning." We have about seven Legion Posts.

Farny: Utilize the planning organization. Help them along.

Rubidge: We have to be directed from a higher source.

Farny: The Council or Chamber of Commerce.

Rubidge: No Chamber of Commerce will do it on its own.

Hosking: The planning board, and their citizens, should say whether it is a good plan to adopt the things that come along.

Sloane: You have no factories?

Hosking: We have none. We have told the governing body we want to know about any requests. We will study them in relation to what is going to happen after the war.

Sloane: Every planning board should be working on that sort of thing.[2]

The conversation clearly manifested the political difficulties that would frustrate any attempt by local planners to involve themselves in local defense planning. "Industrial preparedness" was a much more promising venue for the boards. Local planning boards would deal with the appropriate location of factories, as well as conduct studies of community infrastructure and housing patterns. In 1940, the directors still believed that individual municipalities had the ability to control the effects of the outside world on their own community. A town like Livingston could therefore decide whether it wanted factories or not based on its peacetime needs. Such notions would soon lose their relevancy, if not their desirability.

When New Jersey organized a State Defense Council, Harry Hosking immediately approached Governor A. Harry Moore, offering the Federation's support. The governor accepted his offer, and Federation representatives were placed on the council committee on "surveys and fact-finding." Unfortunately, the organization's elation was short-lived since the committee, which had not received any problem to study, was not activated for quite some time.

The Federation, however, did take the initiative and turned the afternoon session of its fall conference into a defense council meeting jointly sponsored by the Federation and the State Planning Board. Villanueva's address on "The Military Value of Planning" was extremely well received. Its text was published in the *New Jersey Municipalities*, and the Federation received numerous requests for copies, including one from the Public Roads Administration in Washington, D.C. After surveying the role of planning through the centuries, Villanueva had attempted to acquaint his audience with the concepts of European strategic planning, emphasizing the centrality of communication and underground protection. He claimed that "the European principle was to plan for peace-time convenience in a manner that would be of military value in times of war. This principle may well be ours also."[3] New Jersey had an urgent need for a strategic network of military roads connecting its large population centers (there was no direct link even between the first and third largest cities in America, namely, New York and Philadelphia). There was a further need to zone carefully the land surrounding airports in order to improve their accessibility. "The time has come," concluded Villanueva, "for New Jersey to have a Master Plan."

Events soon outpaced planners. This country became the "Arsenal of Democracy" through the cash-and-carry and lend-lease programs. This is how Russell VanNest Black described the conditions in the state as of March 1941:

> Not for decades have the urban parts of this Country (and most of New Jersey is urban) been in such a state of flux. New and expanded industries engaged directly or indirectly in defense activities may strike almost anywhere without warning; so too may defense structures—airports, cantonments, and other essential facilities. With most such new or enlarged activities and projects must come new houses to take care of the increased number of workers; new streets and roads; new sewers and water mains; and many other extended public facilities and services. Such a prospect may be a chamber-of-commerce dream. To the governmental official, and subsequently to the taxpayer, it may well be a nightmare.[4]

There was no conceivable way in which local planners could stem such a tide of defense-related activity. Insistence on home rule became not only futile but even unpatriotic. Localities had to fall in line with regional and national programs. However, as Black pointed out, all was not lost. Though Livingston could no longer decide if it wanted a factory, it could and should determine where to put it:

> One of the few undertakings that can be initiated and carried through by the locality, and by the locality only, is that of providing itself with all the information and plans likely to be needed in any probable eventuality. . . . The gathering of such information and the preparation of such plans can best be done by a planning board.[5]

The planners' nightmares were not only the result of uncontrolled economic expansion but also the envisaged certainty of a postwar depression:

> So shaky is the footing of the mounting waves of prosperity upon which we are now riding that only miraculous public management will succeed in directing the subsequent certain ebbing flow into the usual and more normal channels— smoothly and without serious disruption. In other words, 1930–1936 may come again more oppressive than before.[6]

Based on past experience, planners were positive that at the end of the conflict, defense contracts could immediately be cancelled. As an interim measure during the transitional period from war to peace, public works would again take center stage and a smart municipality with well-thought-out plans would be in a position to take advantage of the money that would become available in order to effect community improvements. A well-rounded plan could serve both current and future needs. Black therefore suggested that localities should (1) appoint planning boards (if they had none), (2) supply them with technical assistance or with funds to acquire such assistance, and (3) develop a master plan to control present development and define future needs.

Unfortunately, many local governments were not in a hurry to follow these suggestions. In his article "A Wasted Resource of Local Government," Black attempted to dispel some governmental fears that "these boards may usurp some of their [the elected officials'] powers, duties and responsibilities." Planning boards, Black assured them, are only advisory bodies whose recommendations could be ignored or rejected. In addition, the appointment of a planning board extends the powers of local government, as the latter can exercise certain powers only with a planning board and not without one. Furthermore, not only could the boards concentrate on the future but, due to their unique nature, such boards "may escape censorship for not showing spectacular results the first year in office."[7]

Not all such appeals fell on deaf ears. *The New Jersey Planner* reported on a growing interest in planning, especially in new areas, such as South Jersey (Camden County established an active planning board in March 1941) and the Jersey Shore (Ocean City created a planning board in February 1941). The difficulty arose with the cities. The city fathers claimed that as their areas were fully developed and had no empty spaces left, a planning board was of no use. Actually, no city in New Jersey with as much as a population of 75,000 had either a planning board or a city plan.[8] Newark, the state's largest city, not only did not have an official planning board but, in June 1941, it even disbanded its Advisory Planning Board and in October of that year discontinued the Newark WPA Planning Project. The Federation's leadership was aghast! Benjamin Taub, editor of *The New Jersey Planner*, expressed the position of the organization:

> We all know that every large city in the State has experienced a problem of migration to the suburbs, leaving declining residential areas within city limits.
>
> We are now, according to Frederick L. Ackerman, New York Architect and Planner, in the replacement era in our cities. He believes that municipalities must take advantage of this period to develop the stagnated areas into desirable resident districts.
>
> The mistakes made in the past must be eliminated or corrected. The agency best fitted for this job is a planning board. That is the reason we feel that an official planning board in every city in the State of New Jersey is a necessity.[9]

In 1941, urban rehabilitation emerged as a central issue along with defense and the building of small houses. What are the connections?

The decade between 1930 and 1940 witnessed a drift from large cities to the fringes and the suburbs. In New Jersey, sixteen of the twenty-nine urban centers with a population of 25,000 or more lost from 1% to 15.4% of its inhabitants.[10] This process was exacerbated by the rapid development of defense industries, which were usually located in the suburbs due to lower tax rates. Defense workers followed the workplace and created a growing demand for low-income housing in the suburbs. The new small houses were viewed with great dismay by the suburbanites because they added to the tax burden of longtime residents. Hosking, whose township of Livingston felt the pressure from ex-Newark residents, strongly opposed the building of small houses in the suburbs. In a series of speeches and articles, Hosking claimed that small houses in rural areas would end up hurting not only old-time residents but, in the long run, also place a heavy tax burden on the small house owner who could least afford it. The attempt to make industry pay for the added burden, as John Sloane had been suggesting, would only result in the loss of industry to more hospitable areas. Furthermore, why underutilize existing facilities in the cities while necessitating the building of new ones in the suburbs? Urban renewal could be the solution to the problems of the suburbs as well as to those of the city. The following papers were presented at the Federation's fall conference: "The Burden of the Small House on the Municipality" by Hosking; "Long-Range Rehabilitation of Urban Areas" by James S. Taylor; and "Discussion of New Legislation in New Jersey for Urban Rehabilitation" by Black. Thus, the drive for urban renewal legislation and programs resulted from the pressure exerted on the outlying areas by the housing needs of the defense industry. Hosking wrote:

> A recommendation has recently been made through the auspices of a Joint Defense Committee of the Planning Federation of Municipal Engineers and Building Inspectors that some relief for the defense housing program may be found if a program of rehabilitation of existing neighborhoods in large cities is carried out. A program of this nature might have a far-reaching effect on the small house program. If adequate housing can be provided for defense workers in areas of the cities already provided with public utilities, schools, and the like, then there

should be no need to provide for defense housing in the small home class in the outlying districts.[11]

The joint defense committee, to which Hosking referred, was created on June 6, 1941, at the suggestion of the New Jersey State League of Municipalities (the League) and was composed of three of the League's own affiliates. The Federation, which was bitterly disappointed by the inaction of the New Jersey committee on surveys and fact-finding, gave its enthusiastic support to the new committee. Such a coordinating body with high visibility suited the organization to a tee, and the Federation participated in quite a number of such committees before the war ended.

The purpose of the joint committee was to study means of improving contacts between the various local defense councils, as well as to guarantee the cooperation of municipal and state officials with state and local defense councils. The committee, which enjoyed the full backing of Governor Charles Edison and the State Defense Council, met monthly, and its subcommittees prepared various studies intended for the use of local civilian workers in time of emergency.

On October 10, 1941, the joint committee organized a state conference in Newark, which was well attended and received wide-ranging coverage. A defense program for cities was outlined, including plans by the Newark Defense Council to establish a rescue and clearance organization similar to the one used in London. Sloane offered a program to produce a map of the entire state that would give data and show the location of all points that would figure in defense schemes.

Despite a reminder by the chairman of the State Defense Council that the task of reconstruction would be transferred to other hands at the end of the emergency, urban rehabilitation took center stage. C. Roy Swain presented a plan to remodel dilapidated dwellings, and Villanueva discussed rehabilitation and reconstruction of old towns.[12]

Villanueva pointed out that "from a town planner's angle, the destruction by fire and demolition by bombs of large sections of our sub-standard areas would greatly simplify the task ahead of us."[13] Like Black, he further explained that since the postwar period would witness mass dislocation of workers, the government was sure to

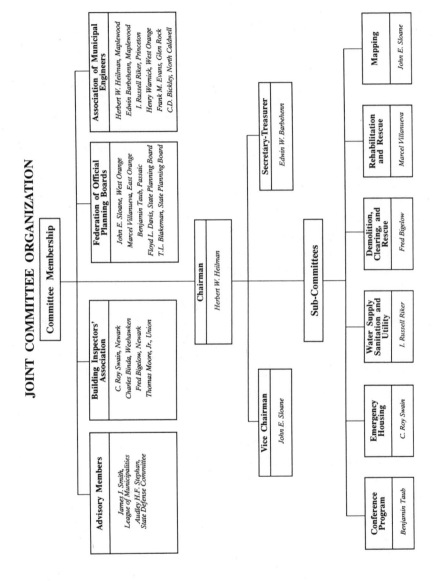

JOINT COMMITTEE ORGANIZATION

Committee Membership

Advisory Members

James J. Smith,
League of Municipalities
Audley H.F. Stephan,
State Defense Committee

Building Inspectors' Association

C. Roy Swain, Newark
Charles Binda, Weehawken
Fred Bigelow, Newark
Thomas Moore, Jr., Union

Federation of Official Planning Boards

John E. Sloane, West Orange
Marcel Villanueva, East Orange
Benjamin Taub, Passaic
Floyd L. Davis, State Planning Board
T.L. Blakeman, State Planning Board

Association of Municipal Engineers

Herbert W. Heilman, Maplewood
Edwin Barbehenn, Maplewood
I. Russell Riker, Princeton
Henry Warnick, West Orange
Frank M. Evans, Glen Rock
C.D. Bickley, North Caldwell

Chairman

Herbert W. Heilman

Vice Chairman

John E. Sloane

Secretary-Treasurer

Edwin W. Barbehenn

Sub-Committees

Conference Program

Benjamin Taub

Emergency Housing

C. Roy Swain

Water Supply Sanitation and Utility

I. Russell Riker

Demolition, Clearing, and Rescue

Fred Bigelow

Rehabilitation and Rescue

Marcel Villanueva

Mapping

John E. Sloane

embark on an enormous public works program, and city reconstruction would receive major attention. To this end, Villanueva recommended immediate action in two interconnected areas. First, each city should use all its available resources to assemble the necessary data and to construct a long-range public improvement program based upon actual need. Second, the state legislature should follow Albany's leadership in New York and enact the necessary legislation to enable municipalities to initiate large-scale redevelopment programs. Thus, urban rehabilitation became a major theme in postwar planning.

Long-range planning became a national concern as President Franklin D. Roosevelt instructed the National Resources Planning Board to assemble all useful plans for significant public and private action in the postdefense period. A new federal agency named the Public Works Reserve was created to provide technical assistance and guidance to state and local governments in the preparation of six-year programs based solely on state and local finances. These programs would be activated when and if needed to relieve serious unemployment caused by postdefense deflation.

Again, the Public Works Reserve was a reaction to past and present failures. Black claimed: "Remembering 1934–1936, planners are more than ever actually aware of the weaknesses and dangers of planless public works programs, usually amounting to little more than blue-sky inventories of uncoordinated and, often times, ultimately unjustified improvements."[14]

As postdefense planning gave way to postwar planning, Taub reminded his audiences:

> It is just as important to plan the peace while war is on as it would have been to adequately plan for war while there was yet peace. Obviously, much of the confusion that had attended America's swing over to a wartime economy could have been avoided by more planning beforehand.[15]

Therefore, as the Federation leadership continually insisted, cooperation with the Public Works Reserve did not mean making a list of desirable improvements. It did mean the appointment of a planning board and the formulation of a master plan. The more comprehensive the master plan, the better the chance the locality would have to partake in the monies that would surely become available to finance the projects. Furthermore, professional help was becoming available.

In New Jersey, the State Planning Board was designated by Governor Edison as the coordinating agency for all state units in formulating a public works reserve program. The services of a planning engineer would even be made available to assist in the preparation of forms and the development of a long-range program. In addition, Princeton University set up a new Bureau of Urban Research, which was not only research oriented but also offered "advisory assistance to governmental officers and agencies, on request, without charge or commitment."[16]

Nevertheless, more comprehensive planning required fundamental changes in the state's legal structure. To the old demands for a constitutional amendment to enable municipalities to zone land were now added demands for legislation enabling the planned rehabilitation of large urban tracts and the construction of limited access highways. The Federation became involved in highway legislation through its participation in the Roadside Council.

The war, which for the United States began in December 1941, brought on a change of emphasis more than a change of direction. Planning acquired a new popularity. Edna A. Hampson, the Federation's chairperson of the education committee, observed: "We should feel encouraged that the transition between pioneer planning and universal knowledge of planning is at hand because today even school children, who are the future home-makers, know about Armament Planning, Civilian Production Planning, Post-war Rehabilitation and the like. Furthermore, the whole world is planning along a scope that ranges from personal victory gardens to allied victory in the war."[17]

The new opportunities were fully matched by the enormity of the problems. New Jersey experienced a population increase of 2% between 1940 and 1942. With only 3.2% of the country's population, New Jersey contributed 7.7% to the war effort. There were seven thousand war-related manufacturing concerns in the state, and these had from 6% to 8% of the total war contracts allocated throughout the United States (with a cash value exceeding $8 billion); 1 million persons were engaged in war production, and fifty thousand persons entered the state in search of work during the first half of 1942.[18]

Here, finally, was the planner's nightmare. An uncontrollable economic expansion followed by a possible disastrous depression. How should planning boards react?

The Federation leadership did not hesitate. It called upon its members to give their full cooperation to the federal bodies and to postpone future planning in favor of present needs. Villanueva, the organization's second president, stated:

> As the nation now swings wholeheartedly into the war effort the planners will have to readjust themselves, temporarily, to fit their endeavors in harmony with the times. At first we took a quick victory for granted. We directed our main efforts towards a post-war period. . . . The serious setbacks already experienced justify a greater concern for the immediate outlook. Instead of blockading Japan we find ourselves blockaded by Japan and instead of enthusing about our tremendous schedule output after 1943 we should make sure that we won't lose the war in 1942. Therefore, we must preach speed and more speed.
>
> The Planning boards should be concerned now with *immediate problems*, with all due respect to what must be planned later on.[19]

The meaning of the war to municipalities became clear rather quickly. Local zoning regulations and ordinances were ignored or had only lip service paid to them. Defense housing no longer referred to small houses but to temporary dwellings built of inferior materials that would probably have to be pulled down at the end of the war. Villanueva did not relent:

> New Jersey municipalities will be urged to cooperate in approving the construction of these temporary projects where critical needs exist. Because of their nature, much of the ghost-town objections raised in the past should be dismissed as a municipal contribution to the war effort.[20]

Planning boards were not quick to accept such advice, as the question Stuart D. Currier posed to the boards implied: "Have they made sincere efforts to place what information they may have in the hands of those that need it now for the war effort or have they kept it locked securely in the safe so it may not be stolen by the enemy?"[21] The kind of information to which Currier referred included maps and tabulated data mainly concerning possible locations for temporary housing and transportation maps showing local bus routes. Currier argued that the information should not just be supplied, it should be volunteered. Postwar planning should not be neglected, but planning boards had an important role to play as well. Such cooperation was an opportunity to demonstrate the pertinence of their past work.

In 1942, the Federation became extremely active. The directors participated in numerous committees. The facts and survey committee of the State Defense League was revived (Hosking even made a preliminary survey of how to protect state records). The joint committee held a second statewide conference in Atlantic City and its members later met with the new head of the State Defense Council. A new war economy committee, organized by the Federation, cooperated with the state Taxpayers' Association in devising a program of priorities on public spending. The Federation also had representatives on both the new urban rehabilitation committee and the New Jersey war transportation committee.

The last two committees were concerned with the formulation of new legislation (urban renewal and limited access highways), and the Federation's participation in them was probably responsible for the letter the organization received from Assemblyman C. Colburn Hardy of Essex County requesting its assistance in improving the state's planning legislation. In 1942, there was also a resurgence of the long-time attempts to revise the state constitution, and the Federation's legislative committee not only kept a watchful eye on the proposed changes but also forwarded its own suggestions.

Hampson, the Federation's only female director during its first decade, insisted "that in planning as in everything else 'it pays to advertise', and that all of us are Planning Board salesmen."[22] She concentrated her efforts on organizing and publicizing a statewide essay contest on the "Relationship of Planning to Community Development." The prize of a $50 war bond was awarded to the winning essay, and the high caliber of the judges was rather amazing. They were Dr. Charles P. Messick, chief examiner and secretary of the Civil Service Commission, Dr. Charles R. Erdman and Dr. William Carpenter of Princeton University, and Dr. Marshall Miller of Columbia University. This was how the *Paterson Morning Call* covered the contest:

> Benjamin M. Taub of Passaic has learned a few things from Hitler, but he intends to beat the dictator at his game. It all has to do with putting the accent on youth, getting youth to participate actively in the problems of today and the world of tomorrow.

> "Why there is so much brain power laying around dormant in high schools and colleges—taking dead subjects, like algebra, Latin, physics," Taub declared, indicating that he expected good, workable ideas to develop from student participation.[23]

An important change was also made in the structure of the organization. The county regional organization was replaced by a tripartite structure, consisting of northern, central, and southern zones, with a regional vice president in charge of each one. The goal was increased efficiency, as it would enable the gathering of larger regions than was previously possible.

Unfortunately, the new regional balance was reflected only in the appointments to the regional vice presidency (the northern region was represented by George Strong of Montclair, the southern region by Albert N. Molt of Camden, and the central region by Dr. Robert McKiernan of New Brunswick). The membership of the committees, and all officers and directors, remained exclusively northeastern. The active leadership also remained unchanged. Hosking gave up the presidency in April 1941 in order to create a democratic tradition within the organization and became its secretary. Villanueva served one year as president, then reverted to an active directorship. Taub was elected president in 1942 and remained at the helm until 1945.

Taub was truly a public citizen. He was also a man of boundless energy, who remained the chairman of the Passaic City Planning

Commission for twenty years and was hailed upon his retirement as the city's "first planner" and a man who made a "religion" of his work. Taub edited *The New Jersey Planner*, participated in numerous committees, publicized the Federation's activities as well as his own, and still found time to remain an active member of the New Jersey Bar Association and the Republican party.

Taub met with the executive secretary of the League and initiated the official participation of the Federation in the League's annual conference, which was held in November of each year. Gasoline rationing made it especially difficult to assemble people (the Federation had to cancel its annual meeting in April 1943). Even the League had to hold its conferences during the war in New York City's New Yorker Hotel instead of its traditional meeting place in Atlantic City. This participation opened up to the Federation a whole new audience of municipal government officials, who would not have bothered to come to a solely Federation assembly but did at times wander onto the panels run by the planning organization. Actually, the Federation's panels proved to be so popular that, by 1944, they were scheduled to take place in the Grand Ballroom of the New Yorker.

The Federation membership reflected the wide scope of activity engendered by the directors, as well as the improved quality and consistency of its newsletter (eight of them were published in 1942). The number of boards affiliated with the Federation increased from forty in 1941 to sixty-four by 1943.

National planning suffered a major blow in 1943. The National Resource Planning Board was abolished in such a way as would preclude its future reemergence. New Jersey was electing a new governor, and the State Planning Board was again in financial difficulties due to a lack of appropriations. As a result, only two *New Jersey Planners* were issued that year, and the state board did not hold a yearly conference. When conditions failed to improve by February of 1944, the directors decided on the following action:

> The matter of the State Planning Board was brought up and it was decided that in addition to the action already taken by President Taub the members should contact their legislators to request favorable action. The basis of the request to be the necessity of giving the State Board funds to set up a Planning

Advisory staff which can be used and which is so much needed by the local boards. Messrs. Currier and Paterson will cover Bergen County, Davis and Johnson, Essex, Rabkin, Union, and Taub, Passaic.[24]

The results were mixed. The new governor began a reorganization of the state government, and the State Planning Board became a bureau in the Division of Planning and Engineering (along with the Bureau of Rehabilitation and Housing and the Bureau of Public Works Reserve). The division was in the new State Department of Economic Development. However, despite the demotion of the State Planning Board in the governmental hierarchy, funds to encourage local planning were allocated.

The war was winding down and the state's apprehensions concerning postwar economic conditions were growing. Postwar planning assumed a new urgency due to the expectation that returning veterans were about to join the soon-to-be-displaced workers of the defense-related industries. Carpenter expressed the conventional wisdom:

> It is unlikely that the people of the United States will be willing to pay for the production of war goods beyond the time when these are required to defeat the enemy. Compulsory military service and the accoutrements of war may become a part of the political scenery in the United States, but nobody can believe that the American people will find this prospect pleasing. The people of the United States will have to do with war only what they are obliged.[25]

It became the new department's task to "determine what private industry contemplates and, with its own carefully listed and at all times up to date plans for a program of public works, to have a single coordinated program for the future development and improvement of the whole state."[26] A 1942 law enabled municipalities to set aside funds for future public works. So, in order to encourage adequate local planning for future capital expenditures, the legislature earmarked $500,000 to be shared equally by counties, municipalities, and school boards to help meet engineering and other planning costs by defraying one-half of the cost of preparing detailed plans and specifications for the proposed public works.

The Federation developed an excellent working relationship with the Department of Economic Development. The director of the Division of Planning and Engineering, William T. Vanderlipp, became a director of the organization, and the new department commissioner, Dr. Charles R. Erdman (a 1942 judge of the Federation's essay contest), was the guest speaker at the organization's 1944 fall conference. However, the days of jointly sponsored conferences and joint publications were over, and *The New Jersey Planner* ceased its publication in November 1943.

As the number of new planning boards increased, the Federation leadership felt that the new lay planners were in dire need of improved legal tools and educational opportunities in addition to adequate finances. Regrettably, the renewed attempt in 1943–44 to revise the state constitution ended in failure, though the work of the Federation's special committee on the new planning provision earned the praise of the legislators. Following this failure, the organization turned its attention to the amendment of the Planning and Zoning Enabling Acts, the preparation of model subdivision rules, and the development of a Model Building Code for the state (the latter in coordination with real estate boards and building inspectors). The Federation was justifiably delighted when the state's first Parkway Bill was signed in early 1945.

In order to provide the new lay planners with much-needed direction, the Federation ran two postwar clinics in 1943 and initiated roundtable forums at its conferences in 1944. The new format provided board members with the opportunity to discuss specific problems with planning experts, as well as fellow board members, and to receive practical help in dealing with their difficulties.

A Federation committee began to investigate the possibility of sponsoring a course for members of planning boards at Rutgers or Newark universities, and Currier was instructed to collect "data valuable to planning boards which would show them how to go about this job of planning."[27] The Federation was beginning to show its potential as a service organization.

In 1944, the *New Jersey Municipalities* published the following editorial:

ARE YOUR PLANS AND PROJECTS READY?

"New Jersey should not anticipate and should not desire a return to the subordination of the States by huge federal subventions as a means of financing the reconversion period." The State Commission on Post-War Economic Welfare makes this sound observation in its initial report to Governor Walter E. Edge and the legislature.

The program outlined will go far to avert the mistakes of the 1930 depression years. The public works portion of the report, which emphasizes that projects be necessary and useful, points the way for definite participation by municipalities.

Whatever the Federal and State Governments do, certain phases will remain for local treatment. The beneficial result to the municipality as a unit will be in direct proportion to the amount of time and effort invested in setting up a well thought out and coordinated program. The time is now. The preparation and plan are vitally important.[28]

Beyond the obvious yearning for the reassertion of state and local power after years of decline, there was fear and hope. Black said that the "biggest and most difficult fight will come after the last gun has fired. This fight will be on the field of depleted treasuries, diminished natural resources, threatened unemployment, and world unrest." Therefore, in order to assure that the country would not lose the peace after winning the war, the plans (besides providing stopgap employment) should be "directed towards stabilizing the peace through the years by minimizing chronic unemployment and removing some of the circumstances of present day living that engender social unrest and war."[29]

In the same vein, Taub, the Republican activist, published a two-part article in the *Passaic Herald News* translating the Bill of Rights "into modern terms applicable to the life of the United States" in the following way:

THE RIGHT TO WORK, usefully creatively through the productive years;

THE RIGHT TO FAIR PLAY, adequate to command the necessities and amenities of life in exchange for work, ideas, thrift, and other socially valuable services;

THE RIGHT TO ADEQUATE FOOD, CLOTHING, SHELTER, AND MEDICAL CARE;

THE RIGHT TO SECURITY, with freedom from fear of old age, dependency, sickness, unemployment, and accident.[30]

How could planners anticipate a Cold War following the hot one, the Marshall Plan, or American acceptance of continuous defense spending? In short, history was not repeated and prosperity, not recession, followed the war. Planners were proven wrong, as their warnings had been unwarranted. They therefore suffered the consequences:

By 1945, nearly three-fifths of the original 47 state planning agencies had unfortunately disappeared or were no longer recognizable as functioning planning agencies. When the post-war recession which many had anticipated did not come about, the special post-war planning and readjustment agencies which had been authorized in almost half of the states also were dissolved. Slowly at first but later with alarming rapidity, the principles of "development" pushed the "planning" functions of state government into the background. . . . States were now emphasizing industrial development rather than agricultural-economic development of the nineteenth century.[31]

The Federation did not escape the general trend. Though it still held one conference per year in 1945 and 1946 (as part of the League's conference) and published a single copy of *The New Jersey Planner* in 1946, the organization lost much of its vitality. In the prosperous aftermath of the war, zoning kept its popularity, but it was generally used as an instrument to prevent undesirable development and was not based on a comprehensive plan. Planning boards were mostly ignored and lacked the financial backing of the local authorities. The Federation had also lost many of its leaders. Some, like Andrew Faure and Henry Pond, moved to other states; others, like Farney, died; while yet others, like Taub and Hosking, simply curtailed their activity due to other obligations.

Sloane became the president of the Federation in November 1945 and watched the membership shrink to a measly twenty-one boards. The organization was at a point of crisis. It would have to be revitalized or it would simply wither and die.

Notes

1. Marcel Villanueva, "The Military Value of Planning," *New Jersey Municipalities* (November 1940):25.
2. Federation's Minutes, July 8, 1940, pp. 8–9.
3. Villanueva, *op. cit.*, p. 26.
4. Russell VanNest Black, "A Wasted Resource of Local Government," *New Jersey Municipalities* (March 1941):14.
5. *Ibid.*, p. 14.
6. *Ibid.*, p. 15.
7. *Ibid.*, p. 14.
8. Russell VanNest Black, "Urban Redevelopment—Principles and Procedures," *The New Jersey Planner* (February 1942):6.
9. Benjamin M. Taub, "Are City Planning Boards Necessary?" *The New Jersey Planner* (July 1941):1.
10. Carl H. Chatters, "Municipal Revenues Shift with Population," *New Jersey Municipalities* (May 1942):15.
11. Harry Hosking, "The Small House Problem," *New Jersey Municipalities* (March 1942):27.
12. "Defense Program for Cities Mapped," *New York Times*, October 12, 1941.
13. Marcel Villanueva, "Rehabilitation and Reconstruction," *The New Jersey Planner* (October 1941):2.
14. Russell VanNest Black, "The Planner and Post Defense Preparedness," *The New Jersey Planner* (September 1941):2.
15. "All Municipalities Require Planning Units, Taub Says," *Paterson Morning Call*, July 10, 1942.
16. "The Bureau of Urban Research—Princeton University," *The New Jersey Planner* (September 1941):6.
17. "Taub Elected President," *Paterson Morning Call*, April 20, 1942.
18. Dr. William Carpenter, "Post-War Planning," *The New Jersey Planner* (November 1942):3.

19. Marcel Villanueva, "A Message," *The New Jersey Planner* (February 1942):2.

20. Marcel Villanueva, "The Housing Situation," *The New Jersey Planner* (August 1942):3–4.

21. Stuart D. Currier, "Function of a Planning Board in the War Period," *The New Jersey Planner* (November 1942):7.

22. "Annual Conference," *The New Jersey Planner* (May 1942):2–3.

23. "Accent on Youth," *Paterson Morning Call*, October 9, 1942.

24. Federation's Minutes, February 17, 1944, p. 1.

25. Carpenter, *op. cit.*, p. 4.

26. Paul G. Tomlinson, "Post-War Planning in New Jersey," *New Jersey Municipalities* (October 1944):22.

27. Federation's Minutes, February 17, 1944, p. 1.

28. "As We See It," *New Jersey Municipalities* (August 1944):3.

29. Russell VanNest Black, "Planning Post-War Capital Improvements," *The New Jersey Planner* (April 1943):2.

30. Benjamin M. Taub, "Post-War Planning," *Passaic Herald News*, June 18, 1943.

31. Alan W. Steiss, "Three Decades of State Planning," *Jersey Plans*, vol. XI, no. 3 (1960):11.

4

Which Way to Turn?

The attempts to rejuvenate the organization commenced on Thursday evening, February 20, 1947, at 8 P.M. A general meeting of the New Jersey Federation of Official Planning Boards was held at the Robert Treat Hotel in Newark. In attendance were nine members of the organization, including its vice president, Sam Rabkin, and two of its longtime directors, A. Thornton Bishop and William McDowell. Following a broad discussion of the responsibilities of the Federation, the group elected the organization's officers for 1947, with Rabkin being chosen president.

The next meeting took place a month later. It was to have been a conference with state planners concerning future relations between the two organizations, but, curiously enough, members of the press were also invited. The need for the reactivation of the Federation was discussed, and a future plan of action was delineated. It is impossible not to compare this revitalization meeting of ten individuals and a handful of newsmen to the 1938 foundation meeting of the Federation and to realize how much the original enthusiasm for planning had waned. So the following questions come to mind: Who needed such an organization? What would be its nature? Who would lead it? Some of the answers to these questions would not be found for seven years, as it was not until the mid-fifties that the nature of the organization took final shape. As will be demonstrated, it was not necessarily the shape envisioned by at least some of the people who attended the 1947 Newark meeting.

Rabkin directed his opening statement to the first two questions: "The Federation had become less active in recent years, but that many planning boards throughout the state had expressed a desire to have the Federation re-activated because they feel there is a definite need for the organization as a clearing house for planning information, and an interchange of ideas and opinions."[1] Henry Atkinson of Alpine further elaborated:

> I represent a community that is large in area, but small in population, and, therefore, is unable to undertake a major planning problem because of the cost involved. I feel that an organization such as the Federation can build up a spirit of co-operation between the planning boards of the state to a point where an Advisory Bureau can be established, through which the planning problems of smaller and poorer municipalities can be cleared.[2]

By 1947, New Jersey had 7 county planning boards, 171 municipal planning boards, and 256 zoned municipalities.[3] This newfound enthusiasm for planning was the result of localities recognizing that planning offered them powerful tools for the active control of their own future. Unfortunately, much of the planning activity was rather amateurish since neither the necessary expertise nor the means to attain it were within the easy reach of many localities. There were few professionally trained planners, and their services were far too expensive for the smaller communities. Would it be possible for the Federation to offer some help?

While a town like Alpine probably wished to maintain its identity by fending off unwanted development, cities like Newark had quite a different problem. Once World War II ended and the country's economic life no longer needed to be controlled by a powerful central government, a sigh of relief was heard throughout the land. The rigidly suppressed civilian consumption of the war years created large savings accounts and a pent-up desire for consumer goods (cars and houses led the way), which in turn fueled a long period of economic growth and prosperity. The availability of federally insured mortgages and the increase in highway construction resulted in a suburban housing boom and industrial decentralization that in turn caused traffic congestion and further deterioration of older urban centers. Leslie Williams, a city planner, delivered the following address before a joint meeting of the League and the Federation on November 14, 1947:

> Housing and highways, designed in a vacuum, unrelated to each other or to plans for the communities they are to serve, will aggravate uncontrolled decentralization—bad for cities, suburbs and the surrounding countryside.

> Unless effective steps are taken to consciously guide urban growth along sound lines before the forthcoming housing and highway building booms reach their full tempo, our cities will be destroyed as effectively from within as bombing destroyed the cities of Europe and Asia.[4]

At the heart of the matter was the ruthless competition that commenced once the need for the marshaling of all resources to a common cause ended. It was a competition between states, regions, and localities to secure as large a share of the economic pie as possible. Such an open economic warfare required the gathering of all available resources and an adequate plan of attack. The Department of Economic Development led the way. In 1946, it organized the New Jersey Land Use Advisory Commission, whose members came from various institutions and organizations concerned with the physical development of the state, such as banks, utilities, and railroads.

The committee's first assignment was to study industry because, insisted its chairman: "There is little sense in discussing commercial and residential progress until the pattern of industry is established. Both follow from industrial trends."[5] His executive director added that not all development was desirable, only "types of industry that will round out the community picture and be best adapted to its resources, physical and human."[6] Although advertising was essential, since "other districts were telling their stories dramatically and effectively, sparing no expense,"[7] planning had to come first.

Planning was not only necessary to determine the optimum areas suited for various types of development but was also vital for the successful wooing of desired industry.

Building or relocating a major industrial plant entailed a large investment. A company had to be secure in the knowledge that it had taken into account all the major variables of the area to which it committed itself. T. Ledyard Blakeman, chief of the Bureau of Planning, told the following story:

> I know of an industry in one of our central Jersey communities which selected a site very carefully with relation to existing highways only to have a new highway run right through the plant grounds with a resulting loss to them in efficiency of plant operation and a considerable cost to the Highway Department than would have been necessary had they known of this projected highway before it was built.[8]

A preponderance of such incidents would obviously have destroyed the state's reputation within industrial circles.

It so happened that the needs of state development corresponded to both the ideological and bureaucratic needs of the state planners. The State Planning Section was searching for a new role to take the place of its previous assignment as the coordinator of postwar planning. Also, throughout its existence, the State Planning Section had been gathering information in the hope of devising a state master plan. Such a tentative plan was completed in 1947, and close contact with local planners was required for the plan to have any chance of becoming realized. Local planning input was needed to finalize the plan, as well as to secure the necessary political backing of local government.

In addition, planners and industrialists had some new ideas to sell. Many suburban townships were wary of industry or airports. Convincing residents that a factory could be beneficial to their community entailed teaching local planners some new ways of zoning land. Basically, planners and industrialists agreed the key to happy cohabitation between residential and manufacturing areas lay in the complete separation between the two. Traditionally, zoning was based on incremental restriction of use. Thus, a residential area would only include homes while a commercial zone could also include residences; an industrial zone was usable for any purpose. "Such a set up," claimed Evan Spalt, longtime Federation director and then a young executive of Ortho-Pharmaceutical Corporation, "included a built-in disappointment for all involved since the activity which inevitably surrounds an industrial plant (such as noise, pollution or commercial traffic) is not conducive to a satisfactory quality of life and causes unavoidable clashes between the plant management and the surrounding residents."[9] A well-designed industrial park would give the plant management room to expand, as well as protect the quality of the community's residential area. The same logic had to be applied to airports.

Thus, a federation of planning boards could serve the needs of (1) lay planners as a clearinghouse for information and possibly as a source of technical information; (2) cities as a center for political support for regional planning and urban redevelopment; (3) state planners for political support, as well as a provider of a forum in which planners could present their ideas; and (4) commercial and industrial interests that required the presentation of their case to local planners.

As the Federation directors met with the state planners to discuss a revitalization plan for the organization, it became clear that another postwar reality had to be taken into account. States and municipalities were reasserting their political independence following years of subservience to the federal government during the depression and the war. In New Jersey, there was a resurgence of the movement to rewrite the state constitution in a way that would strengthen the state government by streamlining its operations and giving greater power to its chief executive. Governor Alfred E. Driscoll remarked: "We sought a new constitution so that New Jersey could become a more effective member of our republic, so that we could help to restore in this nation of ours the federal system."[10] In order to secure the consent of the governed, municipalities had to be assured that the governor's gain would not be their loss. Thus, the governor continued: "One of the significant things about this new constitution of ours is that it reaffirms our faith in home rule."[11]

Obviously, the symbiotic relationship that characterized the Federation's relations with the old State Planning Board would not be acceptable in this new period of municipal assertiveness. A memorandum from Robert Burlingham to his chief, Blakeman, categorically stated: "A state-wide organization, representing local planning effort would be more effective if it functioned independently of state government."[12] Though a permanent seat on the Federation's board of directors was reserved for a representative of the state, any suggestion of the renewal of the tradition of a joint publication was dismissed, and the organization directors proudly declared:

> Note that The Federation Planner is not jointly sponsored by Ecodevelopment. That state department now publishes its own bi-monthly, *New Jersey Plans*. We feel this enables us to be freer and more frank in constructive criticism of local and state planning efforts.[13]

This was rather unfortunate as the Federation, with the exception of its first year of reactivation, was not able to sustain an independent publication until the early sixties.

Other parts of the rejuvenation program included regular monthly board meetings open to all members, which might end with a discussion of any individual planning problem affecting a state community. The minutes of the meetings would be sent to all member boards. In addition, the Federation was to hold a series of regional meetings to deal with problems of concern to particular areas. Since no copies of the original organization's constitution or bylaws were to be found, new ones were written opening the Federation's membership to civic organizations and individuals (though the latter did not have voting rights). Annual membership fees ranged from $15 to $25, depending on the size of the community's population, and officers (president, vice president, treasurer, secretary, and nine directors) would be elected for one-year terms at an annual May meeting. Later on, in 1950, the position of associate director was added for an individual who by reason of his or her background or training could be of definite use to the organization but who was unable to attend regular

THE FEDERATION PLANNER

To Promote Public Interest in PLANNING and Coordination of PLANNING BOARDS in New Jersey

Volume 1 Number 5	PATERSON, NEW JERSEY	November 1947

Published by
**NEW JERSEY
FEDERATION OF
OFFICIAL
PLANNING BOARDS**
Room 300
County Administration Bldg.
Paterson, N.J.
DONALD J. IRVING, Editor

OFFICERS
President
SAMUEL RABKIN
#10 The Village
Union
Vice-President
GEORGE E. DAVIS
28 Ridgewood Avenue
Irvington
Treasurer
WILLIAM G. McDOWELL
152 North Avenue
Plainfield
Secretary
JOHN R. BURNETT
Room 2800
Raymond-Commerce Bldg.
Newark

DIRECTORS
HARRY HOSKING
Livingston
MARCEL VILLANUEVA
Orange
BENJAMIN M. TAUB
Passaic
JOHN E. SLOANE
West Orange
A. THORNTON BISHOP
Teaneck
WILLIAM T. VANDERLIPP
N.J. Dept. of Economic
Development
R.D. PATTERSON
Haworth
ROBERT J.B. FLEMING
Clifton
PROF. EDWARD B. WILKENS
Rutgers University
HENRY G. ATKINSON
Alpine

board meetings or was ineligible for directorship due to lack of membership in an official planning board.

Prominent among the new Federation leadership were John Burnett and Mariano Rinaldi, Newark Central Planning Board members and future presidents of the organization in whose offices many Federation board meetings were held; Harold Buttenheim, the editor of *American City* magazine; Harry Alexander, the man responsible for Newark's new master plan; C. McKim Norton, the executive vice president of the Regional Plan Association (RPA); and, last but not least, Dr. Edward B. Wilkens, a Rutgers planning professor. Beside volunteering his own time and energy to the Federation's activities, Wilkens was instrumental in recruiting into the Federation talented young business executives, as well as in initiating programs for the training of professional and lay planners.

The first pressing item on the organization's agenda was the soon-to-be-convened 1947 constitutional convention. The Federation immediately organized a special committee, chaired by Buttenheim, which included such old activists as Sloane and Biro, along with new faces like Burnett, Wilkens, and Blakeman. To the old demands for making constitutional the zoning of land and large-scale urban renewal were added demands for the protection and conservation of state-owned lands and rights of way from deleterious uses of abutting property; for zoning intended to conserve natural beauty and structures of historical significance; and for provisions for low-rent housing.

The proposed constitutional amendments[14] were mailed to each delegate to the convention, and further personal contacts were initiated by the directors. Also undertaken was an organized writing campaign of the Federation's membership. The results were rather impressive, as a side-by-side comparison is sure to illuminate. It is important to note that previous attempts to strengthen county planning boards by allowing them to approve subdivisions in townships without master plans were not repeated nor was there a dedication of highway funds that planners had been advocating for years. The League successfully opposed those demands as infringing on home rule, and the support of home-rule proponents was crucial to the passage of the new constitution. Still, from this constitution forward, the

JERSEY PLANNERS

C. McKIM NORTON
EXECUTIVE VICE-PRESIDENT
REGIONAL PLAN ASSOCIATION

AN ATTORNEY BY PROFESSION AND A YACHTSMAN BY AVOCATION, EDUCATED AT GROTON AND HARVARD WHERE HE ROWED ON 1929 VARSITY CREW. ATTORNEY FOR NATIONAL RESOURCES PLANNING BOARD WHICH LED TO HIS INTEREST IN THE REGIONAL PLAN ASSOCIATION SERVING THE NEW YORK – NEW JERSEY – CONNECTICUT AREA.

C. McKIM NORTON

EXECUTIVE VICE-PRESIDENT AND BOARD OF DIRECTORS MEMBER OF REGIONAL PLAN ASSOCIATION, INC. SINCE 1940. CITY AND REGIONAL PLANNING STUDIED IN WORLD TRAVELS. SAILED FROM NEW YORK TO SPAIN IN AN OCEAN RACE IN THE WINNING SCHOONER "NINA" IN 1928. FORMER CHM., PRINCETON PL. BD.

-GARRITY-

1943 TO 1945 SERVED ON ACTIVE DUTY IN SOUTH PACIFIC AS NAVIGATOR OF LANDING CRAFT COMPANY IN U.S. ARMY AMPHIBIAN ENGINEERS IN NEW GUINEA.

BOARD OF DIRECTORS OF AMERICAN SOCIETY OF PLANNING OFFICIALS, THE AMERICAN INSTITUTE OF PLANNERS AND THE CITIZENS HOUSING COUNCIL.

JERSEY PLANNERS

DOCTOR EDWARD B. WILKENS
of
NEW BRUNSWICK

RECEIVED DEGREES IN ARCHITECTURE FROM COLUMBIA UNIVERSITY WHERE HE ROWED WITH THE CREW. HAS A "DOTTORE IN ARCHITETTURA" FROM THE UNIVERSITY OF ROME.

MEMBER OF THE NEW BRUNSWICK CITY ZONING BOARD AND AUTHOR OF THE PUBLIC ADMINISTRATION SERVICE BOOKLET "MAPPING FOR PLANNING".

WAS THE FIRST DIRECTOR OF THE MIDDLESEX COUNTY PLANNING BOARD – PREVIOUS PLANNING EXPERIENCE IN HENRICO COUNTY, VIRGINIA; NUTLEY, N.J.; PHOENIX, ARIZONA AND BUFFALO, N.Y.

KNOWN TO EVERYONE AS "DOC"

PROFESSOR OF REGIONAL PLANNING AND DIRECTOR OF SPECIAL SERVICES AT RUTGERS UNIVERSITY.

FOR A HOBBY HE COLLECTS RARE PHONOGRAPH RECORDS – HAS ALMOST A TON OF THEM. TOOK PART IN ROMAN CITY EXCAVATIONS AT LEPTIS MAGNA.

FEDERATION
PROPOSED CONSTITUTION

At its final meeting April 24th, the Federation's Special Committee for State Constitution Revision recommended to the Federation the following "proposed Sections for New Jersey Constitution." Chairman of the committee was Mr. Harold J. Buttenheim of Madison.

ZONING

The Legislature may enact general laws under which municipalities, other than counties, may limit and restrict to specified districts and regulate therein buildings and structures according to their construction and the nature and extent of their use, and the nature and extent of the uses of land. Such general laws shall be deemed to be within the police power of the State.

SIGHTLINESS, ORDER AND HISTORIC ASSOCIATIONS

The natural beauty, historic associations, sightliness and physical good order of the State and its parts contribute to the general welfare, and legislation may be enacted for the conservation and enhancement thereof as a part of the patrimony of the people.

PROTECTION OF PUBLIC INTEREST IN PUBLIC PROPERTY

The State or any agency or political subdivision thereof which is empowered to take or otherwise acquire private property for any public purpose or public use may be authorized by law to take or otherwise acquire the fee or any easement or rights therein, and may be authorized by law to take or otherwise acquire a fee or rights in, easements upon, or the benefit of restrictions upon, abutting property to preserve and protect the public interest therein. No such taking shall be without just compensation. When the fee is acquired for property in excess of that needed for direct public use, such excess may be sold or leased, with restrictions for the preservation and protection of the public interest therein.

ERECTION OF STRUCTURES IN THE PROPOSED LOCATION OF STREETS
OR OTHER PUBLIC WAYS OR PLACES

The Legislature may authorize municipal corporations to adopt an official map showing the location of the public streets and other public ways or places which it is intended to establish in the future, and no compensation shall be paid for any building or structure erected in such location after the adoption of such map.

LOW-RENT HOUSING

The Legislature may provide, in such manner, by such means and upon such terms and conditions as it may prescribe, for low-rent housing for persons of low income as defined by law, and for recreational and other facilities incidental or appurtenant thereto.

PRESENT CONSTITUTION

Article IV Sec. VI-2: The Legislature may enact general laws under which municipalities, other than counties, may adopt zoning ordinances limiting and restricting to specified districts and regulating therein, buildings and structures, according to their construction, and the nature and extent of their use, and the nature and extent of the uses of land, and the exercise of such authority shall be deemed to be within the police power of the State. Such laws shall be subject to repeal or alteration by the Legislature.

Article IV Sec. VI-3: Any agency or political subdivision of the State or any agency of a political subdivision thereof, which may be empowered to take or otherwise acquire private property for any public highway, parkway, airport, place, improvement, or use, may be authorized by law to take or otherwise acquire a fee simple absolute or any lesser interest, and may be authorized by law to take or otherwise acquire a fee simple absolute in easements upon, or the benefit of restrictions upon, abutting property to preserve and protect the public highway, parkway, airport, place, improvement, or use; but such taking shall be with just compensation.

PROPOSED CONSTITUTION (continued)

SLUM AND BLIGHT ELIMINATION

The acquisition and assembly of real property to facilitate the development or redevelopment of a wholly or partly substandard, deteriorated, abandoned, or insanitary area in accordance with an official adopted master plan, whether the uses to which such area is to be devoted (according to the plan), be either public uses or private uses or both, is hereby declared to be for public uses. The Legislature shall make laws governing the acquisition, use, and disposal of such property by an agency of the state or a political subdivision thereof.

REDEVELOPMENT CORPORATIONS OR AUTHORITIES

The Legislature may authorize the organization of corporations or authorities to undertake the development or redevelopment of wholly or partially substandard, abandoned, deteriorated, or insanitary areas, and may authorize municipalities to exempt their improvements from taxation, in whole or in part, for a limited period of time, under conditions as to special public regulation to be specified by law or by contract between any such corporation or authority and the municipality provided that, during the period of such tax exemption, the profits of any corporation and the dividends paid by it shall be limited by law.

PRESENT CONSTITUTION (continued)

Article VIII Sec. III-1: The clearance, replanning, development or redevelopment of blighted areas shall be a public purpose and public use, for which private property may be taken or acquired. Municipal, public or private corporations may be authorized by law to undertake such clearance, replanning, development or redevelopment; and improvements made for these purposes and uses, or for any of them, may be exempted from taxation, in whole or in part, for a limited period of time during which the profits of and dividends payable by any private corporation enjoying such tax exemption shall be limited by law. The conditions of use, ownership, management and control of such improvements shall be regulated by law.

Federation would be intimately involved in formulating all legislation related to planning.

In New Jersey, home rule meant political independence for municipalities, including the control of basic and expensive functions (such as education, general relief, and highways) along with a limited ability to raise funds. A locality had three sources of income: (1) property taxes, which were by far the primary source of funds; (2) the local share of seven tax levies (for example, on public utilities, railroads, or transfer of inheritance), which the state collected but shared with localities mostly according to the location of the tax base; and (3) conditional state grants given for stated purposes, based on need but often requiring matching funds.[15] Such a system benefited communities that were already developed but left cities (with a shrinking tax base as a result of the growing exodus of industry and wealthy individuals) and the newly developing suburbs (with the ever-rising demands for services) in a financial bind. While some cities were still able to marshal the resources necessary to pay for competent planning advice, developing municipalities simply could not afford the expense.

While the Federation's leadership recognized the needs of the smaller communities, it also heeded Williams's warning: "We seem faced with a choice: Continue our piecemeal and negative approach of applying palliatives and prohibitives or take a positive approach of consciously guiding the development of the entire city and suburban areas as a unit."[16] Thus, when the directors were asked for their opinion of the appropriate program for an RPA conference, they recommended that "top priority should be given to a discussion of the gradual elimination of county and municipal lines in favor of modern integral areas."[17]

After an exhaustive study of the state's planning needs, the Federation finally came up with an ingenious plan intended to solve the financial problems of developing municipalities, as well as to ensure better interlocal planning coordination. The Federation called for the establishment of regional planning advisory staffs that would provide industrial municipalities with basic planning data, along with specialized studies on a pro-rata cost basis. These technical staffs would be financed by the state (at least during the early phases of their operations) and its local membership (which would be voluntary):

> The primary objective of the Regional Staff set-up is to meet the planning needs of all the various political subdivisions within the state, thereby making it possible to substantially reduce the cost to any individual governmental agency of having prepared current and comprehensive plans. This scheme provides that all plans be coordinated one with the other, into a Regional and State plan, which is sadly lacking under present conditions and accounts for the many towns and city plans within the State which have no relationship to conditions beyond the immediate corporate limits.[18]

While such sentiments would appear blasphemous in the home-rule State of New Jersey, it is interesting to note that the plan enjoyed the enthusiastic support not only of the state planners but also of the League. During its annual 1950 conference, the League passed the following resolution:

> RESOLVED, by the New Jersey State League of Municipalities that the plan recommended by the New Jersey Federation of Planning Boards for the establishment by the state, on a regional basis, as outlined hereto, providing technical advisory staffs for the purpose of making available advisory consulting services to all political subdivisions within the state of New Jersey and any other member bodies, be, and the same is hereby approved; and be it further

> RESOLVED, that a copy of this resolution and of the annexed plan be forwarded to Hon. Alfred E. Driscoll, Governor, to Hon. Charles R. Erdman, Jr., Commissioner of the New Jersey Department of Conservation and Economic Development, to Hon. William T. Vanderlipp, Director of the Division of Planning and Development, and to each Senator and Assemblyman of the State of New Jersey.[19]

From 1950–52, the Federation tried to get its plan implemented, believing that it was just a matter of time before the needs of the municipalities would have to be acknowledged. No wonder the organization rejected the suggestion of the state director of planning and development to forego the regional approach and replace it with an enlarged state planning office that would provide directly the necessary help (the state planners could have used the assignment). Instead, it passed a resolution to remain faithful to its original purpose and to endeavor to effectuate the program by enlightening the local planning boards as to its objectives and by securing their support for its implementation.

These were difficult years for the Federation. Planning was considered too expensive and too slow a tool for effective community control; zoning seemed much simpler and quicker a medicine. Russell VanNest Black published during the summer of 1951 an article called "Why So Much Zoning and So Little Planning."[20] The Federation's directors reported that zoning panels were much better attended than discussions on planning in general. In addition, state planning seemed to be in as poor a shape as local planning.

New Jersey was going through a period of austerity (these were the years of the Korean War), and the state planning unit, having been demoted from a bureau to a section in 1948, was not only in a lonely bureaucratic position but also in a desperate financial one. Nothing demonstrated its budgetary constraints more than the events of 1951. That year, under the dynamic leadership of Herbert H. Smith, the first state plan was finally published. Its proposals included the construction of the Garden State Parkway, the New Jersey Turnpike, and the Round Valley Reservoir site, as well as the acquisition of the Wharton and the Worthington tracts and the development of Island Beach as a state park (these proposals were adopted despite the planning section's apparent weakness).[21] The state planners were anxious to present their plan at a statewide conference. However, it was impossible for the planning section to assume responsibility for any deficits that might occur. The Federation was asked to cosponsor the conference, that is, promise to underwrite any such deficit. The Federation consented and was gratified when the conference, which was attended by the governor and many members of the state legislature, turned out to be a great success. The Federation continued its efforts on behalf of state and regional planning but with little success. Burnett expressed the board's frustration: "We are getting the runaround on any recommendation we make to the governor or the state on behalf of planning. There have been so many excuses for not endorsing our proposals, that they are becoming contradictory."[22] The leadership embarked on a membership drive in order to increase its political clout.

By November 1952, the Federation came to believe that "unless something is done immediately to provide aid and guidance to the planning boards that are anxious to serve their municipalities and be effective within their areas of operation, planning within the state will be at a standstill, and the reputation of planning suffer considerably."[23] Therefore, the leadership agreed to retreat from its previous position. While affirming the establishment of regional staffs as its ultimate goal, it recommended sufficient appropriation for the state planning section to enable it to give adequate technical aid to planning boards within the state.

"What were the problems of planning that confronted us? We found planning in a paradoxical situation in that the courts gave liberal aid by judicial determinations, while the Legislature attempted to negate the progressive plans adopted by many New Jersey communities."[24] Harry Bernstein, a municipal attorney and a new Federation activist, was referring to a series of court decisions favorable to municipal zoning that culminated in the case of *Lionshead Lake* versus *Wayne Township*, in which the State Supreme Court upheld the right of a municipality to establish a minimum dwelling size. The courts, accepting the fiscal realities of municipalities and operating in a home-rule atmosphere, granted communities the power to pass ordinances "reasonably designed, by whatever means, to further the advancement of a community as a social, economic and political unit."[25] The legislature was less hostile than inconsistent. In 1951, after twenty years of only minor tinkering with the Municipal Planning Act (which was passed as Chapter 235 of the Public Laws of 1930), the lawmakers turned their attention to the new hot topic of subdivision control. They adopted an amendment to the act that included a penalty clause of far-reaching consequences. The new provision permitted the setting aside of illegal transfers of lots and placing of a lien on the entire property from which the subdivision was created any time within a two-year period.

Any division of land into two or more lots was considered a subdivision, and almost all land sales resulted in a title question. Furthermore, no one knew whether the penalty provision applied to all communities or only to those with a planning board.

Planners, while thrilled by the acceptance of their principles, were apprehensive. Smith represented their thinking in his editorial response to the court's ruling:

> Our Municipalities have been granted broad powers by our Constitution and our Legislature. . . . We are now crossing into what might be referred to as the "twilight zone" of zoning in that we are touching deeply into the question of individual rights. An abuse of this trust that has been given to our municipalities can result in a serious setback to zoning and possibly a reversal of our legislative thinking. No one wants to return to the days that zoning was being declared unconstitutional in New Jersey. Neither do we want to go on and find our communities busily engaged in the pursuit of "snob zoning" with little justification for their ordinances other than the desire to "keep certain people out."
>
> Zoning in New Jersey has been handed a "hydrogen bomb." Just as is the case with the real bomb, it must be handled with care by properly trained and instructed people or it can destroy its creators and many others with it.[26]

Subdivision control was second only to zoning in its importance to planners. In October 1952, in the case of the *City of Rahway* versus *Raritan Homes Inc.*, the Superior Court held that municipalities could control subdivisions only if they have a planning board. So, municipalities were appointing planning boards, and the latter were using powerful planning tools, just as planning enthusiasts had always hoped. Unfortunately, these new planning boards were inexperienced and at times arbitrary in their actions. Professional help was expensive and scarce (only in 1951 did Rutgers University start offering planning as an undergraduate option). The planning laws were vague, had contradictory elements, and did not require established standards to be followed by the planning boards. No wonder the Federation leadership was worried.

Sure enough, during the 1952 session of the legislature, three separate antiplanning bills were introduced, and one of them passed by an overwhelming majority in both houses despite the strong opposition voiced by the League, the Institute of Municipal Attorneys, and the Federation. This particular bill would have enabled developers to bypass all subdivision controls and thus would have practically eliminated meaningful planning in New Jersey. The planning community was appalled. It pleaded with Governor Driscoll to veto the bill. The governor agreed but not before he made sure that he would not be put in a similar position in the future. Fred G. Stickel III remembers: "I made a promise to the Governor as President of the New Jersey Institute of Municipal Attorneys and with the assistance of Carl Erdman, my former Professor of Political Science at Princeton who was then serving as Commissioner of Economic Development as well as Herbert Smith who was State Planning Director, that I would form a committee of all parties interested in planning whether pro or con and try to hammer out a realistic bill."[27]

Actually, since 1951, a Federation committee consisting of Wilkens, Norton, and Robert Edwards had been studying the needed legislative revisions in the planning law, as was a committee of the Institute of Municipal Attorneys. The two committees merged and were later joined by the municipal engineers. This group prepared a bill that was later amended by a supercommittee that included building and real estate interests. The result was a compromise bill that did not satisfy everyone but enjoyed the support of all the organizations that participated in its formulation. Smith wrote: "During the sessions of the legislature our work on the Legislative Committee paid dividends, for each of the groups lent full support. Both the Real Estate Association and the Home Builders did a great service in assisting with support for the passage of the bill, with Mr. Stickel leading the battle for all of the group."[28]

The bill clarified the relationship of planning boards to municipal bodies, provided firmer legal control of subdivisions, redefined the scope and aims of master plans, clarified the purpose of an official map, added new definitions to the planning statutes, detailed the procedures and standards to be used by the planning boards (which

Governor Driscoll signs the new planning legislation. Seated, left to right: Alexander Feinberg, Counsel, New Jersey Home Builders Association; Governor Driscoll; Fred G. Stickel III, President, New Jersey Institute of Municipal Attorneys, and Harry Bernstein, Legislative Chairman of the Institute.

Standing, left to right: Herbert H. Smith, Chief, State Planning Section; Mariano J. Rinaldi, President, New Jersey Federation of Official Planning Boards; C. McKim Norton, Vice-president, Regional Plan Association, Inc.; Warren Evoy, Counsel, N.J.H.B.A.; I. Russell Riker, New Jersey Municipal Engineers Association; Bruce M. Larrabee, Society of Professional Engineers; Robert Scott, President, New Jersey Real Estate Association; Herbert Campbell, N.J.M.E.A.; John Wright, Executive Director, N.J.H.B.A.; Charles R. Erdman, Jr., Commissioner, State Department of Conservation and Economic Development; Raymond E. Hanly, N.J.H.B.A.; and Mrs. Madeleine S. Frost, Assistant Director, New Jersey League of Municipalities. Ten members of the Committee were unable to be present at the signing.

were made automatically into zoning commissions), and, last but not least, was an entirely permissive home-rule bill. Municipalities were not required to have planning at all or could have as much as they wanted, and planning boards could be as strong or weak as individual local governments wished. Furthermore, local government always had the final say, and the delegation of legislative authority to boards had been avoided. The *Newark Evening News* explained the importance of the bill to municipalities:

> The law thus enhances municipal home rule, which has been clouded by a succession of ambiguous amendments to the present 19 year old statute. Most interpretations of the law held that planning boards created by municipal ordinance automatically possess all powers granted such boards by the state.
>
> Paradoxically, planning experts see in the opportunity offered municipalities to set up weak planning boards under strong local control, a way to set off a movement for more state planning and development at local levels.[29]

The Federation viewed the passage of the bill with great satisfaction. Although the Federation had only one official representative (its president, Rinaldi) on the committee, at least five other Federation directors representing other organizations participated in the drafting of the legislation. In addition, the Federation established close working relations with sister organizations, especially those of the municipal attorneys and engineers. These three affiliates of the League ran joint convention panels in Atlantic City, prepared model ordinances, and became allies in subsequent legislative battles. Some of the engineers (such as Russell Riker) and even more attorneys (such as Stickel and Bernstein) became active members of the Federation. The growing involvement of lawyers with the organization is not at all surprising since the formulation and the exposition of the planning law became a major function of the Federation following the passage of the 1953 bill.

Local planning in New Jersey was thriving: Between 1949 and 1954, the number of zoning ordinances grew to 371, the number of planning boards reached 320, the number of municipalities exercising subdivision control rose from 115 to 249, and the number of completed master plans increased from 20 to 119.[30] As the editorial of *Jersey Plans* claimed: "The basic principles of municipal planning are now on firm legal grounds and are accepted as a normal function and a service to be rendered to the citizens of our communities."[31]

Still, more than just a few flies remained in the ointment, as John B. Moore's story clearly demonstrates:

> I would like to cite the case of a community planning board, call it "x". It is a rural municipality, approximately 95 square miles, with 2500 citizens. They have a planning board and a subdivision control ordinance. Builders are currently moving into that municipality, building between 100 and 200 homes at a time.
>
> They had no tax map, no base maps. The subdivision plat under consideration involved a lake; the planning board had no topographic information. . . . In this particular "municipality x" their municipal attorney lives 15 miles away in another municipality and can only get down perhaps once a month to see them.
>
> Can the county be of assistance? . . . In this particular "county x" there is no county planning board. . . . Can the State do something to help these municipalities? Well, I started out by saying that there are only three of us down there and the state planners are hard-pressed to keep going as it is.[32]

Clearly, the central issues of technical planning assistance to small communities, the inadequacy of state planning, and the lack of regional coordination of local plans remained unsolved. The governor's signature on the new bill had hardly dried before the sound of saber-rattling between planners and developers was renewed. The controversy centered on the question of who should bear the cost of new development, that is, would it be possible to build moderate-income and low-income housing in the suburbs if municipalities retain the right to practice subdivision regulation and control?

In November 1954, the *American Municipal News* reported the creation of a special committee of the National Association of Home Builders aimed at convincing state legislatures "that responsibility for public education and the provision of community facilities belongs to the entire community." Therefore, municipalities should lose the right to place "restrictive tax and zoning regulations on new construction which boost the cost of new housing to the home buyer and hamper building expansion."[33]

In New Jersey, the nonconfrontational methodology adopted in the formulation of the 1953 planning bill proved its value. When the Federation called a special meeting to deal with the perceived threat to the planning legislation, its directors were greatly reassured by the resolution passed by the New Jersey chapter of the Home Builders Association. The resolution reaffirmed the builders' support of the new planning act, which they had helped to write.

Nevertheless, all was not rosy. The Jersey builders were far from satisfied. Their president, in his keynote address to their 1954 convention, made the following statement:

> This convention will see the greatest mobilization of Home Builders ever to take place in the State of New Jersey, meeting en masse on Saturday to wage a vigorous fight against the ruthless, arbitrary action exercised by local municipalities in their function of planning, zoning and the establishment of subdivision regulation.
>
> This action has practically stopped the building of houses under $14,000.
>
> It has already created a dangerous and serious housing shortage for a large segment of New Jersey's citizens.
>
> We, as builder, cannot stand by and allow snob zoning by local planning boards and municipal bodies to deprive our best citizens of the privilege of owning their own home, regardless of size.[34]

These were not empty threats. A new avalanche of antiplanning bills started to be introduced in the legislature. The Federation directors readily acknowledged that some laws and procedures still needed ironing out, and they were prepared to help write the necessary amendments. However, the leadership also believed that without adequate technical advice and assistance, planning boards were abusing their newly acquired powers and consequently were jeopardizing the hard-fought gains of the planning community.

The directors did not want to realize that the problems were the outcome of a serious clash of diverging interests. They continued to assume that planning was a science and that difficulties were the result of its misapplication. Therefore, as a stopgap measure, the Federation considered the establishment of an arbitration board for the purpose of reviewing and settling differences between municipalities and developers on subdivision applications. President William A. Sutherland suggested the idea to the representative of the home builders, and the latter not only accepted but offered to promote it in the hope that some workable plan could be devised by the Federation.

The establishment of an arbitration board might have had an effect similar to that of the previously suggested regional technical planning centers in that it would have had to base its judgments on some acceptable regional standards. Ironically, it was the indefatigable proponent of regional planning, Norton, who articulated the practical difficulties inherent in the arbitration proposal. In a letter sent to the directors, he wrote:

> Different municipalities set different standards of subdivision and development. This is an essential element of local home rule. To come as a volunteer peacemaker between a local planning board or the governing body of a municipality with high standards and a developer with lower standards is an untenable position.
>
> I wonder if a local planning board with full subdivision powers could contract to stand behind the decision of an arbitration board. The planning board's powers stem from a legislative act by the local governing body. Lacking an amendment to the subdivision regulation law, can the board vary its terms?[35]

The Federation's leadership had to agree with Norton's analysis. It withdrew the plan, instead concentrating its efforts on two fronts: (1) ensuring that that legislature would withstand the pressure to limit the powers of planning boards and (2) providing local planners with the information necessary to deal effectively and responsibly with developers, the public, and local governments.

Building upon the successful cooperation of the various interest groups that had produced the 1953 planning law, the Federation urged the state government to appoint a similarly structured committee to formulate the necessary amendments to the law. Such a committee would be sure to preclude any radical changes in the law. The Federation's position enjoyed the active support of the League (which viewed any attack on municipal planning as an attack on home rule) and especially its affiliates, the engineers and attorneys.

Such a corporate solution had a distinct advantage for the beleaguered legislature, which would rather not be caught between opposing pressure groups. Joint Resolution 13 created a special committee to study and review the planning laws, both municipal and county, as well as the pending amendments before the legislature pertaining to planning. Sutherland would represent the Federation. The attacks on the planning law had been successfully deflected, and time was bought for the educational efforts of the organization to ameliorate the worst abuses of the lay planners.

The educational efforts generally followed the established patterns: area meetings and Atlantic City conferences that included consulting periods along with informative panel discussions. These periods proved so popular that their number was increased from nine in 1953 to thirty-one in 1955, and no wonder, since the list of consultants reads like a Who's Who of the planning community in New Jersey, with some healthy sprinkling of experts from New York and Pennsylvania. If free advice was not enough of an allure, in 1955 there was the added attraction of a mock zoning hearing, with the successful participation of Rutgers University planning students.

The Federation also joined forces with Rutgers University to co-sponsor an in-service course on the "Principles of Local Planning." A similar in-service course on planning law was offered to municipal attorneys. These were the modest beginnings of an activity that became one of the central thrusts of the organization.

Beneficial as these educational activities were, they could not erase the need of small municipalities for technical planning assistance. The Federation's plan for regional staffs remained on the books but did not seem to have much chance of being implemented. State planning was in desperate shape. In 1954, following the election of a new state administration, Edwards, the Federation's secretary, called for an urgent meeting of the organization:

> All board members are requested to give attention to the matter of a reorganization of the Planning Section in the State Government. At the present time the Planning Section is without a Chief Planner and it is understood that one of the Assistant Planners has resigned his position. The starting salary, as well as other conditions relative to these two positions, make it very doubtful that the positions will be filled. . . . Any elimination of existing positions in the Section would result in a further cut in the already meager Planning budget. . . . Please come to the February meeting prepared to enter into an intelligent discussion on this matter.[36]

A Federation delegation met with the new governor, Robert B. Meyner, but was unable to extract any promises.

Again, it was the federal government that came to the rescue. The 1954 Federal Housing Act included Section 701. This section provided federal matching funds for technical planning assistance to communities with fewer than 25,000 residents, to be administered through state agencies. Catching two birds with one stone, the sponsors of the act ensured that small communities would be able to receive some competent help, and state planning agencies would be able to reassert their position within the state bureaucracies as a consequence of the agencies' renewed ability to attract federal funds.

By September 1955, the status of the planning section was elevated to that of a bureau. A new chief state planner was hired, and a $50,000 conditional appropriation (conditional on the bureau's success in obtaining federal funds) soon followed. State planners finally found their place within the state government, and small communities would receive some necessary assistance. Almost lost in the general euphoria were the less favorable consequences of the federal legislation.

It was Louis Mumford, who, in his speech before the 1957 American Society of Planning Officials (ASPO) conference, warned: "The aid to small municipalities which though valid in itself, is currently siphoning our limited reserves of planning talents into myriad little jobs of rewriting suburban zoning ordinances while the big job of metropolitan development coordination goes undone."[37]

The Federation did not, and indeed could not, oppose this trend. Planning came to mean suburban municipal planning. In contrast to the earlier years of the Federation, there were very few planning panels to be found discussing city problems at Atlantic City conferences after 1951. Planning in the cities came to mean slum clearance and urban renewal, and those were controlled by various official redevelopment agencies. The New Jersey legislature did attempt to assure a role for the planners in its 1949 Redevelopment Agencies Act. The act gave planning boards the power to determine whether blight existed in an area slated for renewal, thus granting planners veto power over all proposed renewal projects. Also, the federal law required an approval of the redevelopment agencies' plan by the local planning board. However, as Harold Kaplan's study of Newark's redevelopment program aptly demonstrated, lay planners lacking professional staff and political support could easily be outmaneuvered and rendered impotent.[38] No wonder that the Federation asked Leo Carling, the director of public works in Newark, to speak in Atlantic City on the topic, "Why Planning Does Not Work in Cities Like Newark."[39]

The northern area of the Federation did collaborate with the Hoboken Planning Board and the Stevens Institute in sponsoring a meeting to discuss the impact of the 1954 Housing Act on urban redevelopment. The act shifted the emphasis from the clearance of specific blighted areas to the comprehensive upgrading of blighted neighborhoods. At the meeting, a member of the Philadelphia regional office of the Federal Urban Renewal Administration explained the content and the application of the new law while a professor from the Brooklyn Polytechnic Institute advised city officials to develop a good working relationship with business and industry in order to compete more effectively with the fringe areas.[40]

A 1954 study conducted by Commissioner Joseph McLean revealed an acute shortage of low-priced and middle-priced housing for purchase or rental. The situation was going to be further aggravated by the stipulation of the new housing act, which limited federal support for public housing to communities engaging in urban renewal and redevelopment. Of New Jersey's forty-seven communities engaging in public housing, thirty-four were in danger of losing their funding.[41]

Surprisingly, the alarm bells that had sounded in the forties could not be heard in the fifties. Perhaps planning, which was developed as a response to the problems of the cities, ended up providing the tools enabling the suburbs to escape the consequences of the deterioration of the cities. Municipal planners were able to prevent the building of the small houses, which Hosking so dreaded, as well as outlaw the trailer camps Carling so abhorred.

By the mid-fifties, the Federation had come of age institutionally as well as functionally. The organization's high-profile activities on behalf of planning legislation, along with its emergence as an educational service organization that addressed itself to the needs of the developing areas of the state, contributed to an increase in its membership (from fifty-seven members in 1954 to one hundred sixty-four members in 1956).

After years of struggling to find the right balance between grassroots activities and statewide leadership, the Federation adopted a new constitution in 1955. During the early fifties, a decision was made to decentralize the activities of the organization in order to enable various areas to develop indigenous leadership and local involvement. The result was the establishment of a very vital central area, along with various less successful attempts by the northern area to follow suit.

Unfortunately, there was very little in common between the activities of the areas and those of the leadership. The areas were embroiled mainly in the minutia of zoning and planning, while the leadership was interested in having an impact on the planning trends of the state. For example, while the deficiency of state and regional planning was a vital concern of the directors, a survey conducted in an area meeting of the central Jersey group revealed that only 20% of its membership favored regional planning and only 4% felt that efforts should be made to strengthen the state planning section.

In its new constitution, the Federation was divided into three areas: northern, central, and southern (though the latter was only in planning stages), and it was recognized that the activities of the organization would emanate from these three areas. Effective coordination would be provided by means of an executive committee and an annual meeting. The membership would elect twenty-one directors, a president, vice presidents representing the areas, a council, a treasurer, and a secretary. The executive committee would consist of the officers, along with seven representatives elected by the directors. To ensure leadership continuity, only a third of the directors would be elected each year.

As the Federation's income was rising along with its membership, the organization decided to incorporate and to establish some orderly budgetary procedures. In addition to a decision to attempt to bring the south into the union, there was also talk about the need for an office, a publication, and more women directors (in 1955, Mrs. Frances Cocchia of Newark found her way into the organization and was promptly elected to the executive committee).

The Federation's leadership reflected the new emphasis of the organization. While men concerned with the cities as well as the larger issues of planning were prominent in the leadership of the late forties, suburbanites took their place by the mid-fifties. The places of the Nortons, Burnetts, and Buttenheims were taken by the Sutherlands, Carlings, and Stickels, young business executives and lawyers bent on fashioning their own suburban utopia. Resigned to the impossibility of rectifying the mistakes of the past, they intended to ensure that their own communities would not repeat them. Meanwhile, as Norton commented: "They would come to RPA meetings as if to touch the holy grail."[42]

Finally, this new local bias of the organization's membership and leadership found its formal articulation in the Federation's official definition of purpose. The 1948 Federation Constitution read as follows:

> OBJECT: The object of the Federation shall be to promote public interest in municipal and regional planning, and to foster the co-operation of planning boards throughout New Jersey in furthering the aims of planning.[43]

In 1955, there appeared a need to add this qualification to the definition: "to assist local planning boards with advice, and to encourage the development of regional, county, and state planning *as an aid to local planning.*"[44]

JERSEY PLANNERS

FRED G. STICKEL, III
OF
CEDAR GROVE

FRED IS A MAGNA CUM LAUDE GRADUATE OF PRINCETON UNIVERSITY AND HE RECEIVED HIS L.L.B. FROM COLUMBIA UNIVERSITY LAW SCHOOL. IS ATTORNEY FOR THE BOARDS OF EDUCATION, AND COUNSEL FOR THE PLANNING BOARDS OF CEDAR GROVE AND ROSELAND. PAST PRESIDENT OF THE CEDAR GROVE ROTARY CLUB. CHAIRMAN OF LOCAL RED CROSS AND COMMUNITY CHEST CHAPTERS.

A SPECIALIST IN MUNICIPAL LAW, PARTICULARLY ZONING AND PLANNING MATTERS, HE RECENTLY RECEIVED THE NATIONAL AWARD FOR MUNICIPAL SERVICE IN LAW. WAS CHAIRMAN, OF THE COMMITTEE THAT REVISED THE PLANNING ENABLING LEGISLATION AND VARIOUS STUDY COMMITTEES OF THE LEAGUE OF MUNICIPALITIES.

DIRECTOR OF THE COUNSEL TO THE NEW JERSEY FEDERATION OF OFFICIAL PLANNING BOARDS, PAST PRESIDENT OF THE NEW JERSEY INSTITUTE OF MUNICIPAL ATTORNEYS, AT PRESENT A TRUSTEE OF THAT ORGANIZATION AND THE NATIONAL INSTITUTE OF MUNICIPAL LAW OFFICERS TO WHICH HE IS ALSO CHAIRMAN OF THE COMMITTEE ON ZONING AND PLANNING

FRED

HIS HOBBY IS FISHING - PRIMARILY FOR FRESH WATER BASS, BLUE FISH AND OTHER SALT WATER FISH. ALSO A CAMERA ENTHUSIAST, AND ACTIVE WITH THE LITTLE LEAGUE BASEBALL TEAM FOR WHICH ONE OF HIS FIVE CHILDREN PITCHES.

JERSEY PLANNERS

WILLIAM A. SUTHERLAND
PRESIDENT OF THE NEW JERSEY
FEDERATION OF OFFICIAL PLANNING BOARDS

EDUCATED IN SCOTLAND AND ENGLAND — GRADUATE OF CAMBRIDGE. POST GRADUATE WORK AT LONDON POLYTECHNIC AND LEEDS UNIVERSITY. BECAME A CITIZEN OF U.S. IN 1942 IN THE SOMERVILLE COURT HOUSE.

PLANT ENGINEER FOR AMERICAN CYANAMID COMPANY, ORGANIC CHEMICALS DIVISION, BOUND BROOK WHERE HE HAS WORKED FOR 19 YEARS. SMOKES ROPE CIGARS — HAS A HABIT OF TUCKING THEM BEHIND AN EAR BETWEEN LIGHTS.

"Bill" TO EVERYONE.

GARRITY

HIS HOBBIES ARE ARBORICULTURE AND BOOK BINDING ALONG WITH CONSIDERABLE SAILING IN THE NORTH SEA, WESTERN ISLES OF SCOTLAND AND LONG ISLAND SOUND. MADE A SINGLE HANDED CANOE TRIP DOWN MISSISSIPPI RIVER IN 1934.

ACTIVE IN LOCAL, COUNTY, AND STATE ENDEAVORS. A MEMBER OF BERNARDS TOWNSHIP BOARD OF EDUCATION. HAS LONG BEEN INTERESTED IN PLANNING — CONSIDERS IT THE MOST ESSENTIAL AND COMPLETE TOOL FOR THE TOTAL DEVELOPMENT OF OUR STATE.

Notes

1. Federation's Minutes, March 18, 1947, pp. 1–2.
2. *Ibid.*, p. 3.
3. "Local Planning News," *Jersey Plans* (January 1947):14.
4. Leslie Williams, "Our Number One Domestic Problem," *New Jersey Municipalities* (January 1948):25.
5. Charles R. Erdman, Jr., "An Industrial Program for New Jersey," *Jersey Plans* (March 1947):5.
6. Edwin L. Gerber, "Good Industry Can Be Promoted," *Jersey Plans* (March 1947):12.
7. *Ibid.*
8. T. Ledyard Blakeman, "The Master Plan and the Municipality," *New Jersey Municipalities* (May 1946):7.
9. Interview with Evan Spalt, July 10, 1986.
10. Alfred E. Driscoll, "Our New Constitution," *New Jersey Municipalities* (January 1948):7.
11. *Ibid.*
12. Memorandum from Robert Burlingham to T. L. Blakeman, March 17, 1947.
13. "The Federation Planner," *The Federation Planner* (April 1947):4.
14. "What Should State Constitution Say About Planning?" *The Federation Planner* (May 1947):2; and Julian P. Boyd, *Fundamental Laws and Constitutions of New Jersey* (New York: D. Van Nostrand Co., 1964), pp. 203, 224.
15. Norman H. Leonard, Jr., "State-Local Fiscal Relations in New Jersey," *New Jersey Municipalities* (June 1948):11.
16. Williams, *op. cit.*, p. 25.
17. Federation's Minutes, September 24, 1948, p. 1.
18. R. F. Edwards, Letter of Transmittal, August 25, 1950.
19. "Conference Resolutions: Regional Planning," *New Jersey Municipalities* (December 1950):14.
20. Russell VanNest Black, "Why So Much Zoning and So Little Planning," *Jersey Plans* (August 1951):3.
21. Alan W. Steiss, "Three Decades of State Planning," *Jersey Plans*, vol. XI, no. 3 (1960):11.
22. Federation's Minutes, February 26, 1952, p. 1.
23. Federation's Minutes, November 19, 1952, p. 2.
24. Harry E. Bernstein, "The Background of the New Planning Legislation," *Jersey Plans* (August-November 1953):2.

25. H. H. S., "Editorial: The Case of Lionshead Lake Versus Wayne Township," *Jersey Plans* (August 1952):1.

26. *Ibid.*, p. 2.

27. Fred G. Stickel III, a letter to Evan R. Spalt, May 12, 1987.

28. Herbert H. Smith, "Joint Committee Produces Municipal Planning Act," *The American City* (November 1953):105.

29. "New Planning Statutes Prompt Many Queries," *Newark Evening News*, November 23, 1953.

30. John Brewer Moore, "Subdivision Activity Since Adoption of New Legislation," *New Jersey Municipalities* (March 1955):30.

31. "A New Leaf Is Turned," *Jersey Plans* (August-November 1953):1.

32. Moore, *op. cit.*, p. 31.

33. "Campaign Opened to 'Break' Municipal Subdivision Regulation and Control," *American Municipal News* (November 1954):1.

34. Joseph McLean, "The Challenge of Planning," a speech before a meeting of NJFPB, Atlantic City, November 17–18, 1954 (as quoted in the Federation's Minutes).

35. Federation's Minutes, February 28, 1955, p. 2.

36. Federation's Minutes, February 8, 1954, p. 1.

37. Louis Mumford in a speech before the ASPO 1957 conference, *Jersey Plans*, vol. XII, no. 3 (1962):48–49. However, Budd Chavooshian maintains that Mumford's criticism did not apply to New Jersey.

38. Harold Kaplan, *Urban Renewal Politics: Slum Clearance in Newark* (New York and London: Cambridge University Press, 1963).

39. Federation's Minutes, September 25, 1951, p. 1.

40. "Summary of Panel Discussion on Urban Renewal," *New Jersey Municipalities* (May 1955):38.

41. Moore, *op. cit.*, p. 30.

42. Interview with McKim Norton, June 28, 1986.

43. "Federation Constitution," *The Federation Planner* (January-February 1948):3.

44. Federation's Minutes, November 15, 1956, p. 7.

5

Life Amidst the Clover

The decade between 1955 and 1965 was a period in which planning achieved a place of permanence and influence within the governmental structure, and planning practitioners came to be acknowledged as members of a separate professional grouping. Dr. Mason Gross, the president of Rutgers University, remarked: "The pendulum has completed its swing, and 'planning' from being a dirty word, is now almost the best of all possible words."[1]

Regrettably, in New Jersey, comprehensive planning was solely limited to municipal planning and zoning, and the only government with the power to implement its own plans through zoning ordinance and subdivision regulations was the municipal government in conjunction with its planning board. It seemed as if ideological, political, economic, and judicial forces all united in enabling planners to use the Garden State as a laboratory in which the effects of placing powerful planning tools exclusively in the hands of local planning boards could be studied.

As the results of the experimentation became progressively clearer, the need to terminate the experiment, or at least reevaluate and readjust its components, became apparent. The following decades then were to be marked by power struggles between levels and types of governments and by salvage operations of varying degrees of success, but the innocence and the consequent assurance of this decade would be lost forever.

Ideologically, the country was reaffirming its belief in a free enterprise system combined with grass-roots democracy. A parallel was
drawn between the right of the individual to determine his or her
fate and the right of the community to do so. Each was entitled to
make the choices deemed best suited to itself. The enactment of
planning-related regulations was the modern and rational way for
communities to exercise the right of self-determination, that is, practice effective home rule. This was the ideological basis of Leo J.
Carling's comments concerning the regulation of trailer camps:

> People who are living in trailer camps and in trailers are living
> there because they want to. It's their way of life. It has not
> been forced upon them, except in rare instances. Generally
> speaking, that is what they want to do.

> In summation, then, I might say that if you are unhappy about
> trailer camps that are now within your boundaries it is not too
> late to enact improved legislation.[2]

Economically, New Jersey was growing at an unprecedented rate.
The state population increased 25.5% during the fifties and averaged
an additional 100,000 persons a year during the sixties. It was also
the only state in the union in which the number of bank accounts
exceeded the population.

The new highways opened up vast new areas to development, and
modern two-level industrial plants, giant shopping centers, and new
residential neighborhoods were being constructed across the state. A
completely new infrastructure to accommodate the relentless growth
had to be built.

In New Jersey, home rule meant that the state was content to let
local officials run their communities as fiefs. The state assumed only
minimal responsibility for providing services or financing them. The
municipalities had the right to collect property tax and use the
proceeds to finance their own development costs. As a result, the
state ranked forty-eighth in the country in state tax collections but
third in local government tax collection and second in property tax
collection.[3] Planning enabling legislation permitted localities to direct
and control their development in any way they chose, but it stipu-

lated that the only way municipalities could exercise their power over subdivisions was by appointing a planning board.

The federal and state government actively encouraged such use of municipal "police power" by helping to finance the cost of the design and implementation of such controls. The federal 701 program, through the good offices of the State Planning Bureau, assisted about four hundred municipalities with the drafting of their master plans and the formulation of their zoning ordinances. Other programs helped underwrite various local redevelopment schemes, such as the purchase of parklands and the building of libraries.

State courts followed suit and repeatedly upheld the right of municipalities to use the available planning tools, especially zoning, in any way they chose. The court held: "That the role of the judiciary in reviewing zoning ordinances is 'narrow', the court cannot pass upon the wisdom or unwisdom of an ordinance, but may act only if the presumption in favor of the validity of the ordinance is overcome by an affirmative showing that it is unreasonable or arbitrary."[4] The philosophical reason for this latitude was the belief that the board represented the public health and the general welfare, which "is broad and inclusive. The values it represents are spiritual as well as physical, aesthetic as well as monetary."[5]

Judges did place two limitations on the powers of planning boards: (1) planning regulations had to be comprehensive ("Injustice and vice emanate from haphazard zoning. Discrimination, spot-zoning and re-zoning by variances are the negation of planned zoning and impinge upon property rights protected by constitutional guarantees."[6]); and (2) individual property rights had to be protected ("A zoning ordinance limiting the use of one's property for a school or for public parks and playgrounds is unconstitutional and deprives the property owner of the value of his property."[7]).

The Federation leadership was well aware of all the aforementioned trends. The future of planning depended on the success of the municipal planning board, and thus the protection and guidance of these boards became the paramount concern of the organization. After all, the future of the Federation could not be severed from the future of municipal planning boards. As the power and the prestige of these boards grew, so did the power and the prestige of their association. The organization increased its membership from 71 boards in 1955 to 329 boards in 1965, its area of operation was extended to cover the whole state, its legislative clout grew, its educational programs were greatly extended, and various organizations sought its cooperation in their own efforts to influence the state's planning community.

The Federation had excellent relations with county planners and worked hard to spur counties, such as Union, to appoint planning boards, as counties could conduct various studies, pave roads, or even employ professionals who could help local planners with their growing difficulties. Many county planners were active members of the Federation, as were state planners.

During the fifties, the reinvigorated State Planning Bureau (under the able directorship of the ever-popular B. Budd Chavooshian) also functioned mainly as an aid to local planning. The administration of the federal 701 program was the sine qua non of its existence. No conflict of interest between state and local planning was possible since the State Planning Bureau had neither funds to prepare a state plan nor a mandate to implement one.

Like the courts, the State Planning Bureau did use its clout to encourage comprehensive municipal planning by insisting that only communities prepared to complete a comprehensive master plan would be eligible to receive federal and state funds. In addition, the bureau used the 701 program to prepare for better times when state-wide planning would again be possible. It acquired its own professional staff (albeit to prepare municipal plans), acquainted its staff with the divergent needs of the state by choosing a varied sample of localities for the federal program, and secured most of its state funds under a general appropriation. The bureau then proceeded to convince most of the municipal participants of the federal program to underwrite the full 50% of the necessary planning cost instead of requesting state funds for that purpose. As a result of this success, the bureau was able to use its general appropriations to prepare special regional studies, including the Meadowlands Development Study, the Pinelands Region Study, and the Newark Area Transportation Study. Preparations for a statewide plan took on a broader scope in 1960 as a result of the new availability of federal funds for that purpose.

The Federation was delighted with the bureau's success in providing the much-needed technical assistance to its constituency and job opportunities for the professional planners (many of whom were active members of the organization). Just as valuable was the bureau's readiness to provide the Federation with administrative help. Each of the Federation areas, as well as the state organization, had an administrative secretary at its service, and the distribution of the Federation's mailings was handled through the bureau (the Federation contributed $750 toward the purchase of an addressograph for the bureau). The two organizations continued to cosponsor an annual state planning conference and collaborated in promoting various planning-related legislation (like the 1958 water bill) and programs. The Federation constantly backed the bureau's appropriation requests, and the bureau used its newsletter to promote membership in the Federation and support its activities.

The ease with which the two organizations collaborated was as much a function of their shared philosophy as their shared clientele. Dr. Edward Wilkens, one of the state's most important linchpins, succinctly summarized the basic planning tenets of the period. In an address entitled "How to Get Started in Planning," which he gave at numerous Federation forums and which was consequently published in *Jersey Plans*, Wilkens explained:

> To the average planning board facing the problem of getting started in a local planning program, the problem is very similar to that faced by any business man who is about to get started in a commercial enterprise. There would appear to be five indispensable factors in getting started in either activity.
>
> First, the business man should know his product, what it is, and what it can do, the extent to which it is meeting a popular demand and the basic elements which must be put together to assure a sound marketable product.
>
> Second, the business man must be clear in his own mind about the objectives of his business.
>
> Third, the business man must begin where he can. . . . He must build up "a following"—a group of satisfied custom-

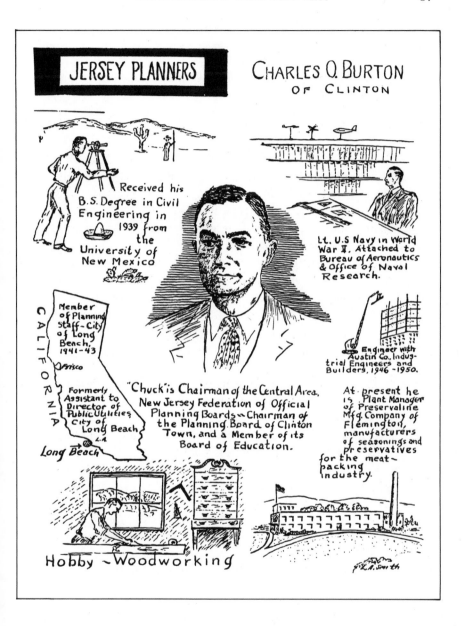

JERSEY PLANNERS

CHARLES Q. BURTON
OF CLINTON

Received his B.S. Degree in Civil Engineering in 1939 from the University of New Mexico

Lt. U.S Navy in World War II, Attached to Bureau of Aeronautics & Office of Naval Research.

CALIFORNIA

Member of Planning Staff - City of Long Beach, 1941-43

Frisco

Formerly Assistant to Director of Public Utilities City of Long Beach

L.A.

Long Beach

Engineer with Austin Co., Industrial Engineers and Builders, 1946 -1950.

"Chuck" is Chairman of the Central Area, New Jersey Federation of Official Planning Boards ~ Chairman of the Planning Board of Clinton Town, and a Member of its Board of Education.

At present he is Plant Manager of Preservaline Mfg. Company of Flemington, manufacturers of seasonings and preservatives for the meat-packing industry.

Hobby ~ Woodworking

J.L.A. Smith

ers. . . . Furthermore, he must begin where he can be sure he can remain "in the black ink."

Fourth, the modern business man must be prepared to use all available instruments and tools to accomplish his objectives.

Fifth, the business man must have the courage of his convictions.[8]

The businessman was the lay planning board member, his enterprise was one of the state's 567 municipalities, his objective was the building of a suburban utopia, his customers were the members of the local community who had to be pleased by the provision of adequate services without additional demand for higher property taxes, his instruments were the planning-related ordinances, and his courage was his ability to work "with inadequate knowledge and incomplete standards" fully prepared "to face opposition from selfish interests, who may try to sow seeds of doubt and confusion in order to protect selfish rights. Opposition will undoubtedly be forthcoming from the ignorant and the apathetic as well as the malicious and the vicious."[9]

This philosophy had to be sold on two parallel tiers. Experience showed that while state conferences were an excellent way to reach governmental officials and professionals with planning-related jobs, and as such ideally suited for the discussion of statewide problems and planning innovations, lay planners could only be found in local meetings where their particular concerns could be addressed. William A. Sutherland vividly described the atmosphere of such an area meeting:

We find that quite a large proportion of the people attending these sessions are new planning board members and they are our most valuable assets, I believe, for the future and we try not to appear too high-brow with them and scale everything to the beginner, the neophyte, the chap who simply doesn't know and wants to know. We don't laugh at any questions that come up. If you were to see them—just this last time I think 98 people turned out; we have had as many as 150, and all working their heads off right around the table; and when you stop to interrupt them to tell them that it is time to change or time to go home, they want to hang on. We made a mistake one night of saying reserve your questions and we will wind up the meeting and ask them later. Later was about quarter past twelve, and Rutgers threw us out.[10]

Since the power to implement planning rested exclusively in the hands of such lay planners, the Federation embarked upon a program to apply the lessons it learned in the organization's central area to the rest of the state. The directors decided to revitalize its northern area and constitute a southern one. The two areas presented vastly different organizational problems. The northern area suffered from factionalism, which frustrated many area chairmen. Only Henry Williams (the Federation's president from 1956–1958) was both forceful and diplomatic enough to assure the appropriate functioning of the area for quite some time.

It was Williams who insisted on organizing the south. Distance and lack of contacts were the main problems confronting the directors. The unusual dedication of three men was responsible for the eventual success of the southern endeavor: Henry Vaughn-Eames, Herbert Smith, and, interestingly enough, Harry Hosking. However, the success of the expansion did not depend solely on individuals. At least as important was the organization's commitment to a geographical power-sharing. The central area continued to be an inspiration for all, but a strict official and unofficial territorial balance permeated the whole structure of the organization.

Each area had its own vice president, its own representative on each of the committees, its own directors and associate directors, and two representatives on the executive committee. A rotation system was established for the Federation's presidency (William Gillett was the first southern president), and turns were taken in hosting the Federation's annual meetings. Even within the areas, there was a tendency to rotate the location of the meetings, so as to assure maximum participation and minimum inconvenience to the lay planners. By 1963, a series of fringe meetings was organized in which problems unique to the border areas were addressed.

Since each of the area chairmen was expected to present the central leadership with a list of activities and related budgets, and also to report on his programs during the organization's annual meetings and even at times host such a meeting, a good-natured competition brought added excitement to the proceedings. Similarly, when the Federation became actively involved with the Regional Plan Association (RPA) programs in North Jersey, the southerners demanded and received similar cooperation with the newly formed PenJerDel (Pennsylvania–New Jersey–Delaware) program.

For years the directors had been aware of the Federation's need for a paid staff, but the projected cost of such a move was prohibitive. It was estimated that a budget of $15,000 to $25,000 would be needed to provide the organization with the required staff and office at a time when its annual income did not exceed $2,500.

However, with a newfound confidence buoyed by the recent membership growth, the leadership decided it was time to prepare its own plans for the future. In 1958, President Carling appointed Evan Spalt to head a planning committee, with the following mandate:

> This committee shall prepare a master plan for the future of the Federation including, but not limited to, such projects as an executive director, office and equipment, clerical help and a monthly newsletter. The plan should include an estimate of costs involved and suggested means of financing.[11]

The committee soon discovered that the Federation, in its eagerness to promote planning any way it could, failed to provide any special benefits for its own membership. This situation had to be remedied if the Federation wanted to continue its growth. The committee recommended securing "seed money" from an interested foundation in order to hire a full-time executive secretary. The secretary would (1) produce a newsletter, (2) promote good planning legislation, (3) help municipalities solve individual problems, and (4) organize educational and promotional activities in order to enlighten the members of the community at large in the advantages of planning. In the meantime, the Federation would use its meager resources to hire a part-time executive secretary.

The directors accepted the committee's report, and an intensified membership campaign was immediately launched to beef up the organization's income. As a willing foundation could not be found, the leadership embarked on another scheme: the establishment of a new class of corporate membership (with dues of $100 and no voting rights). A goal of one hundred corporate members was set, but, at its peak, the number of corporate members was only eleven. The directors never gave up hope of attracting more corporate money, but in reality the Federation could only rely on its membership dues.

The Federation found itself in a classic catch-22 situation: It needed additional funds to hire a staff in order to be able to provide a more efficient and complete service to its membership; it needed a large membership to supply the necessary funds, but it could only attract the necessary members if it supplied the services that required a staff.

It was the idealism of a planning enthusiast that saved the day. Horace A. Vanderbeek, a retired structural engineer from Watchung who had served for two years as the secretary of the central area, agreed to accept the position. His monetary demands were extremely modest ($970 plus expenses), as the acceptance of a higher salary would have jeopardized his Social Security benefits. The new secretary even agreed to use his home as his office, and William Garbe furnished him with a set of filing cabinets. For a year and a half (May 1960 to December 1961), the Federation had at its disposal an almost full-time professional for a very part-time salary.

The first issue of the regenerated *The Federation Planner* appeared in November 1960, and its distribution, despite the misgivings of some of the directors, was strictly limited to members. It carried information concerning upcoming Federation-sponsored events, State Planning Bureau activities, the legislative committee's evaluations of pending bills, a summary of recent pertinent court decisions, news of past and future area meetings and state conferences, some practical advice concerning the appropriate relationship between planning boards and the citizenry, and, finally, an invitation: "Your executive secretary is an experiment, for him, for you and for the Federation. Try him out to see if he can get the answers for you."[12] The Federation had reached yet another milestone.

In American history, 1960 is noted as the year John F. Kennedy was elected president and announced that the mantle had passed on to a new generation. In the Federation's history, 1960 is marked by the emergence of Thomas A. Hyde as the unchallenged leader of the organization, first as its president and then as its part-time and eventually full-time executive secretary. This individual would become "Mr. Federation" for the next two decades. As Harry Maslow, past president and longtime treasurer of the organization, accurately remarked: "Tom ran the Federation and we all helped him."[13]

Some helped more than others. Chavooshian, the able chief of the State Planning Bureau, could always be counted on, as could the self-effacing Maslow; the fierce home-rule advocate and Rutgers professor, Sam Owen; the brilliant and committed attorney, Harry Bernstein; and the energetic Gillette, to name just a few.

This new leadership concentrated its efforts on (1) increasing the power and effectiveness of the Federation by activities designed to sharpen its organizational identity; (2) serving the membership by enhancing the power of the local planning boards; (3) cooperating with various organizations in tackling new statewide concerns and keeping the membership abreast of the new developments in the planning field; and (4) using the leverage gained from the previous activities in order to encourage the passage of legislation that would help improve upon the quality of life within the state.

As usual, many of the activities undertaken by the leadership served multiple purposes, but none superseded the scope of the ambition of the organization's commitment to sponsor the 1962 national American Society of Planning Officials (ASPO) convention.

It all began on December 18, 1958, when President Williams informed the directors that it might be possible to get the ASPO to hold its 1962 convention in Atlantic City under the auspices of the Federation. During the following few months, Williams and Smith contacted various groups and New Jersey ASPO members in order to test the waters. Finally, with the promised support of twenty organizations, an official proposal was formulated, and on November 20, 1958, the Federation's tenth president, Carling, reported that the ASPO had officially accepted the Federation's invitation.

No debate or soul-searching accompanied this enormous undertaking. Obviously, exposing the state to the latest thinking of the country's planning community would be a superb educational experience for the local planners and a high-profile activity for the Federation. In addition, the directors were proud of the strength of their own organization and viewed the ASPO's willingness to have their conference sponsored by the Federation as equivalent to the receipt of a medal of honor.

Little attention was paid to the financial commitment that such an undertaking required. The need to guarantee a sum of $5,000 was mentioned, but the leadership did not dwell on this figure even though it represented double the annual budget. The directors were confident that the burden would be carried by the other twenty organizations that participated in the invitation. Carling's submission of a bill totaling $400 spent on the invitation activities did raise some eyebrows, but all rejoiced at the positive outcome. After all, the conference was three and a half years away.

In the ensuing years, two directors carried the ball for the organization: Smith, one of the state's foremost professional planners, who headed the steering committee from its inception in July 1959 through the final accounting in late 1962, and Carling, who represented the Federation in its dealings with the national organization. When the ASPO nominating committee searched for a new director, preferably from the northeast, the Federation recommended Carling as the state's best representative and agreed partially to underwrite his expenses. Carling became a director of the ASPO in 1960 and was instrumental not only in advertising the achievements of the Federation but also in focusing attention on the role such a state organization could play in the future of planning.

Carling was appointed as the chairman of an ASPO committee to promote state planning associations (there were eighteen such associations in the country, but New Jersey's was considered the strongest). At the ASPO conference in Atlantic City, his committee organized a panel on "State Planning Associations" in which President Hyde spoke about New Jersey's experience. The strong impression made by the Federation was one of the pertinent reasons for the consequent interest shown by the ASPO in such organizations, and, in 1963, the ASPO board of directors authorized a detailed study of state association structure, finance, and operation to be compiled in a manual as a guide to new organizations.

By the middle of 1961, when preparations for the conference had to begin in earnest, the Federation found itself otherwise occupied, national interest notwithstanding. Frustrated, Smith had to emphasize time and again: "The basic thought is that the 1962 conference is a conference of the Federation with the ASPO being our guests. Never before has a state organization taken over with grass roots leadership and operation."[14] Again, he stressed that "the big thing to realize is that it is *our* conference."[15]

As always, money turned out to be a major stumbling block. Many of the organizations that joined in the original invitation were unprepared to offer any financial assistance, and the Federation had to fulfill its original commitment and advance $5,000 to the finance committee.

In July 1961, the following item appeared on the front page of *The Federation Planner:*

> THE PRESIDENT HOPES FOR A MIRACLE! It seems to me everybody must know about our big Statewide Planning Conference for A.S.P.O. in Atlantic City on April 29 to May 3 next spring. It's the biggest thing your Federation has ever done, even with the help of many, many people, such as the State Division of Planning and other agency associations, and it *has* to go over! There'll be people here from all over the country and New Jersey will be under the microscope (It'll look good, too!).
>
> But did you know we need money? . . . Still reading? We've looked into professional fund raising organizations to raise a few thousand and there aren't many who can on a state-wide basis. And we'd have to do the campaigning any way.
>
> So a suggestion came up at the last Directors' meeting—why can't every member board get a donation of just $50 for the '62 convention? From a business firm, an industrial organization, a civic association—or just a friend. This is a "grass roots" Federation—Let's get the money in a grass roots way! And the idea grew.
>
> So here it is (we've never done a thing like this before and we just hope it works). A "grass roots '62 Convention Campaign" is hereby inaugurated. Any planning board member—or individual member—who gets someone or something to give $50 to the Convention will be listed in the Convention program, along with their donor's name. Perhaps two donors at $25 each? or several at more than $50?[16]

As important as the money raised by the grass-roots fund was ($1,810 was collected), the leadership was just as interested in involving its membership in the affairs of the convention. When President Hyde met with the ASPO steering committee, he raised the issue of special registration fees for the state residents. It was agreed that a record of the proceedings should be made available through the Federation to Jerseyites attending the conference, even if they were not ASPO members. There would also be a one-day registration fee of $5 instead of the full $20 for New Jersey residents.

The convention attracted 1,700 participants: seventy of them came from Canada while the rest represented almost all of the fifty United States. The program was well received, the entertainment was greatly enjoyed, and, in the end, the Federation not only recouped its financial investment but also added to its nest egg.

The Federation Planner was happy to observe that "it is interesting to note how much was said of immediate pertinence to New Jersey problems. We suppose that this wasn't deliberate but merely demonstrates again how similar problems are all over the world."[17] Unfortunately, few of the state's residents were present to appreciate the relevance. Only one hundred sixty-eight persons from New Jersey attended the conference, including eighty volunteer staff members. The special one-day registration attracted all of six enthusiasts.

The directors did not dwell on their disappointment, as most were justifiably pleased with their ability to execute such a complex undertaking. The members of the old guard, like Carling and Williams, were proud of the Federation's and their own national exposure, while some members of the new guard, like Vanderbeek (whose sudden death on December 10, 1961, was a heavy blow to the organization) and Hyde (who had to function both as president and as the executive secretary for the following six months), did not care much for the whole affair and were glad to be able to refocus their attention on the local scene. They deemed it much more important, not to mention far less precarious, from a financial point of view.

Actually, the national conference was successful in exposing the state's planning community to the new emphasis placed by the national planning vanguard on social and spiritual aspects of planning. (Such emphasis would become relevant to the state much sooner than many thought possible.) In addition, the conference fitted neatly into the directors' efforts to forge in its individual board members a sense of pride in belonging to such an important association. Such feelings were particularly important in the constant quest to increase the size of the Federation's membership. Such an increase became even more essential due to the untimely death of Vanderbeek and his replacement by Hyde as the new part-time executive secretary, with a salary triple that of Vanderbeek's.

In 1962, the Federation's membership was broadened to include boards of adjustment, and the organization's name was changed to the New Jersey Federation of Planning Officials. This move was not welcomed by many directors who had successfully opposed it for years, as they saw the addition as symbolic of the organization's growing immersion in zoning minutiae. Nevertheless, following years of delay and study, the majority reached the conclusion "that boards of adjustment and planning boards, insofar as the local community is concerned, together are the planning function of that municipality."[18] Boards of adjustment grew in stature as the result of a growing tendency of some zoning ordinances to allow almost nothing as a matter of right but only through variances and special permits. Under such circumstances, municipal planning could only succeed if the two types of boards were made aware of each other's objectives. After all, improved communication between various planning boards had been an established goal of the Federation. Of course, the hope that the move would result in additional member boards, and thus help ease the organization's financial difficulties, was not far from many directors' minds.

During the sixties, the Federation's coming of age was marked by an increasing preoccupation with the organization's own past. When the Federation started presenting certificates to retiring officers, it attempted to present them to all past presidents and secretaries. Hosking was the guest of honor at the 1961 annual meeting, providing a symbol of all the past officers of the organization. By the November 1961 meeting at Atlantic City, seven of the ten past presidents of the organization were honored, and, in May of the following year, it was decided to award free individual life memberships to all past presidents (with the last two presidents to act as voting members of the board of directors). All these activities led up to the quarter-century celebration that took place at the November 1963 members' luncheon in the presence of state officials and Senator Clifford P. Case. The guest speaker was again Hosking, who, after reminiscing about the past, analyzing the problems of the present, and setting the agenda for the future, offered the following toast:

> And now I dedicate this Federation to its second 25 years—to a full half century of service to the people of New Jersey. When the end of that time is reached, I and some of the others will not be here but we know now that a proper and successful job will have been done. We have faith that planners who follow after will do their part to keep the people of this country free from oppressive regimentation arising from too much concentrated power. Keep faith with us and with our Colonial Forefathers who started it all one hundred and eighty seven years ago.
>
> The Melting Pot will boil, as it always has, let us just be sure it does not boil over and put out the flame of the greatest country that ever was. So mote it be![19]

Hyde ruefully noted that almost twenty-four hours to the minute following Hosking's speech, the melting pot did boil over as President John Fitzgerald Kennedy was assassinated.

Jersey Plans and *New Jersey Municipalities* commemorated the Federation's anniversary with the publication of a short history of the organization written by Hyde, and Governor Richard J. Hughes issued the following proclamation[20]:

PROCLAMATION

WHEREAS, the New Jersey Federation of Planning Officials, consisting of the statewide organization of citizen-planners, members of our Municipal, County and Regional Planning Boards and members of municipal Boards of Adjustment, has completed its first quarter century of service to the planning officials, municipalities, counties and regions and the State for "Better Planning in the State of New Jersey"; and

WHEREAS, for the benefit and improvement of our State, a great number of citizens of our municipalities and counties have been engaged for a period of years in active planning and recommendation for the betterment of their communities, counties and regions, without recompense except for the certain knowledge that they will leave their communities in an improved economic, social and cultural climate;

NOW, THEREFORE, I, RICHARD J. HUGHES, Governor of the State of New Jersey, do hereby proclaim the week of

FEBRUARY 2–8, 1964
AS
NEW JERSEY STATE PLANNING WEEK

AND FURTHER, I wish to express the appreciation of the State to its citizen-planners for their unselfish efforts, through the New Jersey Federation of Planning Officials, in educating both themselves and the general public in the responsibilities of Planning as it affects the future of our State;

AND FURTHER, I call upon the people of our State to recognize the untiring efforts and countless hours of service of members of Planning Boards and Boards of Adjustment who have, with sympathy and understanding, improved the position of their communities;

AND FURTHER, I ask the full cooperation of all citizens, as well as all corporations in the furtherance of the work of the Federation of Planning Officials of New Jersey and citizen-planners.

GIVEN, under my hand and the Great Seal of the State of New Jersey, this twenty-second day of January in the year of Our Lord one thousand nine hundred and sixty-four, and in the Independence of the United States the one hundred and eighty-eighth.

/s/ Richard J. Hughes
Governor of New Jersey

Valuable as the identity-forging activities were to the leadership and membership alike, the directors were constantly striving to improve the services they offered to individual members, as well as to the membership as a whole. The help offered a board member ranged from the willingness of the executive secretary or the Federation counsel to address a specific problem a lay planner encountered to the appearance of a Federation director at a town meeting in support of a beleaguered planning board. The director would not only offer his or her moral support but would be ready with a hard sell. An example of the nature of such support could be found in Vaughn-Eames's appearance at a Delaware Township meeting on June 29, 1961, which was described by a local reporter as follows:

> A battle raged over planning and zoning in Delaware Township Monday night, amid a barrage of words covering sovereignty of the state, lawyers, legal language, legislative red tape, and the fall of ancient Greece and Scranton, Pennsylvania. Opposing forces and non-partisans gathered in numbers that caused the transfer of the regular meeting place of the Township Committee, from its cozy customary room, to the auditorium of the Township Hall. Approximately 100 were present.[21]

Under fire was Edna Horn, the planning board chairperson (and future Federation president) and her proposed subdivision ordinance. Her opponents questioned the township's very need for planning and zoning. They believed that an updated building code would have sufficed.

When one of the citizens finally asked the right trigger question: "What will zoning cost us taxwise, five years from now?"[22] Vaughn-Eames had his answer ready:

> The purpose of planning and zoning is to create a source of taxes. Medium priced homes do not pay school bills while a profitable farm or other business more than pays the school bill. Proper zoning will attract industry where living conditions are pleasant, but even with land and industry contributions, our taxes will still go up. Nevertheless, having zoning and planning will cost us less, tax-wise than not having them.[23]

A different kind of support was offered to Fairlawn's planning board, which was summarily dismissed following the election of a new mayor and municipal council. Harry Bernstein, the Federation's counsel, filed an amicus curiae brief in support of the abolished board, as the Federation feared that such an action might have severe ramifications on planning boards throughout the state. (The original trial judge found against the planning board, but he was reversed by the state Supreme Court.) Actually, the Federation's ability to involve itself in litigation was severely curtailed by its own limited budget.

Much more important was the watchdog role of its legislative committee. This committee vehemently opposed any attempt by the legislature to limit the powers of municipal planning boards. It objected to attempts to exclude private schools from planning and zoning ordinances (public schools were already excluded) or abolish the need to obtain approval for minor subdivisions. The Federation's records are replete with comments such as: "Mr. Owen reported that the County Planners Association has decided to request that the County Planning Act be amended to strengthen the powers of the county concerning development and construction fronting on county roads. The legislative committee is working with the County Planners Association to recommend a law which will aid the counties and yet not infringe upon 'home rule' principle."[24]

However, the organization's support for the local planning board did not mean that it viewed the actions of such boards through rose-colored glasses. Many leading planners, including numerous directors, believed that the unreasonable actions of lay planners remained the greatest threat to the future of planning. In his 1962 article, "Problems of Planning Legislation," Owen illustrated the problem:

> Let us take the history of A-487 as an example. . . . A developer began assembling parcels of land in an area that was zoned commercial, for the purpose of developing a shopping center. After he had almost completed assembling the parcels the local planning board rezoned the area from commercial to residential without hearings prior to the change. Similar reports of capricious and precipitous action of other planning boards stated that the owner or purchaser of *any* land in a municipality would be exempted from any change in a zoning ordinance for a period of one year provided he filed a statement with the county clerk that he intended to build with conformance with the existing provisions of the ordinance. This, of course, could nullify all of the amendments of zoning ordinances in the state.

It could create chaos in the county clerk's offices as well as in the municipal clerk's offices if a sizable number of people filed their intentions to build according to existing ordinances.

The Legislative Committee wrote to the sponsors of the bill asking that it be withdrawn. The Committee asked the N.J. League of Municipalities to oppose the bill, also the Advisory Planning Commission. They did so. In spite of this the bill was not withdrawn but was amended to eliminate single family residence zones from the exemption privileges. It was sent to the Assembly floor where it was defeated 21 to 15. A bill similar to this one can be introduced again and it may pass, especially toward the end of a session, without anyone being aware of what is happening.[25]

To prevent the feared backlash, the Federation pursued a triple strategy:

1. It emphasized the lay board members' need to be well versed in planning and urged them to participate in the various educational area meetings and the numerous courses, which the organization co-sponsored with Rutgers University. Introductory courses were offered each winter for the benefit of novice board members, and advanced courses were offered each autumn. Some municipalities made participation in such courses a condition for planning board membership, and the Federation greatly encouraged the trend.

2. It attempted to bring about a revision of Title 40 (the land-use law) so as to provide more precise guidelines to local boards and thereby stem the growing tide of litigation that threatened to overwhelm the state court system. From 1960 to 1965 five attempts to revise the law were bogged down, "each victim to local and special interest."[26] By September 1965, the Federation was alarmed enough by the new federal Housing and Urban Development Act to embark upon a new course of action:

> The Federation has, in this past month, evolved action in our planning crisis, authorizing a study committee to report on our entire planning legislative situation. A deep and comprehensive review will be made and the committee will examine all points of view in the needs and mechanics of municipal, county and

state-wide planning. It will meet with all organizations and act
as catalyst for a movement to originate the best possible Act for
present and future planning and zoning.[27]

3. Last but not least, the Federation played a pivotal role in
encouraging the legislature's recognition of planning as a separate
profession. The directors had been urging their membership to make
use of the services of professional planning consultants. The Federation believed that an official recognition would promote the respectability and permanence of planning in general, but even more importantly, it would protect municipalities, counties, and other employers
from unqualified practitioners.

The first bill to license professional planners was introduced in
1958, and it received the support of the Federation and the State
Planning Bureau. However, the engineers, architects, and land sur-
veyors strongly opposed the bill and even introduced their own
counter bills. Members of the established professions, many of
whom were planning pioneers, were afraid of losing their right to
practice planning. The Federation, in whose ranks all these professions were well represented, decided to follow its long tradition of
acting as an honest broker and asked all the parties to collaborate in
the drafting of a compromise bill. This attempt was successful, and,
on June 10, 1962, Governor Hughes signed into law the act creating
a State Board of Professional Planners. The law regulated the licensing of professional planners as those with planning degrees or
degrees in related fields with several years of experience who had to
pass a written examination. On the other hand, it permitted the
award of licenses to applicants with engineering, architectural, or
land-surveying licenses merely on the basis of these licenses. Most
importantly, the act defined a planner for the first time as a member
of a separate and distinct profession.

However, the Federation's euphoria was short-lived. Professional
planners who were at first delighted by the new dignity acquired by
their profession soon became incensed by the law's inequities. Not
only were planners alone subjected to an examination, but the licensing board was inundated with applications from practitioners in fields
as remote from planning as ceramic and chemical engineering. The
Jersey chapter of the AIP (American Institute of Planners) filed suit

to prohibit the board from issuing licences on the ground that the confinement of the examination to those with planning or related degrees and experience was grossly unfair. The president of the state's AIP, Douglas Powell, who was an active member of the Federation, asked the Federation to support the suit in the interest of protecting planning boards from bogus practitioners.

The leadership was aware of the act's shortcomings and would have welcomed the introduction of some clarifying amendments. However, following various consultations with representatives of the established professions, a decision was reached to remain neutral as long as the court case remained unsettled. The directors regrettably had no other choice. All four professions were well represented among its membership, and their associations had collaborated with the Federation in many legislative battles. Most importantly, the act represented a compromise reached under the Federation's auspices, and if the organization renounced its neutrality at this stage, it would lose its future effectiveness as an honest broker. A cooling-off period was also mandated by the hurt feelings of the architects and the engineers, who believed that the planners used them to gain professional recognition and then proceeded to break the gentlemen's agreement by refusing to give the statute a fair test. After all, the AIP got its injunction before the licensing board had a chance to issue a single license. As the battle raged, the planning boards' best bet was to rely on the recommendations of various planning organizations, including the Federation, when choosing a professional consultant.

As the Federation's membership and prestige increased, various organizations became interested in joining in an effort to address mutual problems. The Federation joined the ASPO in 1961 and, in addition to its traditional cooperation with the state planning agencies, it accepted an invitation from the state's industrial development committee to cosponsor yearly industrial planning conferences. The resultant industrial planning conferences, which were initiated in 1960 in Forsgate, consistently attracted hundreds of participants from all over the state (including the governor). They dealt with such subjects as industrial parks, the relationship between regional planning and industrial development, and the effects of planning and zoning practices on the state's industries. It was during the 1964

Forsgate Conference that Smith examined New Jersey's fluctuating industrial growth from 1950 onward and warned that the state was following patterns of decline observable in such areas as the New England states. He then proceeded to place the blame squarely at the feet of the local planning boards:

> Obviously something has seriously gone wrong beginning about 1956, and that something appears to be a policy subject to our control more than outside influences. One is that this is the period during which true tax assessment began to accelerate and the scramble for ratables began in earnest. The other is that the period between 1956–1964 may well be termed the "age of sophistication" of planning and zoning boards in New Jersey. This is the period in which it has become stylish to zone out all housing development which would adequately house employees and turn to "campus-type, Johnson and Johnson like" research parks as indicating an encouragement of industrial development.[28]

The Federation's cooperation with the state's industries was not limited to a yearly conference. Many corporate executives became active members of the organization, participated in its various functions, put corporate meeting rooms at the disposal of area groups (they even supplied the refreshments), helped distribute the Federation's press releases, and even designed a new emblem for the organization. Some industries and utility companies saw such cooperation as part of their public relations activities while others wanted the opportunity to acquaint planners with the industry's needs and aspirations.

Access to its large lay membership across the state was the Federation's most valuable asset. The Federation was willing to place this precious commodity in the hands of any organization whose causes it found commendable. Regional associations, such as PenJerDel and the RPA, received as much cooperation as the New Jersey industrial development committee. The Federation was represented on the board of directors of both regional organizations and advertised their activities in *The Federation Planner*.

The various departments of the state government received similar cooperation, as did Rutgers University. When concern for pollution brought forth the need of planners to be aware of the growing health hazards that resulted from the state's increased population density, the Federation joined with the Rutgers Bureau of Conservation and Environmental Health and the United States Public Health Service in sponsoring a statewide conference on "Planning for the Environment."

As a result of this conference, the Federation appointed an environmental health committee to further the cooperation between planners and health officials. However, the organization refused to support the demand to mandate the placement of a health officer on planning boards for fear that such a requirement would open the door to similar requests from other interests (such as school boards) and eventually result in the lay planners' loss of control over the planning process.

Similarly, the Federation joined forces with the state Division of Aging, the Bureau of Housing, the Division of State and Regional Planning, and the Department of Conservation and Economic Development to sponsor the first conference on the problems of local planning for housing the elderly. In New Jersey, the rate of growth of the elderly population was almost double the rate of growth of the population as a whole, and the new wealth and independence of the new geriatrics made them an asset to the community. George Greier pointed out the consumer value of this group:

> Older people spend more . . . per capita for food and startlingly more for food away from home, more for reading, less for education, less for transportation overall but more for transportation other than auto. . . . They spend more per capita in these respects than all families with heads aged 35 through 44.[29]

After establishing the ratable value of the housing for the elderly, the conference speakers proceeded to list the appropriate assumption necessary for proper planning in this field.

Interestingly enough, so successful were the presentations that the director of the Division of Aging soon reported that she was deluged with enough applications for such developments to house not only New Jersey's elderly but those of three other states as well. In an attempt to stem the tide without being called impractical, the organization began to point out that whatever expenses could be saved by not having to provide the elderly with educational facilities would be balanced by the cost of special health services, especially in the large developments. "A community consists of all age levels of people living together. The elimination of certain age groups will inevitably increase the intensity of the problems of those who inhabit this unnatural environment," it warned.[30]

Establishing appropriate standards for housing for the elderly, freeing the state of air and water pollution, and even addressing housing and transportation problems were all part of the organization's quest for securing a high quality of life for the citizens of the state. After all, concern for the physical environment was the essence of planning. The Federation never tired of searching for ways to use its clout to bring about "the day our municipalities will say, 'Here is beauty where there was ugliness.' "[31]

In the late forties, planners had objected to the intrusion of billboards on their landscape; in the fifties, "look-alike" and "nonlookalike" ordinances attempted to enhance the aesthetic values of the developing communities; and in the sixties, historical preservation had become the tool chosen to secure the state's visual variety. The Federation was in the frontline of all these battles but was especially proud of its sponsorship, along with various historical groups, of the 1962 law that exempted from taxation certain sites owned by nonprofit organizations. Later, the Federation succeeded in amending the law to extend the exemption to the content of the site as well. This success owed much to the renewed interest in history engendered by the preparations for the state tricentennial celebration. The theme of the 1964 Annual State Planning Conference was "Preserving New Jersey's Heritage through Planning." The conference explored the opportunities and benefits of utilizing urban development projects, aesthetic ordinances, the new public enthusiasm, and (obviously) the availability of federal grants in an effort to protect the special character of some of New Jersey's localities.

Preserving the unique character of the state involved more than just preserving its historic buildings; it entailed the retention of its right to be called the Garden State. Already at the Federation's 1955 meeting in Atlantic City, John Brewer Moore pleaded for the maintenance of a second shade of green. He pointed to the growing state problem of vanishing farmlands (the land was becoming too valuable to farm) and called upon the public policymakers to adopt the British theory of agricultural greenbelts and garden cities. Moore advocated a novel idea:

> In contrast to existing park programs which acquire land in FEE, this program would acquire only certain public rights and assign ALL remaining rights to the property owner. In effect, the rights acquired would amount to a prohibition of structure; commercial, industrial and nuisance uses.[32]

Of course, no one heeded his advice, and "the state's farmland was lost at the rate of about 41 acres per day in the period 1950–1955, 104 acres per day in 1955–1960, 115 acres per day in 1960–1965 and was well over 200 acres per day in 1966."[33] Finally, in 1963, a serious effort was made to stem this tide with the Farmland Assessment Amendment. The amendment provided that farmland in active use could be assessed at farm-use value. The Federation supported the amendment in the hope of preserving the farm industry, providing additional open space, and "at the same time protecting the municipality in the tax picture."[34]

Concern for the disappearing farmland was only one example of the Federation's consistent support for environmental legislation. In 1958, the organization threw all its energies into assuring the passage of the Water Supply Bill, and, in 1960, it worked just as hard to secure the adoption and consequent success of the Green Acres Program (Hyde represented the organization on its citizen's committee).

In pursuing these goals, the Federation was never satisfied with a few standard conferences and resolutions. New ideas were given comprehensive coverage in the *Planner* and were discussed in the various area meetings and roundtables. Nor was the leadership reluctant to use its clout and call on its members to support actively or reject various pieces of legislation.

In 1962, the RPA published a report entitled "Spread City, 1960–1985" and sent shock waves through the planning community. "Spread City" was the term used to describe low-density, acreage-zoned, highway-oriented bedroom communities. The report concluded that if the zoning patterns would remain constant, they would result in a continuous city about a hundred miles across covering everything as far as Riverside on Long Island, Danbury in Connecticut, and Lake Hopatcong and Lakewood in New Jersey. More land would be used up in the ensuing twenty-five years than in the past three hundred and thirty-six years. Furthermore, a population increase of 38% would be accompanied by a 78% increase in the number of cars, and, by 1985, more money would be spent on highway construction than school construction.

The following argument was recorded at the January 9, 1963, regular meeting of the Federation's directors:

> Clark stated that RPA had been advancing an official position that low-density zoning is all wrong; this is not what we have been advocating. Is the RPA premise correct? We should have a committee to look into this matter of whether low-density or high-density is better and make recommendations for a policy.

> Bernstein observed that he felt this motion was a mistake. He was not under the impression that RPA advocated rigidly one way or another. He pointed out that there were legal cases on both sides. The Federation, he added, cannot make recommendations of what is right for a particular community—all the Federation should do is to encourage by every means studies in the community for best planning.

> Clark held these opinions as specious and held RPA was publishing dangerous propaganda and that we should find if their recommendations are damaging.

> Spalt said that we were impressed with RPA's program and its statements have become extremely important. But it might be good to investigate how best to encourage thinking on the elements of planning.

> Williams declared that RPA preaching of high density is bad.

> Moskowitz said he thought the solution lay in between the two densities and that it would do no harm for the Federation to talk to RPA.

DeMartini said that if RPA was doing something wrong they should be told about it. It seemed very simple.[35]

Interestingly enough, it was in Somerset County, the county that was frowned upon by RPA because 85% of its vacant land zoned for residence was in one-acre and two-acre zones, that clustering was tried. The Federation heralded the new Hillsborough development and extended its congratulations to all the people involved in developing what it termed "the first new concept in residential layout in the state since Radburn."[36] In May 1963, it presented Hillsborough Township's planning board with the award for the best subdivision planning. Ironically, the planning board had to revert to its previous large-acre zoning due to the enormous development pressures that resulted from the success of "the village green." Cluster developments were not good enough ratables, and ratables were the name of the game in the New Jersey of the sixties.

Farms were good ratables and so were commercial establishments and so were "clean" industries and even luxury apartments, provided 80% of the apartments were limited to one-bedroom units. Any attempt to question the state's zoning practices, which placed economic considerations in a paramount position, were deemed highbrow, impractical, futile, and highly controversial. However, in order to maintain the prevailing conditions, a solution had to be found to the growing transportation and housing problems.

The Federation, under the leadership of William Gillette, proceeded to mount a campaign for "a proper mass integrated transportation system."[37] A series of conferences around the state was followed by the appointment by Governor Hughes of the Transportation Study Commission, the Tri-State Transportation Commission, and, finally, the creation of a new Transportation Department.

Similarly, Gillette threw up the following trial balloon in October 1962: "I would like to hear from our members on this subject: A STATE DEPARTMENT OF URBAN AFFAIRS (or URBAN AND SUBURBAN). . . . Where do I stand? I think it's long overdue."[38] A year later, the Division of State and Regional Planning presented Governor Hughes with a report recommending the establishment of a new Department of Community Affairs. In 1964, the

Federation passed a resolution in support of the creation of such a department despite the worry of some of the directors that such a department could potentially circumvent "the home rule concept." After all, this new department was expected to tackle such issues as housing and urban renewal and planning and local finance, in addition to providing a central clearinghouse to all state and federal programs relating to various communities.

Proponents of home rule were not being paranoid. Calls for a regional approach to the worsening difficulties created by the state's rapid urbanization were multiplying at an alarming speed. During the 1963 Atlantic City convention, Senator Case discussed federal legislation (which he helped sponsor) designed to encourage communities and counties to join in areawide or regional solutions to problems. A major feature of the new law would be a provision that each application for a federal loan or grant affecting a metropolitan area would have to be accompanied by the comments of a planning agency performing regional planning for the area. More than 80% of New Jersey's residents lived in a metropolitan area.

The issue of regional versus local planning was so controversial that the Federation generally preferred not to express any opinion on the matter. Instead, it used its forum to explore the issue. At the 1965 annual meeting, the commissioner of the State Department of Conservation and Economic Development, Robert Roe, made the following comments:

> I think we are entering an era which our future historians will label as the regional era. Perhaps we might call it cooperation comes of age. Regardless how we describe it, unified concerted action involving groups of municipalities is becoming more commonplace particularly with respect to water supply, pollution abatement, land, air and water transportation, industrial development and planning. New Federal legislation for resource development and conservation, planning and pollution control emphasize and strengthen the regional approach towards solving these problems.
>
> There is no disagreement on the need for cooperative, coordinated and concerted action. The question is how to achieve the regional cooperation.

The most important and most meaningful step is the need to lay to rest the mythical legend that regional cooperation destroys home rule and adversely affects the democratic process.[39]

Convincing municipalities of the need for regional action in the fields of transportation and environmental protection was difficult enough, but attacking the municipal zoning practices was considered political suicide. Though the RPA did it in 1962 (and incurred the fury of some of the directors) and Smith, one of the state's foremost professional planners, did it in 1964, the Division of State and Regional Planning suggested a regional approach that would have in fact strengthened local planning and home rule. The following article appeared in the February 1965 issue of *The Federation Planner:*

A SLIGHT DIFFERENCE IN MEANING. The recent study of the Division of State and Regional Planning has received extensive news coverage. . . . However, there were some news stories and editorials that took a negative position, attributing conclusions to the study which, according to the Division's director, were neither explicitly nor implicitly stated in the report. . . . Rather than "urging" a revision of local zoning codes as some editorials suggest, the report concludes that local zoning ordinances should be re-evaluated to reflect "informed planning and a balance of housing types."[40]

The article continued its hairsplitting, claiming the report was not critical of large-lot developments; it only maintained that they were costly both in economic and social terms. It ended by reaffirming its belief that local planning should be strengthened rather than diluted, suggesting local practices should be modernized to include a "permissive" approach. Clearly, the state planners believed it most unwise to challenge home rule and local zoning privileges, which would have amounted to political suicide. However, a series of events outside their control would make such a challenge inevitable.

In 1966, Donald Kanouse assumed the presidency of the Federation with the following remarks:

I am sure the months ahead will offer you and me a challenge the founders of the New Jersey Federation of Official Planning

Boards [its original title] never dared to dream. The Regional Planning Association, the state government as well as the federal government and others all point to this little state of New Jersey with a warning: Prepare for Judgment Day!

Each community in New Jersey is part of a metropolitan area threatening to reduce us all to nonentities. In this ever-growing deluge can your community be preserved? We cannot stop this wave of the future, if indeed we wished to do so—we can only prepare for it. If we prepare wisely and well, growth will be nothing more than the fruition of our proper plans.[41]

The reasons for this upheaval and its nature, and the response of the municipalities, their planning boards, and the Federation, will constitute the central theme of the next chapter.

Notes

1. Mason W. Gross, "The Respectability of Planning," *Jersey Plans*, vol. XI, nos. 1, 2 (1960):24.
2. Leo J. Carling, Jr., "Trailers," *New Jersey Municipalites* (April 1953):26.
3. Lyle C. Fitch, "Planning and the Property Tax," *Jersey Plans*, vol. XI, nos. 1, 2 (1960):14.
4. *Ascione* versus *Union City*, 77 N.J. Superior Court, Appellate Division, December 14, 1962.
5. *Berman* versus *Parker*, 348 U.S. 26 (1954).
6. *Ascione* versus *Union City*, *op. cit.*
7. *Plainfield* versus *Borough of Middlesex*, 68 N.J. Superior Court, September 14, 1961.
8. Edward B. Wilkens, "How to Get Started in Planning," *Jersey Plans*, vol. IX, no. 3 (1958):21.
9. *Ibid.*, p. 23.
10. Federation's Minutes, November 15, 1956, p. 18.
11. Federation's Minutes, June 19, 1958, p. 2.
12. "Your Executive Secretary," *The Federation Planner* (November 1960):4.
13. Interview with Harry Maslow, May 15, 1986.
14. Federation's Minutes, June 15, 1961, p. 2.
15. *Ibid.*

16. "The President Hopes for a Miracle," *The Federation Planner* (July 1961):1.

17. "Highlights in Afterthought on ASPO," *The Federation Planner* (August 1962):3.

18. "The Federation Changes Its Name," *The Federation Planner* (June 1962):1.

19. Federation's Minutes, November 21, 1963, p. 6.

20. Federation's Minutes, January 16, 1964, p. 3.

21. Arthur Christensen, "Hot Word Barrage Marks Delaware Discussion," *The Courier-News*, June 29, 1961.

22. "Zoning Opponents in Delaware Twp. Work on Petition," *Newark Evening News*, June 29, 1961.

23. *Ibid.*

24. Federation's Minutes, January 22, 1965, p. 2.

25. Samuel P. Owen, "Problems of Planning Legislation," *The Federation Planner* (June 1962):4.

26. Harry A. Maslow, "From the Federation President," *The Federation Planner* (October 1965):1.

27. *Ibid.*

28. Herbert H. Smith, "Industrial Development," *New Jersey Municipalities* (January 1965):11.

29. "Conference on Housing the Elderly," *The Federation Planner* (June 1964):2.

30. "Are We Selling the Elderly Short?" *The Federation Planner* (June 1964):2.

31. "Harry Maslow Writes," *The Federation Planner* (August 1965):2.

32. John Brewer Moore, "Needed: A Second Shade of Green" *New Jersey Municipalities* (February 1965):5.

33. "Federation Annual Meeting, 1967," *The Federation Planner* (June 1967):4.

34. "The Farmland Assessment Amendment," *The Federation Planner* (October 1963):1.

35. Federation's Minutes, January 9, 1963, p. 5.

36. "An Interesting Cluster-Type Subdivision," *The Federation Planner* (June 1962):5.

37. "From the Federation President," *The Federation Planner* (April 1963):1.

38. William F. Gillette, "The President Writes," *The Federation Planner* (October 1962):1.

39. Federation's Minutes, May 13, 1965, pp. 5–6.

40. "A Slight Difference in Meaning," *The Federation Planner* (February 1965):2.

41. Federation's Minutes, May 19, 1966, p. 10.

An Original Play Program

IF YOU ARE AN

INDUSTRIAL RATABLE -

WELCOME TO NORTH - SOUTH DUMPFORD*

WE WILL DO ANYTHING TO

ACCOMMODATE INDUSTRY

NORTH SOUTH DUMPFORD INDUSTRIAL COMMISSION

OTTO C. DUMPF - MAYOR

*An original play performed on May 17, 1962 during the annual meeting of the Federation at the Far Hills Inn, Bridgewater, New Jersey.

An Original Play Program (continued)

CAST: The following are sample excerpts of the roles assigned to each of
       the planning board members:

Planning Board Chairman - "When the mayor was forced to set up a planning
board he chose you as chairman confident that you would lead the board in
harmless circles..."   Played by Roger Scattergood
                                  Division of State & Regional Planning

Vice Chairman - "Above all you are a yes man and tend to argue in favor of
both sides of any argument... thus complicating many a simple argument..."
                         Played by   (To be announced)

Mayor - "Your ancestors founded the town and you've been running it ever
since. Recently you've come under heavy criticism and you defend your
administration at the drop of a hat..."
                         Played by Harvey Moskowitz, Planning Director,
                         Passaic County

Secretary - "You tend to be bored by business matters, magnify the trivial
and dismiss the important - this is reflected in the minutes..."
                         Played by Miriam Kiss, Division of State & Regional Planning

Building Inspector - "You are a positive "nut" for getting industrial ratables
and have personally issued variances when needed to accommodate a new but
not necessarily popular industry..."
                         Played by John Tomaselli, Planning Director, Camden County

Farmer - "No matter what it is, you are against it, but your only real
interest is how your property is affected... you need reassurances..."
                         Played by Al Gershen of Gershen Associates

Reform Candidate - "Since you flunked law school you've been forced to practice
law as a hobby ... you will seize upon any issue in your conflict with the
major..."   Played by John De Figgos, Planning Director
                         Hunterdon County

Planning Consultant - "As a member of a planning board in true life you will
play the role planning consultant offering his services..."
                         Played by Harry A. Maslow, A.I.A. Chairman,
                         Central Jersey Area N.J.F.O.P.B.

Janitor - Played by Woody Walnut, Division of State & Regional Planning

              The acting talent is provided tonight through the auspices of
the New Jersey Chapter of the American Institute of Planners.

              Skit situation designed by Al Guido, Woody Walnut, and James W. Collins.

NOTE: any resemblance to persons living or dead is purely coincidental-
       the skit is modeled after occurrences in a small town in a nearby state.

An Original Play Program (continued)

Capsule History of North-South Dumpford

Many years ago Josiah Dumpf, while trapping muskrat, stumbled upon a clearing in the wilderness. Looking around, he picked himself up and proclaimed, "If I could build a city here I'd make a mint!" Thus the concept of Dumpford and its suburbs was conceived. Dumpford was to be one of the nation's first completely planned cities with broad boulevards leading in all directions and the whole thing girdled by a greenbelt of parks, forests, golf courses and country clubs. Trees were felled, lots were laid and direction signs were erected. Many people came to Dumpford: some bought lots, some rented rowboats to find their lots, and some came to try and get their money back. By 1926 Josiah's humble one-room log cabin office was surrounded by the seething activities of a thriving business district with law offices, ice cream parlors, hot dog stands and a speak-easy or two.

By 1928 downtown Dumpford was experiencing its first serious traffic jams. In a carefully conceived maneuver designed to save municipal expenses and at the same time bring business literally to their doors, the Downtown Merchants Association prevailed upon the Highway Department to route the new 4-lane highway down Main Street. Unfortunately it was then discovered that 98% of Dumpford's homes and businesses would be in the path of the new, controversial 48' right-of-way. By the time construction was brought to a halt most of Dumpford was gone and the people realized that their city had received a set-back from which it would never recover. Today, one can still poll his way through the streets of Dumpford little realizing that this beautiful refuge of aquatic plants and migratory waterfowl was once a pioneering ground for the planned communities of today.

But while Dumpford no longer exists, its suburbs have survived both the depression and the repeal of prohibition and gone on to prosper. Sensing the impending tax crisis that arose from heavy municipal borrowing and the over-extension of municipal services, Josiah wisely advised his sons, as he left for Florida, to take the family parks, golf courses and country clubs and incorporate a new suburban municipality unencumbered by the burdens of the central city. Thus North-South Dumpford was scooped out, in the form that we know it now.

As one wends his way through modern North-South Dumpford it is hard to believe that its teeming residences and throbbing industries are situated on what once were mere landscaped parks and golf courses. Only an occasional sand trap can now be found and these have been put to practical uses such as school playgrounds and municipal parking lots. Under the watchful eyes of the Dumpf family, our founders mandate to "build a city..." continues to be fulfilled.

Today North-South Dumpford township is a model community demonstrating what can be done when practical people work together to build a city with a tax position second to none. By cutting municipal expenditures to the bone and never turning away a single industrial ratable, North-South Dumpford has been able to reduce taxes to the point that property owners are paid to stay here.

Prunella Dumpf, Township Historian
Room 1403, Town Hall Annex

An Original Play Program (continued)

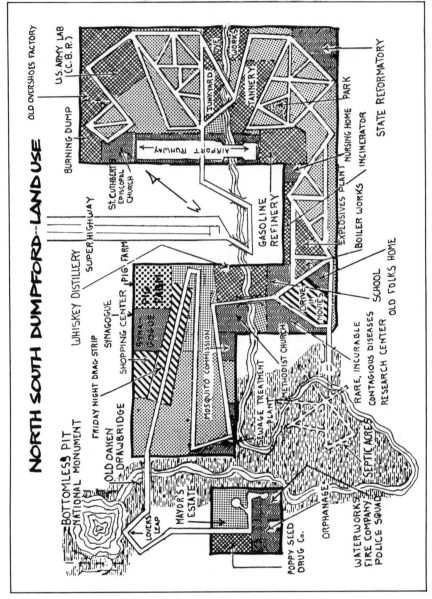

6

"The Times They Are A-Changing"

The sixties and early seventies were a period of upheaval in the American society. Established beliefs, values, and theories were reevaluated and their shortcomings mercilessly exposed. As the confident action of the fifties gave way to the rigorous self-examination of the sixties, and concern with winning was replaced by attention to the fate of the losers, the tenets and practices of the various governments came under close scrutiny and were found wanting. Planning, which had been accepted as an establishment function of government during the fifties, became embroiled in the political and ideological battles that became the hallmark of the sixties and seventies.

Actually, there was very little debate concerning the nature of the difficulties faced by New Jersey. Years of unremitting development left the state's environment in various stages of deterioration, the population polarized by income, race, and location, and local government lacking the means to provide the services its constituency needed or expected. The consensus over diagnosing the patient's ills did not extend to an agreement concerning the definition of good health, the methods of treatment, or even the identity of the doctors best suited to administer the medicine. To put it more plainly, was New Jersey's development to follow a prescribed pattern that would strive to equalize the services provided to its citizenry, redistribute the population, and protect the state's environment? If so, should

119

these goals be accomplished by mandatory or voluntary actions, and who should be in charge of effecting the desired policies?

The federal government and the state courts (which were the central factors in the establishment of the old regime, that is, municipal home rule) changed direction and embarked upon the creation of a new regime in which state and regional government would replace local government as the locus of power.

As such changes can never be accomplished without bloody battles, and as the planning function was one of the central powers local government was in danger of losing, both the ideology of planning and the practices of lay and professional planners came under sharp attack.

Thoughtful musings concerning prevalent planning and zoning practices were beginning to be heard as early as 1959 from men of the stature of Walter Blucher, executive director of the American Society of Planning Officials (ASPO), who expressed his discomfort with some overconfident local planning board actions that blatantly infringed upon the civil rights of individual members of the communities:

> The point I make is that for a considerable number of people the mobile home is a necessary way of life. It is a far superior way of life than living in the slums or blight areas which make up a substantial part of many of our modern cities.

> In the interest of protecting our communities we can go too far in zoning and much as I, as a planner, hope to see an enlightened viewpoint on the part of the courts, as a citizen, I resent the infringement which is now taking place on civil rights in the various parts of the United States.[1]

In 1960, Mason Gross, the president of Rutgers University, expressed a different concern. He worried about the planners' ability to maintain their professional integrity in face of the mounting political pressures:

> The difficulty is that planners are now almost in the position of quack-medicine men or faith-healers. They have got to come up with a solution, and that right quick. If the solution is not

quick enough, you may not be able to get a high enough priority for federal funds, and there is always the horrid possibility that there may not be any more federal funds one of these days.[2]

Quack doctors or not, David Craig, a Pittsburgh attorney, told the national planning conference that planners had lost control over their own tools as a result of their failure to put forward a coherent explanation of their planning philosophy:

Planners don't seem to know that the zoning tool has been snatched away from them and distorted into just one more legal devise for the protection of private property interest. They don't know that the zoning plowshare that could have led to productive growth for all has been beaten into a legal sword used to fend off isolated threats to individual land use units.

Planners have not displayed any consistent fundamental philosophy in relation to zoning. They mentioned it as a possible tool of the broad social and economic plans of the community and then, for the sake of selling it, have switched to the terms of the chap who is interested merely in keeping those nasty prefabs away from his door.[3]

John Holland, director of Cumberland County Planning Board and a Federation director, did not dispute Craig's allegations but insisted that the end was worth the means since "if he (the planner) had not at certain times thrown in his lot with individuals attempting to protect their private property interests, we might not have zoning as a planning tool at all."[4]

Still, most critics believed that the fault was not in the planners or even in the municipalities but in the state's system of taxation. Dr. Lyle Fitch, a New York City administrator, explained the effects New Jersey's heavy reliance on property tax had on planning:

It is an incentive tax, but the incentives it provides are for doing the wrong things.

First, it induces local communities to compete furiously for manufacturing plants and commercial establishments.

Second, the property tax encourages communities to favor higher-income over lower-income residents.

Third, the property tax is unrelated to the profitability of business firms who must pay for it.

Fourth, the property tax often influences the timing or the pattern of land use development in ways distasteful to planners.

Fifth, the property tax discourages improvement and maintenance of property simply because anything that increases property values also increases the amount of tax.

Sixth, the property tax is becoming increasingly less appropriate as a revenue source of older communities, characterized by old buildings.[5]

While the negative aspects of the state's heavy reliance on property tax were consistently addressed by the Federation's sponsored forums, the actions of its directors fell in line with the actions of the planning community as a whole. McKim Norton, the executive director of the Regional Plan Association (RPA), accurately observed that "the planners did not crusade against the property tax nor did they root for an income tax. They [planners] maybe did not want it [the tax problem] solved."[6] Norton believed that the system presented planning enthusiasts with the opportunity to design communities that were superior to the ones in which they had spent their childhood. The tax system only provided a convenient justification for carrying out policies motivated by other considerations.

Norton's assessment was confirmed by the Musto Report (County and Municipal Study Commission), which concluded: "The analysis of fiscal implications of various development alternatives clearly suggests that relatively few municipalities channel their development in any systematic way according to fiscal criteria, despite their impression that they are indeed doing so."[7] This failure to act according to fiscal criteria was not the result of premeditation or incompetence: "The trend of local decision-making suggests that the particular inequities and imbalances of the New Jersey fiscal system are of relative moment. If anything, the imbalances that exist are of greater significance to the degree that they serve as a surface rationale for decisions made on other grounds."[8]

Those other grounds basically amounted to "the sense of what the community is and what it should or should not become."[9] Thus, despite the transformation of many suburban areas into "multifaceted commercial and industrial centers, with few ties to the central cities beyond the utilization of their blue-collar labor pool,"[10] the inhabitants of those same suburbs continued to insist on maintaining a rural self-image based on "the physical similarity of the housing in the community, and the centrality of suburban homeownership, from which, it is believed, stem an entire complex of related social attitudes and values coloring their life in the community."[11]

Perhaps the knowledge of these fundamental realities explains the fact that the Federation's minutes include very few deliberations concerning the state's tax problems. In April 1966, William Gillette raised the issue by observing that "unless we get state money soon, there won't be much sense in planning for transportation, or pollution or educational solution; I hope some sort of a broad based tax will be voted soon."[12] In the discussion that followed, the possibility of an organizational policy in favor of a broad-based tax was considered, but "it was agreed that if a policy statement were called for it should certainly be in favor of an adequate study of state taxes."[13]

Clearly, the extremely controversial nature of the issue was also at the heart of the leadership's reluctance to take a firm public stand in favor of state tax. Privately, the directors were more outspoken. In June 1969, the board authorized the executive secretary "to communicate the feelings of the board to the governor, reiterating our position on the necessary tax solution to planning."[14] Governor Richard J. Hughes promptly replied: "My personal feelings on over-reliance on property taxation are well-known. That is one of the reasons I proposed an income tax in hope that the structure of taxation in New Jersey might be made more progressive and less dependent on property ratables. The support of groups such as the New Jersey Federation of Planning Officials will always be necessary if any New Jersey Legislature is to have the political courage to enact a broader-based and more progressive tax."[15]

This letter was duly read into the minutes as part of the secretary's report, but no further comments were made and the issue was dropped. The organization had never passed a tax-related resolution nor did its president ever discuss the problem in any of his editorials or public addresses. Occasional comments, such as the ones made in reference to other political issues like elections and reapportionment, expressed the hope that the matter would be resolved quickly so that the attention of the legislature could be redirected toward other measures of more immediate concern to the planning community.

The planning enthusiasts, who Holland claimed had no choice but to learn the political game, discovered that not only would it be extremely difficult to disentangle themselves from their former partners (individual property owners) but that many planners, professional as well as lay, developed a vested interest in the existing system. Basically, municipal home rule enabled professional and lay planners to achieve influential positions within the local government system far outstripping the clout planners achieved or were ever likely to achieve in the state or federal government. After all, no one doubted that the power to tax gets inevitably translated into the power to rule.

Meanwhile, justifiably or not, the alliances into which the planners entered were threatening to undermine the very basis of the new discipline. Planners, who justified their right to infringe on individual liberty for the sake of the community, were bitterly attacked for actually serving only one segment of the community (the strongest?) to the possible detriment of others.

Planning theoreticians like Alan Altshuler emphasized the value-ridden and political nature of planning. David Ranney, in his book *Planning and Politics in the Metropolis,* inquires:

> How much land should be devoted to housing for low-income families in a community and what priority should low-income housing have relative to other aspects of a city's physical development? Those low-income people who feel that their present living facilities are inadequate would favor a plan which places a very high priority on the development of housing units that meet their need. The downtown merchants who feel that they need to have more affluent customers living nearby, would favor a plan which places a high priority on replacing "slums" with middle and upper-income housing or with parking garages.

Whose values come first in this case, the low-income slum dweller or the downtown merchant?[16]

Others, like Paul Davidoff, the president of Suburban Action, drew the inevitable conclusions and called on planners to follow in the footsteps of lawyers and openly advocate the interests of a particular segment of the population. Plans resulting from the expert clash of various advocates would be like all other policy decisions— compromises. Of course, such a solution would undermine one of the chief values planners have for government officials, the use of the planners' expertise to provide a nonpolitical or technical facade for what was really a political decision.

The next premise to be questioned was the absolute right of a municipality to self-determination. Professor Norman Williams, Jr., maintained: "The predominant local viewpoint is often parochial, and not infrequently directly opposed to the general welfare."[17] After all, the comparison of a community to a business enterprise, which seemed so apt in 1947, appeared rather callous in 1965, and planners who had turned their backs in the fifties on the old world in order to direct the building of a new one were forced to admit that such a dichotomy could no longer be maintained. The very rationality and efficiency so valued by planners mandated intermunicipal cooperation, as interlocal services could enable communities to be provided with services at a level not attainable by individual municipalities alone. Obviously, as some experts maintained, planning is the least conducive to decentralization of all functions of government.

The move toward centralization of planning was accompanied by one away from purely physical planning in the direction of social planning, especially in urban areas. This was the result of the realization that physical planning has a major impact on the social makeup of a locality. Thus, the Federal Demonstration Cities Act was designed to address the problems of the inner city poor and not just the problems of the inner cities' environmental deterioration.

Paradoxically, just at the time when the urban areas of the state were breaking new planning ground, the rural areas of the state were just discovering the old grounds. The constant population movement from the center to the periphery brought planning and its organizations to the consciousness of a new constituency. New Jersey's rural counties of the northwest and the southeast suddenly found themselves embroiled in development concerns that used to be the monopoly of the metropolitan counties.

The Federation tried to weather the storm by strengthening its own organization, tailoring its services to suit its varied membership, and using its position and its long-term relationship with other organizations to enhance its impact on state legislation and policy. The Federation was still growing, and its membership reached an all-time high of 430 boards in 1972. Beginning in 1966, Tom Hyde ran the organization as a full-time executive secretary and, from 1968, as its executive vice president, since "it was felt that this title would be more prestigious in dealing with other agencies and with municipalities, generally, and would bring the title in line with that of other organizations with whom we are constantly dealing."[18] The income generated by the expanded membership enabled the Federation to move its offices out of Hyde's basement and into the second floor of the Firemen's Exempt Association Building in North Plainfield in 1970. There, Hyde could even employ some temporary help to assist with the ever-mounting paperwork, though, according to his own testimony, it was the voluntary labor of his family that really saw him through.

The membership growth and administrative rationalization were accompanied by geographical expansion. In 1965, in response to the newly manifested interest in planning expressed by rural communities, the Federation joined forces with the State Department of Agriculture and Rutgers University's College of Architecture and its Extension Service in order to organize the first Rural Community Planning Conference. It was geared to the needs of the northwestern counties (Hunterdon, Warren, and Sussex) and was followed (at the insistence of Gillette) by a similar assembly in the southern area in 1966.

These conferences became a permanent feature on the organization's calendar, and in May 1967, after two years of preparation, the three northern rural counties were given permission to secede from the northern area and create the northwestern area. Four years later, the old southern area was reorganized along similar lines with a southern area (consisting of Atlantic, Cape May,

Cumberland, and Salem counties) with a rural emphasis and a Delaware-Atlantic area (consisting of Burlington, Camden, Gloucester, and Ocean counties) with an urban tilt.

In 1966, in an effort to formalize these administrative changes, the constitution and bylaws committee under the leadership of the Federation's counsel, Harry E. Bernstein, embarked upon a complete rewriting of the Federation's constitution. The new constitution was officially adopted in May 1967. It incorporated and reorganized all the amendments and unwritten practices of the previous decade, and it included the addition of the fourth area and the replacement of the commissioner of the Department of Conservation and Development by the head of the Division of State and Regional Planning as the twenty-second director of the Federation. This was done partially out of the recognition that the director of the division, and not the commissioner, was the person who worked most closely with the Federation and partially in order to resolve the awkward situation that resulted from the transfer of the Division of State and Regional Planning from the Department of Conservation and Development to the Department of Community Affairs (DCA). Furthermore, such a designation was deemed appropriate in view of the many services provided by the division for many years, including staff services to Hyde and the area secretaries.

Interestingly, the most important and possibly the most unfortunate organizational change was made in a rather haphazard fashion. The Federation completely abandoned the practice of geographical rotation of both the presidency and the location of its annual gathering. From 1964 to 1970, the Federation's annual meetings were held in Cedar Gardens Restaurant in the central area. The areas no longer had the chance to take turns in hosting the state organization, but no one seemed to care as no discussion of the matter was ever recorded. However, the geographical rotation of the presidency ran into trouble in 1964. Due to personal reasons, Donald Kanouse of the northern area was unable to assume the presidency. It was decided that Harry Maslow of the central area would take his place, and Kanouse would follow him. In 1966, Kanouse assumed the presidency, but, instead of remaining in office for the traditional duration of two years, he served only one and was followed by yet another central area representative, Sam Owen. The principle of

PLANNERS MEET—Pictured from the left, Harry A. Maslow, Roland J. Delfause, and Harry E. Bernstein.

James G. Gilbert

Samuel P. Owen

geographic rotation was dead, replaced by a tradition that the president and the vice president would represent different areas.

According to Hyde (the only person who seemed ready or able to recall these events), the system of rotation fell victim to the unreadiness of the leadership to accept a woman as their president. Despite Kanouse's 1964 remark that "we have a greater number of men, and I am proud to say, women, upon whom we can call for help and who are willing and able to do a good job,"[19] the ascendancy of Florence Griffin, chairwoman of the northern area, was blocked. Griffin remained active in the Federation until 1967, and only in 1969 did she send in her official resignation explaining that she "feels she had better concentrate her activities in women's club work."[20] Five years later, in 1974, the Federation elected its first woman president. She was Edna Horn of Delaware Township, a seventy-two-year-old woman whose consensus-building ability is still remembered fondly by her colleagues (unfortunately, she died unexpectedly during her first year in office).

For a number of years, the Federation escaped the ramifications of its leadership having set aside its commitment to a balanced area representation, perhaps because as long as Gillette remained active in the organization, he continued to ensure that the interests of the southern half of the state would be properly addressed by the organization. The areas continued to hold a minimum of three educational gatherings a year, in addition to an annual meeting that was devoted in the main to administrative matters. The services of the Federation remained conferences, courses, direct advice, and publications. The Federation continued its policy of organizing and participating in conferences in cooperation with various organizations, including a number of departments of the state government and Rutgers University, in an effort to deal with topical issues and to cross-pollinate planning with other fields, such as health, industry, or social work. An attempt to replace these joint gatherings with an independent three-day annual conference was rebuffed by the directors, but the annual meeting was expanded in 1970 into a miniconference that included a presummer planning session followed by a short business meeting, cocktail hour, and dinner with a speaker.

The Federation's publications were also enjoying a growing popularity. *The Planner* was mailed to all the members of the state legislature (at their request), as well as to an increasing number of local libraries. In 1965, the Federation embarked on a new series of publications modestly named the Federation Planning Information Reports (FPIR). Hyde initiated the series as a supplement to the organization's regular newsletter. These reports were written by recognized planning experts and dealt with pertinent issues from a New Jersey point of view. Their length was to be flexible and the language easily accessible to the lay planner. Copies of the FPIR were free to members, but additional copies could be purchased at a low cost.

The new publication turned out to be an immediate success, the issues concerned with the practical aspects of planning being particularly popular. The first issue, a study of "Subdivision Control" by Harvey S. Moskowitz, had to go into a second printing, as did the third issue, "Community Guidelines for Industrial Development," by Herbert H. Smith. The reaction to the second issue, which consisted of reprints of the addresses given by Justices Frederick W. Hall and Joseph Halpern during previous Federation conferences, was rather disappointing. It soon became clear that the FPIRs were not appropriate vehicles for the illumination of theoretical issues. Instead, they provided a practical way to keep up with recent developments in the planning field for both lay and professional planners alike. Through the years, the interest in the publications remained high, and Hyde reported that he had received requests for the material not only from other states but also from faraway places, such as the Soviet Union and Hong Kong.

On the educational front, the Federation continued its collaboration with Rutgers University in offering introductory courses in February (for the benefit of newly elected board members) and advanced courses in October. The number of courses kept expanding as more and more lay board members felt obliged to further their expertise in order to be able to deal with the additional demands placed on them by the courts and the federal and state governments. After all, as Maslow reminded his constituency: "Only an informed body of planning board and board of adjustment members can survive (or ensure their municipality can survive) in this day and age."[21]

On the whole, much of the activity undertaken by the planning leadership was motivated by a combination of survivor's instinct and genuine progressive concern for "doing the right thing." The Federation's directors worked hard to convince the membership that change was unavoidable, as local boards could no longer disregard the world beyond their community. This was especially true following the Newark 1967 riots. The social unrest that swept the cities combined with the growing awareness of the deteriorating environment in forcing planners to reevaluate the established patterns of suburban growth. Still, despite the acknowledged urgency of the situation, many directors continued to place their faith in the voluntary actions of the local planning boards. If local planners failed to show goodwill, home rule would be doomed. Hyde laid it on the line:

> You know as well as I that there isn't any municipal planning any more—it is community planning, taking into consideration the forces surrounding the municipality on all sides: other towns, highways, railways, slums, farms, industries, $50,000 homes and whatnot.

> And we will go much further. Because, my friends, if we don't I imagine someone else will fill the vacuum. Such as the Federal Government. . . . Or the State of New Jersey. This is a State with a basic tenet of Home Rule. . . . Please make a note: Does the law say anything about whether the State cannot plan? Further, industries are ensconcing themselves nicely in our suburbs and leaving all those dirty cities behind. And leaving behind a mounting number of jobless and untrained people.

> Can our suburbs afford this? I am sure our suburbs do not wish to give up funds to that old fogey, the city. But money has to come from somewhere. . . . There will undoubtedly be Federal Funds acts. . . . It is worthwhile to do a little regional thinking and to consider what sores we are innocently planting for which we will inevitably have to pay.[22]

The directors did try to take their own advice and, starting in 1965, they attempted to renew their relationship with the state's urban constituency. For five years, the Federation devoted the opening session of its program in the Atlantic City conferences to a joint session with the New Jersey Association of Housing and Redevelopment Authorities for a discussion of urban problems. In addition, the Federation began to cosponsor the New Jersey Welfare Conference in an attempt to open a dialogue between planners and social workers. It was not easy. "We have learned that social workers have a far different method of problem solution than we," remarked Hyde, "and it might take a great deal of common discussion with countless diverse social welfare groups before a successful connection might be outlined between physical planning and social planning." However, he added the following warning: "It must be realized that within a decade, insofar as urban core-city planning is concerned, a project without the furtherance of social welfare solutions will not be acceptable, by state or federal demand."[23]

Area meetings and courses in the Principles of Urban Renewal followed the conferences but enjoyed a very limited success. Maslow tells how the locations of the urban renewal courses were constantly shifted in a futile attempt to attract lay city planners. Finally, the Federation came to accept its limited appeal to the state's urban constituency. After all, at its core, the Federation has always been an organization of dedicated public citizens who had believed passionately in the Jeffersonian ideals of participatory democracy and were prepared to invest the time and effort necessary to the acquisition of the skills needed to assure that their voices would be heard. Regrettably, such self-confidence is difficult to come by in the city ghettoes and almost impossible to put into use in the highly partisan atmosphere of the city halls.

On yet another level, the communication difficulties the Federation experienced with social workers and city planners were the result of a more fundamental problem. Social planning in the mid-sixties was in its infancy. John C. Bullitt, the director of the New Jersey Office of Economic Opportunity, explained:

> Our most acute problem in this great effort is the almost complete non-existence of a body of theoretical knowledge of trained personnel to do the planning.
>
> In this effort, I believe you can play a significant role, if you wish to. While we struggle to create in our universities and

communities the ability to educate social planners, many of you have, and many more will, fill the gap.[24]

In response to this plea, the Federation in 1968 began to explore the possibility of sponsoring a high-level seminar for the exposition of new planning concepts on an academic plane. Following months of preparation, and with the help of Rutgers University's Department of Urban Planning and Policy Development, a yearly conference entitled "Frontiers of Urban Planning" was launched in March 1969. The first conference dealt with advocacy planning, social policy planning, and cost-effectiveness analysis. Later conferences addressed the problems of pollution, population density, and aesthetics. The gatherings were geared to the professional and advanced lay planner and tended to present the views of experts from outside the tristate area.

Despite the Federation's best efforts, the municipalities were slow to adjust to the changing times, and, as a result, they found themselves under mounting pressure from state and federal authorities. Essentially, local planning was under attack from two distinct, though interrelated, fronts: housing and pollution. The municipalities ended up concentrating all their resources in fighting any encroachment on their right to regulate the type of housing they wished to see in their community, allowing the state an ever-increasing role in environmental regulation. Was it possible that for all their protestations home rule, like fiscal zoning, was only a facade that covered a deep-seated desire by a large segment of the population to build islands of homogeneity in the midst of a great heterogeneous nation, as the Musto Report maintained?

Perhaps so, but municipalities might also have been motivated by their wish to hold onto some role in the planning of their community, and the example of regional planning in the Meadowlands did not help assuage their fear of being completely supplanted. The creation of the Hackensack Meadowlands Development Commission (HMDC) was the jewel in the crown of the Division of State and Regional Planning. Basically, it involved the transference of the planning and zoning rights of fourteen municipalities to a regional planning and development authority. The promise of federal funds played a crucial role both in the financing and timing of the state legislation, as did the prospect of job creation in the socially volatile area of the northeast.

"The passage of a Meadowlands bill this year will enable New Jersey to benefit from a major federal reclamation project which will be of inestimable value to the state as a whole, as well as preventing the increasing stangulation of this vital area within the next few years," declared *The Federation Planner*, and added: "Every effort has been made to ensure the fullest possible protection of local interests."[25] Actually, while the municipalities concerned might not have experienced any financial loss, the local planning boards had completely lost their say in the Meadowlands area. On the other hand, environmental legislation, like the Wetlands bill, only tended to set guidelines for local actions but not replace the need for such action.

To the chagrin of the Federation's directors, the municipal determination to oppose any further diminution of local planning was translated into a series of defeats for the organization's attempts to modernize the state's planning enabling legislation that the Federation deemed essential to the future viability of municipal planning. In 1965, the directors decided to make a concentrated effort to bring about a thorough reform of the planning law. They had in mind a comprehensive set of laws that would define the exact role each level of government was to have in the planning process. Experienced and battle-scarred as the directors were, they could not have imagined that it would take a decade of struggle to achieve the passage of only a municipal land-use law and yet another decade to establish a proper state planning unit, while an effective integration of the county's planning role beyond statutory jurisdiction over roads and drainage remains to be determined.

After a careful examination of the history of past failures to rewrite the law, the leadership decided to repeat the process that resulted in the 1953 planning law. The directors made a successful appeal to Governor Hughes to instruct the commissioner of the State Department of Conservation and Economic Development, Robert Roe, to appoint a broad-based committee for the purpose of overhauling the present planning legislation. However, following the creation of the Department of Community Affairs (DCA), the responsibility for this committee was transferred to its commissioner, Paul N. Ylvisaker. The committee's first meeting took place on December 14, 1967, in the office of the new commissioner, who immediately used the opportunity to express his commitment to regional planning or at least regional cooperative action.

Nine months later, Maslow was happy to report that "he and the rest of the committee were delighted that we advanced so far and so well in bringing these documents up-to-date for some time to come. The new act when formulated will include all planning law . . . : municipal planning and zoning law, the master plan, the capital improvements program, subdivision regulations, the official map, state involvement in planning and development (and it is high time this is defined) as well as a State judicial review board to take the place of the present court system."[26] The directors then passed a resolution expressing their support for the bill in its present form.

The leadership was especially anxious to bring about a revision in the new Planned Unit Development (PUD) legislation. In 1967, a PUD bill, supported by the Home Builders' Association but vehemently opposed by the Federation and the Institute of Municipal Attorneys, was passed by the legislature and signed into law by the governor. The Federation took the unusual step of directly warning its members not to make use of the permissive legislation without the advice of both an attorney and a qualified planning consultant. It even pressured the Division of State and Regional Planning not to issue copies of the act. Budd Chavooshian, the division director, explained that while the division could delay publication, it could not completely evade its responsibility to publish it. Still, fourteen months later, the following entry appeared in the Federation's minutes:

> The secretary brought up the matter of the information bulletin being put together by the Division of State and Regional Planing on P.U.D., previously delayed on request of the Federation until more legal answers had been ascertained. This report has now been rewritten and, according to Mr. Maslow, Chairman of the Federation Planning Statue Committee, now gives ample warning as to possible difficulties of utilizing the present Act. It was moved by Carr, seconded by Marron, that the Division be notified that the Federation's objections to the publication's distribution were now withdrawn.[27]

As work on a new planning bill was progressing satisfactorily, the organization decided to live with the PUD law and concentrate its energies on the passage of the comprehensive planning bill as the best solution for overcoming the failings of the existing law. Unfortunately, by the time the long-awaited bill S-803 was finally introduced in May 1969, controversy replaced consensus.

The Federation leadership tended to blame much of the opposition to the bill on the work methods of Ylvisaker, the DCA commissioner. Instead of introducing the August 1968 draft bill that was developed by the committee (according to Maslow), Ylvisaker played "big daddy" and rewrote the entire bill without any further consultation with the thirty-five organizations that were represented on the committee.

On the whole, the legislative committee was still prepared to support the bill, though it demanded certain amendments and was annoyed enough by the bill's opponents' deliberate spread of misinformation for Owen to include the following observation in his analysis of S-803 in *The Planner:* "Many groups worked together to develop the bill and it is disconcerting to hear attacks which are directed not against the bill as much as against the DCA."[28]

The editor of *New Jersey Municipalities* had a different view of the origin of the hostility with which the bill was met:

> The Commissioner viewed the Garden State's myriad collection of planning and zoning laws as the most logical and obvious vehicle for achieving the broadscale social and economic reforms which he felt were required. Commissioner Ylvisaker's bill became the center of renewed controversy. In addition to offering badly-needed revisions of technical and administrative provisions of the planning and zoning law, Senate S-803 dramatically altered the traditional structure of zoning powers which had been vested exclusively in municipalities and introduced a new and greatly expanded state role in local zoning matters. Senate S-803 consequently died and there was very little mourning on the part of local officials.[29]

Clearly, municipalities were no more prepared to relinquish their zoning power to the state than their residents were ready to increase their own tax burden. The Federation, bowing to political realities, had to resort to damage control, as is evident from the following entry in the organization's minutes: "After much discussion, it was decided it was important for Mr. Owen to ensure that a resolution in this committee [the League's resolution committee] would not block or harm the basic needs of a new planning and zoning proposal and that S-803 were not generally condemned."[30]

Still, something was accomplished. The County Planning Act had been amended to give counties more control over developments along county roads and an additional advisory role. The Federation's legislative committee worked closely with the County Planners Association during the preparatory phase of the bill and consequently threw its support behind its passage. However, Owen could not refrain from commenting: "Most of the new powers granted to the counties are advisory in nature. However, if the municipalities do not respond to the pressures which are being created by the more intensive use of land the act could be further amended to give the county mandatory powers."[31]

While the planning community was debating, a slow but unmistakable shift could be detected in the court's attitude toward municipal planning prerogatives. Three distinct issues came before the court: (1) individual property rights, (2) pollution, and (3) housing. It could be assumed that by the late sixties, the issue of property rights had been settled in favor of planning. Therefore, the challenge of a fourteen-year-old state statute, which gave municipalities the right to delay for one year the development of land for public purposes, seemed symbolic of the new era. When the trial judge found for the plaintiff, the Federation was sufficiently concerned to join with the New Jersey Institute of Municipal Attorneys as amicus curiae in the appeal process. Both organizations were represented by Fred Stickel, an associate counsel of the Federation, who argued:

> The function of the court is to ascertain in each case where there is a clash of public and private rights whether the general benefits to be derived by the public outweigh the disadvantages or limitations on private property owners indicated. In the issue at hand, we submit the property owner, as a part of the community, enjoys and shares in the common benefit secured to all by official mapping and such is sufficient compensation for such

minor interference with his absolute property right for that
one-year period.[32]

The state Supreme Court upheld the constitutionality of the law,
but the court's activism was expressed not only in its insistence that
the property owner be justly compensated but also outlining the
manner in which such compensation should be attained.

In August 1968, the court ordered nine North Jersey communities
to suspend any further building activities until they stopped polluting
the river with their raw sewage. Owen, the Federation president,
noted:

> This court order comes less than a year after the warning which
> was sounded in the August 1967 issue of the PLANNER in
> which it was stated that the unabated contamination of air and
> water will create eventual industrial stagnation and may turn our
> cities and towns into graveyards. If the communities did not
> regulate themselves, it was suggested that the state would have
> to do so. The State has done just that.[33]

Warnings that the courts might be ready to change their liberal
attitude toward municipal zoning were beginning to be heard across
the land as early as 1965. In 1962, Justice Hall still considered the
question whether zoning should be grounded on a geographical base
broader than that of a municipality as an issue of policy "subject to
ultimate resolution by the legislative branch rather than the judiciary."[34] By 1965, in the case of the *Roman Catholic Diocese of Newark*
versus *Borough of Ho-Ho-Kus*, the same justice maintained that while
he was in accord with the state's system of home rule, he felt that
the system "should encompass responsibilities as well as rights" and
municipalities "must take some of the bitter with the sweet when the
public good thereby advanced necessarily transcends municipal boun-
daries."[35]

In 1968, Charles A. Reid, an associate counsel of the Federation,
told a central area audience: "We must understand that the constitutional basis of zoning is the reasonableness of the exercise of police
power. It is a scale upon which the weights are not constant." He
then proceeded with a question he regarded as rhetorical: "Can we
say, and can we, if called upon to defend our zoning ordinances, now

convince a court that we are indulging in comprehensive planning 'without endangering the needs or reasonable expectations of any segment of our people?' "[36]

The shape of things to come was further revealed in December 1969 when Governor Hughes signed into law a bill permitting state residents to challenge local zoning practices on grounds of alleged discrimination in municipalities in which they do not reside. Owen ruefully noted that "this last bill is more liberal than a paragraph in the yet-unpassed S-803 which had offended many conservative administrators."[37]

In August 1970, the *Planner* reported the institution of the first "restrictive zoning" case in New Jersey. The same issue of the *Planner* also told of the Federal Housing and Urban Development Secretary George Romney's advocacy of a bill that would directly prohibit local government from using local land-use controls to prevent federally assisted low-income and moderate-income housing from entering a community. Even more telling were the changes in the 701 program. By 1969, the federal government, which originally had set up the program to encourage planning in small communities, allocated 85% of the 701 funds to the counties and only 10% to 15% to municipalities. Jules W. Marron, the Federation president, drew the following conclusions: "The main point of this discussion, as I see it, is that the area of arguments pro and con restrictive zoning is rapidly widening and the point of 'critical mass explosion' is fast approaching. We must have the power in our state to make our own proper decisions—which is why we press for completion and legislation into action of our revised new land use law."[38]

The year 1970 brought with it a new governor, William Cahill, and a new DCA commission, Edmond T. Hume. Hume, a previous chairman of the Maplewood planning board and a Maplewood mayor, seemed ideally suited for a leadership role in the necessary updating of the state's planning laws. In an attempt to cover all the possible bases, Hume "created three committees composed of representatives from those groups (organizations and interest groups): a small drafting committee, an intermediate-size steering committee, and a forty-member land-use advisory committee."[39]

The small drafting committee included the familiar names of Stickel, Cox, Bernstein, Maslow, Willis, and Norman, all Federation members in good standing. (Sidney Williams had become the director of the Division of State and Regional Planning under Commission Ylvisaker, and Tom Norman was a bright young attorney on the division staff. Both became active members of the Federation.) By June 1970, the working draft of the new bill was completed, and the Federation began to formulate plans for selling it to its membership. In order to save the new bill from the fate of its predecessor, the framers made sure that it contained no provisions concerning housing or building codes. The latter were expected to be treated in separate bills.

One of the more interesting features of the bill was the creation of a State Planning and Development Commission in the Office of the Governor. The commission would be charged with the preparation of a state development plan, an annual six-year capital program, recommendations on land acquisition, and the regulation of critical areas. Owen declared: "We believe this section creating a State Planning and Development Commission . . . will ensure proper protection of our municipal and county governmental needs. This is essential to the success of the entire proposed Act."[40]

To the directors' disappointment, the administration put the bill on hold until after the 1971 elections, and Owen had to report some suggestions to the effect that it might be helpful to sever the articles concerned with the creation of a State Planning and Development Commission from the rest of the bill. The directors steadfastly rejected the idea and decided to wait patiently for administrative action.

The delay in the introduction of the bill was not solely due to election jitters. The governor was embroiled in yet another futile attempt to impose a state income tax, which experts continued to maintain was essential to the accomplishment of any meaningful changes in municipal zoning practices. Also, the governor was awaiting the report of the Housing Task Force he appointed in December 1970 concerning the need for housing and the scarcity of suitably zoned land. In March 1972, the task force's recommendations were translated into a special message to the legislature, which called for: (1) a uniform state construction code, (2) revision of the planning laws, (3) a voluntary balanced housing plan, (4) a community development corporation, and (5) a state planning task force. The first four recommendations were incorporated into legislative bills introduced in July 1972. A-1422, the revision of the Municipal Land Use Law (MLUL), was part of the package.

The planning act received the enthusiastic endorsement of the Federation and the League. The *New Jersey Municipalities'* editorial did not hedge its bet but flatly stated: "It is a badly needed piece of legislation which deserves enactment."[41] There was even talk of mustering bipartisan support for its passage.

Its timing certainly seemed right. On October 27, 1971, Judge David D. Furman of the New Jersey Superior Court had just decided the state's first exclusionary case: *Oakwood at Madison* versus *Madison Township*. The court upheld the state's zoning laws but not the municipal ordinance. "The ordinance under attack must be held invalid because it fails to promote reasonably a balanced community in accordance with the general welfare," said the court.[42] The vague term "general welfare," which the fathers of modern planning used so successfully against proponents of property rights, was suddenly turned against municipal planners. Furthermore, the term was given a positive social meaning, that is, a balanced community.

The *Madison Township* case was just one of a series of exclusionary zoning cases in which the Federation felt obliged to get involved since one of the courts had alleged the unconstitutionality of the state planning law. Municipalities also became greatly interested in legal cases, and the court coverage by the *Planner* was constantly expanded. Special attention was also paid to minute procedural details, as even minor infractions could lead to the loss of a court case. Unfortunately, the incoherent and much-amended land-use law did not help ease pressures, and neither did the story that was broken by the *Newark Star Ledger* on September 3, 1972: "Pervasive corruption in New Jersey Municipal Government, connected with planning and zoning law violations, will be the subject of a series of public hearings in Trenton by the State Commission of Investigation within the month."[43] Apparently, probes into organized crime that began in 1965 resulted in the discovery of the ties between organized crime and corrupt local officials. The investigations resulted in the indictment of more than one hundred thirty public officials between 1969 and 1972. In one case, a Union County grand jury found that the planning board did not receive sufficient legal advice from its attorney, did not establish appropriate procedural rules or uniform standards of action, and was careless in regard to conflict of interest. Bernstein, the Federation counsel, stated: "What has been written hereinbefore are facts given to the general public which can only have the effect of weakening the respect of the average citizen for local government and its administrative agencies."[44]

Still, the embattled planning boards were not about to receive any help from the legislature. Throughout 1972 and the first half of 1973, the Federation spared no effort in its attempts to secure maximum exposure and support for the pending land-use bill, but it soon became apparent that Governor Cahill's gambit failed. The inclusion of the land-use bill in a package of "housing bills" sealed its fate.

While housing and land-use bills were dying in committees, radical environmental bills had little trouble getting the approval of the legislature, regardless of the fact that they represented a major dilution of home rule. Hyde reported in 1973:

> This year, we have seen a gradual movement by the Administration of intrusion on local zoning responsibilities, with a defense of state control as an ecological necessity. In this the administration has had the encouragement of the Federal Administration and William Ruckelshaus, Administrator of the Federal Environmental Agency.
>
> The Wetlands Bill and the Flood Plains Bill, both of good intent, have broken ground in placing large tracts of land under the supervision of a single state agency. The Pineland Protective Act, sanitizing 300,000 acres, has been passed. Opposition to these was, fortunately, small, but with the introduction of a Coastal Protection Bill, an attempt to prevent environmental deterioration in a ten-mile swathe around the State from Monmouth to Camden Counties through prohibitions in development, opposition to an all embracing environmental policy has began to form, and industrialists, developers, builders and employment planners have began organizing on an "economic need" basis to counter the "total environment" case.[45]

The environmental bills passed by the legislature were signed by the governor, while the land-use bill languished in committee. After all, issues related to the quality of life were always dear to the hearts of planners and suburbanites alike. In addition, municipalities hoped to use environmental fragility to justify their zoning practices. Most telling was the reaction to the 1973 energy crisis by Earle Finkbiner, the Federation president. He wrote an editorial called "Virtues of a Gasoline Shortage" in which he mused over a future without automobiles. There will be no need for unsightly gasoline stations, no loss of agricultural lands, and, most importantly, no more suburban shopping centers. People would return to the cities, and urban blight would finally be stopped.

The governor, realizing the probable fate of the planning bill, issued an executive order creating a State Planning Task Force with a mandate to prepare and maintain a comprehensive state physical development plan and to review the planning programs of each state department. The task force took depositions, held public hearings, and, finally, produced a report recommending the creation of a State Planning Council—and then disbanded.

The year 1973 was an election year, so all efforts to get the planning bill off dead center had to be suspended. When the election dust settled and the new administration was safely in place, the League's planning committee (on which the Federation was well represented) began a series of informal meetings with members of the county and municipal government committees of both the Senate and the Assembly. The planners received some unexpected advice: "Everyone agrees that the planning laws affecting municipalities should be brought up to date. Influential members of the Legislature have asked the League and the Federation to draw up a bill independently of the state, promising to work for enactment of a planning and zoning bill which would help our municipalities. . . . The new bill would not include the county act or the state regulations of the last bill, but would apply to municipalities only."[46] In essence, the committee was told that a complete distancing from the state government was necessary in order to secure the passage of a solely municipal planning bill.

Clearly, the backlash feared by Hyde was on its way, but, for the time being, it was directed at the state government as a whole rather than against environmental controls in particular. Horn, the Federation's first woman president, exhibited the same attitude when she suggested moving the annual State Planning Conference out of Trenton and making it less politically self-serving. She clearly expressed her belief that "the Federation should avoid political sides or close identification with State policy, unless it was something on which we could all agree."[47]

The League, which had a broad-based legislative committee that included representatives of its affiliates, appointed a special subcommittee to write the new bill. The drafting committee was chaired by Maslow, the Federation treasurer and past president (who claims in his self-deprecating way that he was picked for the position because the members recognized that they needed an unthreatening arbiter between high-powered attorneys). His vice chairman was Stickel, the attorney behind the 1953 municipal land-use law (formulating the law, claimed Stickel, is easier and more enjoyable than studying it), and the other members were Bernstein, William Cox, Walter Wittman, Stewart Hutt, Phillip Cocuzza, Malcolm Kassler, and James Jager.

After five months of hard work, the committee emerged with a bill that it hoped was "foolproof" since it was purported to be a purely administrative bill that strengthened municipal planning and zoning while being devoid of all previously proposed state and county provisions. The usually mild-mannered Maslow expressed the growing frustration of the local planning activists in his report to the organization's executive committee: "If this updated land use law is not enacted, I am afraid lay planners and their organizations will give up the fight for reform and leave, as the legislature has so often done, the solution of people's problems in communities solely to the Courts."[48]

The new bill, S-3054, was introduced in March 1975, and, as luck would have it, the bill was immediately surrounded by controversy, which, as Owen explained, was due to "the confusion the news media has caused, because the Mt. Laurel decision was handed down at the same time as the bill was introduced, vacant-minded reporters confused S-3054 as a 'housing bill' to answer the decision."[49] Owen was referring to the path-breaking decision reached by the New Jersey Supreme Court in the case of *Southern Burlington County* versus *Mount Laurel*. The court affirmed the lower court's judgment that declared the township's zoning ordinance invalid because it precluded low-income and middle-income housing. The court held that exclusionary zoning violated the due process and equal protection of the state constitution as well as the purposes of zoning enumerated in the state's planning and zoning laws. Furthermore, the majority opinion, written by Justice Hall, maintained that "because Mt. Laurel belongs to a class of municipalities defined as 'developing' it must 'by its land use regulations, presumptively make realistically possible an appropriate variety and choice of housing' so that the opportunity for low and moderate income housing is affirmatively afforded 'at least to the extent of municipalities' fair share of the present and prospective regional need therefore.' "[50]

Despite the new danger posed by this revolutionary (if not unexpected) ruling, the public hearings went fairly smoothly, as only three witnesses opposed the bill, deeming it unresponsive to the recent court decision. Ironically, one of those witnesses was Alvin Gershen, a leading professional planner and a longtime associate director of the Federation. Gershen came to the April 1975 directors' meeting since he said that he felt that he owed the Federation an explanation of his position. The bill, Gershen claimed, should be amended to include housing as a prerequisite of planning and, in defining "housing needs," the terms "regional basis" and "fair share" should be mentioned. Despite his awareness that the bill had been stripped of everything that might obstruct its passage, he still insisted that an inclusion of a housing element had become a necessity in order to alert communities to their new duty. His views were duly reported in the *Planner*.

The Federation threw all its resources behind the bill yet again. It helped finance and distribute copies of the bill despite the organization's precarious financial position (this was a task previously undertaken by the Division of State and Regional Planning), held numerous forums to discuss it, called upon its member boards to send resolutions supporting the bill to their representatives in the state legislature, and, of course, the directors and officers did their part in "discussing the bill" with the lawmakers.

This time, the hard work finally resulted in a well-deserved success. On January 14, 1976, Governor Brendan T. Byrne signed the bill in the presence of Maslow, Hyde, Owen, Stickel, Cox, Harold Feinberg, and Jager.

Despite the constant claims made by the bill's advocates that the new MLUL was only intended to improve the administration of the planning, many of its provisions were intended to strengthen and widen the power of the local planning boards and render the boards' actions more easily defensible in the court of law.

Although the MLUL had a widely permissive nature, while it treaded softly, it also carried a big stick. Municipalities did not have to appoint a planning board, but if they wanted to zone land, they had to have a planning board that prepared a master plan and adopted a land-use element; most significantly, the zoning ordinance had to be substantially consistent with the adopted land-use plan. As the vast majority of the state's municipalities would not dream of abolishing their zoning ordinances, the role of the planning boards was assured.

The centrality of the master plan, which was usually prepared by a professional planner following exhaustive studies of the community, helped localities. Zoning ordinances based on current master plans and adopted land-use plans (the plans had to be updated every six years) would be less likely to be challenged in court and easier to defend. The simplified, unified, and standardized procedures ensured that the boards would have to adhere to the due process of the law and thus help further to limit the grounds for judicial involvement. While the ability of the planning board to adopt the master plan without the expressed approval of the governing body might strengthen the ability of the boards to "act courageously", it also turned the municipal government into the first court of appeal, eliminating in many cases the need to resort to another court.

The following list of administrative changes was meant to ascertain that justice would not only be done but would seem to be done: (1) All interested parties must be notified concerning hearings. (2) There must be verbatim recordings at all public meetings. (3) Maps and relevant documents must be made available for public inspection. (4) The minutes of the meetings must contain all pertinent data. (5) The chairperson must be empowered to administer oaths, to issue subpoenas, and compel the appearance of witnesses and production of needed documents. (6) Testimony has to be taken under oath or affirmation. (7) Decisions are required to be in writing based upon facts and conclusions.

The new MLUL also legitimized the use of innovative planning techniques, such as site planning, time phasing and staging, capital improvement budgeting, and establishing design control districts. The drafting committee noted "that a total of 14 separate, and often conflicting, state laws would have to be repealed in part or in totality."[51] One of those laws was the 1967 PUD law so disliked by the Federation. The new PUD provisions became an integral part of the MLUL and earned the following judgment: "The New Jersey P.U.D. Act is one of the most comprehensive and well written. It provides for a wide variety of land uses including industrial."[52]

Similarly, the law was designed to provide developers with fair and prompt treatment. This was to be achieved also by strengthening the boards of adjustment, as well as the planning board, and giving developers the choice of which board they wished to approach (this provision was found unsatisfactory and was subsequently amended). Thus, the need to petition both boards was eliminated. Furthermore, the failure of a board to act within a prescribed time period would constitute approval of the applicant's petition. After all, by the time this MLUL was deliberated, New Jersey's period of rapid growth had been halted, and the state was no longer interested in limiting growth but in spurring it.

The Federation leadership viewed the passage of the 1975 Federation cosponsored MLUL as symbolic of the new maturity and effectiveness of the organization. Maslow elaborated: "In 1975 the Federation took a major step forward in the leadership of the planning process. Before we were lay people who went along with professionals [the state planners], the Federation just reacted to pressures. After 1975 the Federation became the positive leader in the zoning and planning field."[53]

Unfortunately, the legislative achievements of the organization were not accompanied by increased support from its constituency, at least so far as membership was concerned. After long years of steady growth, the Federation began to experience a significant decline in its membership. General inflation, coupled with spiraling energy, paper, and mailing costs, put a strain on the Federation budget. The organization had to raise its dues periodically, and, while the rise in dues as such had little effect on the size of the membership, when it was combined with the recession-inspired municipal budget cuts (especially in the rural areas), it soon became difficult for budget officers to recommend approval of membership.

Furthermore, there was a constant rise in the number of municipalities that felt obliged to employ professional planners and attorneys in order to cope with the constant barrage of new regulations and the ever-present threat of litigation. The Federation encouraged its members to take just such defensive measures, but it soon became clear that many communities no longer considered membership in the Federation important, and, in addition, the entry of professional planners into a community caused an atrophy of interest among lay planners. While some lay planners continued to take courses, few became interested in wider planning issues. It was also just possible that the activists who were attracted to planning in the fifties and sixties tended to flock to environmental commissions in the seventies. Fairly or not, after a decade of fierce attacks, the image of the lay planner went through a radical metamorphosis. The progressive idealist of the twenties, thirties, and forties had evolved into the provincial conservative of the sixties and seventies.

Such changes seem to have been inevitable in the life of individuals, movements, and organizations, but movements and organizations, unlike individuals, can be rejuvenated by new leadership and new ideas. Regrettably, before such renewal occurs, conflict, confusion, and sadness prevail. Abraham Janz, the 1972 president of the Federation, offered a grace that beautifully mirrored all those negative feelings but added to it a dose of courage and hope clearly indicating that, as profound as the changes had been, they had only just begun:

> Almighty God, King of the Universe, blessed be Your Name: Help me as a servant to my fellow men to seek and find the truths and answers to the perplexing problems which beset us. Guide me in this wilderness of modern times and complicated thinking. Guide those in the judiciary and the legal professions so that they may assist and instruct us in ways to buttress our way of life, rather than erode it.

> Guide the builders to truly serve their fellow men—large profit or small. Guide the citizens' organizations and committees so

that they may be less critical and more informative, helping us all to attain a common goal of meaningful, relevant discourse on the problems that plague us all. And finally, guide us that we may together strive to achieve the paradise lost so many centuries ago.[54]

Notes

1. Walter H. Blucher, "Answers to Current Planning Problems," *New Jersey Municipalities* (January 1960):22–23.

2. Mason W. Gross, "The Respectability of Planning," *Jersey Plans*, vol. XI, nos. 1, 2 (1960):25.

3. John J. Holland, "Inter-Municipal Planning," *Jersey Plans*, vol. XIII, no. 4 (1963):66.

4. *Ibid.*

5. Lyle C. Fitch, "Planning and the Property Tax," *Jersey Plans*, vol. XI, nos. 1, 2 (1960):14–15.

6. Interview with McKim Norton, June 28, 1986.

7. County and Municipal Government Study Commission, "Fiscal and Social Impact of Multi-family Development," *Housing & Suburbs* (October 1974):ix.

8. *Ibid.*, p. x.

9. *Ibid.*, p. xi.

10. *Ibid.*, p. 117.

11. *Ibid.*, p. xiii.

12. Federation's Minutes, April 21, 1966, p. 7.

13. *Ibid.*

14. Federation's Minutes, June 12, 1969, p. 4.

15. Federation's Minutes, September 17, 1969, p. 2.

16. David C. Ranney, *Planning and Politics in the Metropolis* (Columbus, Ohio: Charles E. Merrill Publishing Co., 1969), p. 35.

17. As quoted in Elvin S. Fulop, "Community Planning—Stone Age or Moon Age," *New Jersey Municipalities* (January 1970):16.

18. Federation's Minutes, April 11, 1968, p. 5.

19. Federation's Minutes, May 14, 1964, p. 2.

20. Federation's Minutes, January 14, 1969, p. 2.

21. "Harry Maslow on Education," *The Federation Planner* (April 1966):2.

22. Federation's Minutes, November 17, 1966, p. 4.

23. Federation's Minutes, April 21, 1966, p. 2.

24. As quoted in the Federation's Minutes, May 19, 1966, p. 7.

25. "Regional Planning in the Hackensack Meadows," *The Federation Planner* (August 1968):3–4.

26. Federation's Minutes, September 18, 1968, p. 5.

27. Federation's Minutes, June 11, 1968, p. 3.

28. "Report of Our Legislative Committee," *The Federation Planner* (August 1969):3.

29. "New Jersey's Land Use Revision: Finally, a Realistic Bill Is in the Works," *New Jersey Municipalities* (June 1970):5.

30. Federation's Minutes, October 23, 1969, p. 7.

31. "President Owen Notes," *The Federation Planner* (October 1968):2.

32. Thomas J. Hooper, "State's High Court Hears Defense of Option Statute," *Newark Evening News*, December 5, 1967.

33. "President Owen Notes," *op. cit.*, p. 1.

34. As quoted in "Day and a Half Light," *The Federation Planner* (December 1962):3.

35. As quoted in Harold Feinberg, "Further Ramifications of School Zoning," *New Jersey Municipalities* (November 1966):13.

36. "Changing Concepts of Local Planning Rights," *The Federation Planner* (February 1968):4.

37. Federation's Minutes, January 15, 1970, p. 6.

38. Jules W. Marron, "Federal Assault on Restrictive Zoning," *The Federation Planner* (August 1970):1.

39. Edmond T. Hume, "Land Use and Zoning Developments in New Jersey," *New Jersey Municipalities* (January 1971): 6.

40. "A New New Jersey Land Use Law," *The Federation Planner* (December 1970):5.

41. "New Jersey's Land Use Revision," *op. cit.*, p. 5.

42. "Observations on Madison," *The Federation Planner* (February 1972):3.

43. As quoted in the Federation's Minutes, September 13, 1972, p. 6.

44. *Ibid.*

45. Federation's Minutes, April 13, 1973, pp. 5–6.

46. Federation's Minutes, May 15, 1974, p. 3.

47. Federation's Minutes, May 15, 1975, p. 2.

48. Federation's Minutes, September 12, 1974, p. 3.

49. Federation's Minutes, April 14, 1975, p. 3.

50. *Burlington County NAACP et al.* versus *Township of Mount Laurel,* New Jersey Supreme Court, October 1974, pp. 8–9.

51. Harry A. Maslow and Malcolm Kasler, "The League's Proposed Municipal Land Use Law," *New Jersey Municipalities* (November 1974):7.

52. T. William Patterson, *Land Use Planning—Techniques of Implementation* (New York: Van Nostrand Reinhold Co., 1979), p. 52.

53. Interview with Harry Maslow, May 15, 1986.

54. Federation's Minutes, May 18, 1972, p. 6.

7

The New Guard

John F. Kennedy declared in his 1961 inaugural speech that the torch had passed on to a new generation. That generation spent the sixties busy with consciousness-raising activities in the civil rights, peace, and environmental movements. By the mid-seventies a growing maturity, accompanied by significant changes in the nation's political and economic realities, caused that generation to change its tactics, if not its goals. Consequently, riots gave way to court cases, exhortations to quotas, and hippies to yuppies. In short, romanticism was replaced by realism and amateurism by professionalism. As was evident in the past, neither the state nor the planning establishment could escape its position in the eye of the storm, and the Federation, after all, was an integral part of the planning establishment.

The new sobriety of the late seventies and eighties was caused, at least in part, by the energy crisis, which forced the whole of the western world to come to terms with the realities of diminishing resources. Following decades of consistent growth, New Jersey (especially its populous north) found itself in the center of an "ailing northeast," suffering from an economic recession accompanied by a seemingly intractable inflation. It appeared the American Dream based on the right of each family to a home of its own complete with a two-car garage would have to be abandoned, and nowhere was the psychic shock suffered by such abandonment greater than in the Garden State.

Planners and environmentalists had always emphasized the finiteness of the state's resources; now they finally acquired an attentive audience. Efficiency in resource management and distribution was no longer merely desirable but vital, and, as always, centralization of the decision-making process appeared the obvious way to rationalization. However, in order to appease the home rule devotees, as well as maintain the ideological and practical benefits of decentralized management, a way had to be found to secure effective cooperation between the various levels of government. Eventually, it worked out that such a system had to be based on clear policy guidelines laid down by the federal and state governments but administered by the municipal government, possibly under the supervision of the county or other regional authority. The road to such an ideal state of affairs was far from smooth, especially as no one was sure where it led. Some were skeptical as to its benefits, and many were sure to lose at least some of their power and influence. Thus, the question of the decade was, will the irresistible force triumph over the immovable object?

During the late seventies, municipalities found themselves under severe financial pressures. Inflation made the provision of services more difficult, while a stream of new state laws, including the Municipal Land Use Law (MLUL), and regulations further increased their expenses. The new burdens had to be passed on to already overburdened homeowners. To prevent the recurrence of the California taxpayers' revolt, which gave birth to that state's famous (or infamous) Proposition 13, in 1976 the New Jersey legislature placed a 5% cap on the yearly rise in municipal expenditure (any municipality that wished to exceed this cap had to get the approval of its voters in a referendum). As inflation consistently ran higher than 5%, the communities had to go through quite a tough period of belt-tightening, despite the fact that the new cap law was part of a package that included a state income tax (the new tax was designed mainly to take care of school funding in the wake of a State Supreme Court ruling that invalidated the local funding of education).

The controversial *Mt. Laurel I* decision, which was intended to end exclusionary zoning litigation, ended up giving birth to a whole new series of court cases. Undefined terms like "regional need," "fair share," and "developing communities" had to acquire a more precise meaning. Within six months of that court ruling, 12% of the state's municipalities had their zoning ordinances challenged in the court of law.[1] It was a small wonder that cynics called the decision "the full employment bill for planners and lawyers."

The general economic downturn, and the municipal fiscal difficulties, continued to have a serious effect on the Federation. Membership dropped as communities cut any expenses they did not deem absolutely vital. Participation in area meetings and courses suffered from the same municipal scalpel. Tom Hyde compared life in the late seventies to life during the depression, and he and some of the directors scavenged through the organization's early records in the hope of finding a better way to cope with the hard times. Alas, those early years offered little insight. The Federation of the seventies had greatly outgrown the infant organization of the thirties and forties. Attempts at economizing could become self-defeating. Reductions in the number of area meetings or publications were feared to cause an even greater loss of membership and income, as did the inevitable rises in the cost of membership. Still, years of consecutive budget deficits were eating into the organization's nest egg and threatening to undermine its very existence.

In 1976, the Federation elected Bud Schwartz as its new president, and the battle for the control of the organization commenced. Schwartz was a successful, amiable, self-made businessman intent on saving the Federation by reordering its priorities and modernizing its management. Tragically, he did not fully understand Hyde's unique role in the organization.

The Federation, Schwartz insisted, had to become a forceful spokesman for the needs of local planning boards, the one organization to which the state's powers that be would turn for help whenever they wished to sell their policies to the municipalities. Within months of his ascendancy to the presidency, Schwartz (accompanied by Hyde) met with the commissioner of the Department of Environmental Protection, who suggested setting up regular meetings between Federation representatives and members of his department in order to coordinate priorities and to secure better cooperation between the state and the localities. A decade of radical environmental legislation made such cooperation vital.

In a second meeting, the beleaguered commissioner of the Department of Community Affairs (DCA) secured the cooperation of the Federation with the Housing Forum, which was organized to address the state's worsening housing problems; inflation and high interest rates were causing house prices to skyrocket. Interestingly, Hyde soon found out that, in reality, the Housing Forum had no other immediate goals aside from protecting the DCA from elimination. The Federation, which was one of the motivating forces behind the establishment of the DCA, was vehemently opposed to its dismemberment. Still, Hyde expressed his bitter disappointment with the failure of the forum not only to secure action but even to provide a platform for the discussion of the housing needs of the state on an annual basis.

Important as these leadership activities were, without a large and loyal following, all the Federation's efforts would be rendered meaningless. Therefore, Schwartz set out to convince the local planning boards that belonging to the Federation was worthwhile even during the period of "fiscal misery":

> *WE KNOW WE HAVE WHAT YOU NEED.* As local planning comes more and more under attack, the Federation has taken steps to help local planning boards retain their integrity and their identity. The chairmen of our major committees and I have worked out goals which are intended to give you the kind of services that can only be provided through a state-wide organization whose basic job is to assist and represent you.

> The Legislative Committee, under Sam Owen's guidance, will be preparing regular reports. . . . And you will receive recommendations as to what bills deserve your support and which are objectionable. Planners need to express their views in the most effective and unified way.

> The Environmental Review Committee, under Bob Tatton, expects to concentrate on finding ways to translate the things we preach about into meaningful action. They have been talking about developing model ordinances dealing with ecological problems in a positive way.

The Local Response Committee, directed by Abe Janz, is also on its way. As new court decisions come down, local planners ask "What do we do now?" The mission of this committee is to explore all the possibilities available to you and then to provide you with a digest of the alternatives.[2]

Worthwhile as such elaborations of the Federation's usefulness were, it soon became obvious that the problems caused by a $7,000 budget deficit would not be solved by rousing editorials. The organization had to embark on a major membership drive. Consequently, Schwartz ordered his executive vice president to drop everything except membership solicitation while he, the president, would undertake the job of representing the organization at state functions. Schwartz tried to treat Hyde as an ordinary executive, and Hyde had no intention of accepting such a role. Board members became torn between the inescapable logic of their president's demands and their personal respect and affection for their long-serving executive. Furthermore, the directors were well aware that they would never be able to find anyone as capable, hard-working, and loyal to the cause as Hyde. Thus, following months of open hostility and numerous attempts at reconciling the differences between the two men, when push came to shove and Hyde forced the leadership to choose between him and Schwartz, the board chose the former; the latter resigned.

It was a bruising fight. Hyde retained his position, but according to Budd Chavooshian, neither man ever fully recovered from the wounding battle. The first attempt to unseat Hyde failed, but it was clear that unless the Federation's fortunes were to change, it would not be the last. The directors, who had bought peace in their time, heaved a sigh of relief and refocused their attention on the state's mounting planning problems.

The first item on the Federation's agenda was helping the municipal planning board to implement the new MLUL. The new planning law, which became effective on August 1, 1976, allowed municipalities six months in which to come into compliance, with an additional year (later extended to two years) in which to work out the relationship between the adopted land-use element of the master plan and the local zoning ordinances. Harry Maslow took it upon himself to make sure that municipalities understood the new requirements. During the months of March and April 1976 alone, he conducted six free, informal discussions all around the state in which he explained the changes communities had to make in their planning procedures. Four additional symposiums took place in June, and there were also two specialized meetings for professional planners and municipal attorneys that featured Maslow on their panels. All this was in addition to numerous clarifying articles in the *Planner* and the *Special Reports* issued by the local response committee designed to simplify and illuminate specific aspects of the law, such as the treatment of variances or the necessary changes in the makeup of the planning boards. It was clear that the organization felt that since it was a major instigator of the law, it was its responsibility to assure its successful application; when the first snags began to appear in putting the law into practice, the Federation stuck to the agreement it made with the other sponsoring organization and refused to join in any efforts to amend the law in its first year.

Another major preoccupation of the Federation was the 1976 passage and application of the Uniform Building Code. The organization actively supported the measure in the hope that it would lower skyrocketing construction costs by replacing 567 unrelated codes with a single up-to-date one that would allow the introduction of new construction methods and materials. It was disheartening for the leadership to be deluged with inquiries and complaints resulting from a faulty administration of the code. A new construction review committee was named. It was headed by Sidney Graybar, a noted builder and a longtime director. The committee soon discovered that new requirements, such as energy efficiency and barrier-free construction, together with a shortage of qualified inspectors and time-consuming forms, ended up defeating the purpose for which the code was designed. Instead of lowering construction costs, the effort to unify and centralize ended up increasing them.

The continued "infringement" by the state on municipal prerogatives also remained a constant Federation preoccupation. The Department of Environmental Protection, armed with laws like the Coastal Area Facility Review Act (CAFRA), began to show its claws, and special interest groups succeeded in passing legislation mandating new buildings to be barrier-free and allowing the physically and

mentally disabled to locate in any residential zone. Still, the most controversial and intractable issue of the day remained housing, as young couples, pensioners, teachers, and policemen joined the ranks of poor city dwellers in their inability to afford a suburban home.

In 1976, Governor Brendan Byrne responded to the first Mt. Laurel ruling by issuing Executive Order 35. The order bestowed on the Division of State and Regional Planning the unenviable task of formulating a state housing goal and allocating parts of it to each county or group of counties. The counties in their turn would allocate housing-type spaces to their municipalities. The allocation could then be used by litigants for assessing the reasonableness of a community's zoning ordinances. Further, to encourage municipalities to comply with the new voluntary plan, the order directed state officials servicing various state and federal community-related programs to give priority to those localities that were in the process of meeting their fair share of the state's projected housing needs. When the division produced the demanded allocations in November 1971, the governor rejected its plan and sent the state planners back to the drawing boards along with a list of new requirements, which were completed in May 1978.

On the whole, the Federation's leadership wished to see the issue of housing taken out of the hands of both the judges and the executives and placed firmly in the hands of the legislators. Bills proposing a constitutional amendment permitting binding referendum on the adoption of local planning and zoning regulations were strongly opposed by the organization. The Federation, along with the New Jersey State League of Municipalities (the League), supported S-3139, a balanced housing bill proposed by State Senator Martin L. Greenberg, who, according to Sam Owen, "has leaned over backwards to satisfy the municipalities as to their authority."[3] Owen, a strong home-rule advocate, ended his description of the history and content of the bill in the *Planner* with the following words:

> I strongly recommend that you review the bill which is on its long way through the legislative process. There are, of course, two sides to it: some hold that this is a softening of home rule—others allege that if it is not passed, all municipalities can be subjected to law suits at great expense, and that it is more desirable to have legislative action on the books which has the

combined thinking of local, county and state officials, rather than an executive fiat such as Executive Order 35, or to have to abide by an adverse decision of a court which can involve several thousands of dollars in fees.[4]

His plea fell on deaf ears, and no concrete legislative action was taken despite the numerous conferences dedicated to the bill. As to the executive order, it was never implemented, and, on April 24, 1979, Governor Byrne's chief of staff, Robert E. Mulcahy, told participants at the state's "Fair Share Housing Conference" that "the State's decision to tell towns how many housing units to have for low-income people was not realistic and will be changed."[5] He ended by returning the ball to the legislative court. As the legislators were reluctant to pick it up, it appeared that the battle between the communities and the courts had reached a stalemate; it even appeared to support the judgment of a small group that felt all along that Mt. Laurel would not change matters very much. Few paid any attention to yet another state master plan called the State Department Guide Plan (SDGP), which the State Planning Division, under the direction of Dick Ginman, was preparing, though the Federation did appoint a special committee to keep an eye on the plan. After all, in addition to meeting the division's stated legislative mandate, the SDGP was being formulated in order to satisfy federal requirements as, without an acceptable state land-use element, the state would not be able to continue to receive funds from the 701 program.

Meanwhile, with the new Pinelands legislation, the state was mounting its most radical incursion into a province that local government continued to claim as its sole prerogative, that is, land-use planning and zoning. The view of the Pinelands had undergone a major revision during the past decade, evolving from one of a backward area ripe for modernization to a national trust. In 1964, Carl G. Lindbloom, a planner with the firm of Herbert H. Smith and the director of the Pinelands Planning Project, concluded two years of investigation of the area with the following enthusiastic announcement:

For the first time since the planning of Washington, D.C. 174 years ago, there is an opportunity to build, from raw earth, a completely new major city. Located in the New Jersey wilderness known as the Pinelands (an area now containing pine trees, chipmunks and very little else), the city would have an anticipated ultimate population of 250,000. The rationale for the creation of this new city and its quarter of a million population is a proposed supersonic commercial jetport, serving the twelve-state northeastern region of the United States.[6]

In 1980, the Pinelands Commission opened its Draft Comprehensive Management Plan with a rather different boast: "The New Jersey Pinelands, a million-acre forest expanse in the midst of the country's most densely populated region, have finally been recognized as one of the nation's premier environmental treasures."[7]

No less instructive are the different management styles of the Garden State's two major regional planning authorities, the Meadowlands and the Pinelands. In the case of the former, the municipalities and the counties ceded all their planning prerogatives to the Hackensack Meadowlands Development Commission (HMDC). Such a complete abdication of local power did not happen in the case of the Pinelands. As the commissioner of the State Department of Environmental Protection, Daniel J. O'Hern proudly maintained: "The Pinelands National Reserve Act is a landmark piece of legislation. For the first time, it establishes a local-state-federal partnership in planning and acquisition to protect a nationally significant natural resource."[8]

When Chavooshian, one of the visionaries behind the development of the Meadowlands and a member of the Pinelands Commission, was asked to compare the two regional projects, he immediately expressed his preference for the latter: "In the Pinelands, communities have a stake in the Plan's success. It is their Plan!"[9]

The Federation, to the disgust of many of its affected constituents, maintained a low profile on the subject of Pinelands. Nowhere to be found is the enthusiastic support enjoyed by the Meadowlands legislation nor the crusading rejection of the law requiring all municipalities to permit "community residences" for the mentally and physically disabled. Could it be that the weariness of state intervention was more than balanced by the environmental considerations, the federal involvement, and the regional nature of the venture? Or did the truth belong to those who argued that the leadership (which was heavily tilted toward the northern half of the state) was less sensitive to the concerns of its dwindling southern constituency?

Chavooshian, by now a professor of planning at Rutgers University, claims that the reason for the directors' preoccupation with the northern half of the state was "because that was where the problems were!"[10] However, during the late seventies, the north did not have more problems than the south, only different ones. The south had to cope with an accelerated growth rate while the north saw its population and its industrial and commercial base rapidly declining. Furthermore, southerners bitterly resented the state's attempts to direct their regional development along ecologically sound lines. They interpreted the new environmental legislation as being motivated either by an attempt to limit growth so as to prevent a change in the balance of political forces in the state or as penance for the sins of past mismanagement in the north, which led to such unplanned and unsavory urban-suburban sprawl in that region. Be that as it may, southerners certainly felt that they could use assistance from a statewide organization like the Federation. In 1979, Robert Imler, the southern area chairman, made his area's needs clear: "We are having our problems with growth due to casino gambling and lack of growth due to the Pinelands Decision and we feel that the State Federation can be of more help than ever in helping us during this time of pressure."[11] Imler then continued to express his negative opinion of the management of the Federation: "To put it bluntly, ladies and gentlemen, for people that are charged with regulating the development of a community I think we are doing a poor job of running our own organization."[12]

On the whole, the Federation's fortieth annual meeting on May 17, 1979, turned out to be a rather extraordinary affair. It was planned as a celebration but ended up virtually as a rebellion. A great majority approved a constitutional revision (which was originally initiated by Schwartz in an effort to formalize procedures previously directed by custom and carried out by Bill Cox, the Federation's counsel), a raise in dues, and the creation of a new class-D professional membership (such as lawyers, architects, and engineers); but for the first time in the history of the Federation, negative votes were also cast. More importantly, Imler's criticism was joined by those of the chairmen of the northern and central areas in what amounted to an orchestrated attack on Hyde.

Actually, this unprecedented public reprimand of the executive vice president was the culmination of two years of bickering between Hyde and northern area directors, led by Virginia Koch and Jim Gilbert. Having learned from the failure of Schwartz, these directors preferred a war of attrition to a blitzkrieg. They demanded that the areas be given greater independence from the state organization, criticized the executive's treatment of area officers, and challenged the makeup and procedures of the nominating committee. Koch and Gilbert won a few battles and lost others, but they kept the pressure on, and by 1979, they were joined by the new chairman of the central area, David Ellenberg, and southern area officers Alex Pekarsky and Brian McFadden. This coalition was behind the combative 1979 annual meeting.

Following that fateful gathering, it soon became apparent that not only would the personal attacks on Hyde continue but that the young officers were becoming bolder and better organized. The rebels also proved that they were prepared to pull their weight by serving on committees and attending board meetings. So the officers felt obliged to pay attention when they were being told that the Federation's leadership was aging and badly in need of an infusion of young blood. For a while, it appeared that Hyde just might weather the storm, but when the budget committee's recommendation for a raise in his meager salary was followed by a lengthy discussion "as to whether the executive was worth the price,"[13] Hyde decided it was time to go. On January 16, 1980, Federation President John M. Reuter read a letter he received from Hyde terminating his services:

Gentlemen:

It had been my intention, since the frame-work for a three-year term for the Executive Secretary was set two years ago, to leave the Federation's service at the end of the third year, that is, on December 31, 1980. However, pressures have been sufficiently severe to persuade me to curtail this year's period to six months, ending my services on June 30, 1980. This, then, is official notice of my intentions.[14]

The pressures to which Hyde refers were not caused merely by the young challengers. The appropriate way to deal with the continuous decline in membership was the central point of contention. Hyde believed that if you had a good product (and the Federation did!), there were bound to be buyers. His theory held true for the fifties and sixties but faltered in the seventies. When Schwartz first questioned this assumption, the directors were not prepared to acknowledge that a more aggressive selling strategy was necessary, but when the number of member boards fell to three hundred fifty in 1979, the budget committee faced facts and decided to employ a part-time assistant for membership development. Hyde lost the argument and had to go.

Hyde's departure marked an end of an era in the history of the Federation. For twenty years, his name was synonymous with that of the organization. For Hyde, the Federation was not merely a place of employment but a cause to which he dedicated his life. His monetary compensation was always far from adequate while his workload remained enormous. It was only after he left that the directors came to realize the magnitude of the job he had been performing.

The Federation was unable to find anyone who could fill Hyde's shoes, but perhaps the organization of the eighties no longer had room for such a formidable leader. After all, the very qualities of idealism, dedication, and determination that are so essential for the creation of new enterprises may be interpreted as narrow-mindedness, domination, and stubbornness by the members of an ongoing enterprise. Therefore, the final judgment of such leaders often depends on the timing of their departure, and perhaps Hyde overstayed his welcome by a number of years. Unfortunately, those last years were full of acrimony, which tarnished his image at least temporarily and caused great anguish to him, his friends, and even his opponents. Be that as it may, according to Ginman, the director of the State Planning Division, very few eyes remained dry as Bernstein bid Hyde farewell in a special testimonial dinner. Tom Hyde's place in the annals of the Federation is secure.

Patricia (Pat) McKiernan, a former mayor of Hillsborough and a community activist, was chosen as the new executive of the Federation. Unfortunately, this bright and competent woman, who had just left politics in order to be able to spend more time with her children, was soon disillusioned by her new job. As a Federation executive, she was expected to perform an inordinate amount of routine office work using what she dubbed "nineteen thirties equipment." She told the directors that they were paying her too much money for the clerical work she was busy doing. Actually, it soon became apparent to her that she was required to do two jobs, as there was also a need for an executive who would get involved with the areas, work with Rutgers University on course development, and represent the organization in Trenton. Thus, when a new job opportunity came her way, she gladly took it. Interestingly enough, the values of the organization and the quality of the people involved with it apparently attracted her sufficiently to become a very active director of the Federation and, three years later, its president.

Helyn (Lyn) Beer, a land-use administrator in Park Ridge and the president of its board of education, was chosen as the new Federation executive. She remained with the organization for five years, during which she proved herself a capable organizer, a knowledgeable adviser to local planners, and an able representative of the Federation within the executive and legislative halls of state government.

In order to avoid the traps into which her predecessors fell, Beer was given some clerical assistance, had her office equipment slowly updated, and received strong support from Marie Bradley in membership development. The number of member boards started rising in 1980 immediately following the employment of Bradley as a special assistant responsible for membership and continued to rise at a fast pace to overtake the previous 1972 all-time high of 431 members by 1984. This happened despite the fact that the services supplied by the Federation sharply declined during this tumultuous period, especially in the area of publications. The Federation did not produce any publications from June 1980 to January 1982. When the *Planner* was renewed, it was a much more attractive publication, but it made fewer appearances at indeterminate intervals. The Federation Planning Information Reports (FPIR) was renewed in 1983 and suffered a similar fate.

For a time, the leadership investigated the possibility of replacing the *Planner* and the FPIR with a tabloid-type publication that would carry advertisements, but it soon discovered the cost of such a venture would be too high unless the Federation cooperated with such related organizations as the NJAPA (New Jersey American Planning Association). Concern that such a step would undermine the uniqueness of the Federation caused the directors to reject the project.

The organization's conference record paralleled its publication one. With the exception of the state and Atlantic City conferences, the organization did not initiate or cosponsor any special gatherings. Still, it appeared that direct and repeated solicitation of membership was more effective than services and leadership activities, and Bradley, at times as a paid employee and at times as a director and the chairman of the membership committee, succeeded in retaining and increasing the membership of the organization.

The Federation always had among its directors individuals who were interested not only in the organization for its own sake, though they endeavored to strengthen it in any way they could, but who were especially interested in using the Federation as a base to secure a better future for the state as a whole. The newest addition to this group was Gilbert. He left a high-flying position as an investment banker on Wall Street for a less lucrative but more self-directed one in the Morristown branch of Merrill Lynch. Gilbert freely admits that his activities on behalf of planning had a detrimental effect on his earnings, but he claims that the excitement and feeling of accomplishment generated by this activity more than compensated his loss of income.

Gilbert, a highly ambitious and self-assured man, began his rapid rise within the Federation in 1977 when he became the vice chairman of the northern area. In 1979, he became a director from Bergen County; in 1980, the vice president; and, in 1981, the president of the organization. Around him gathered a group of young activists, such as McFadden, Al Schmitt, Judith Schleicher, McKiernan, Harry Pozycki, Pekarski, Bradley, and Barbara Walsh.

At first, the group concentrated its efforts on revitalizing the areas and restructuring the planning courses. The young leadership felt that the state Federation had neglected the areas and allowed many of them to falter. Probably the best case in point was the almost complete disintegration of the central area, which used to be the bulwark of the organization. Other areas, like the northwest and the

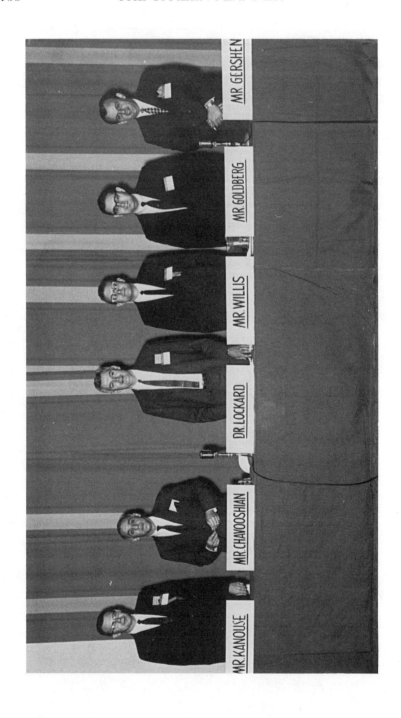

south, were also having difficulties. The directors always knew that the areas were vital to the viability of the Federation, not only as a source of new membership and leadership but also as a forum in which lay board members could express their local concerns to the state leadership, and vice versa. In the past, directors routinely attended area meetings either as lecturers or participants, but, as time went by, other concerns took precedent. Despite earlier criticism, it was Tom Hyde who kept the areas functioning until the mounting pressure of the new leadership (as well as their resentment at what they considered his inflexibility) began to take its toll.

In 1980, the directors appointed an advisory committee on areas to help area officers revitalize their local activities. The committee, chaired by Gilbert, concentrated its efforts on encouraging and helping areas to reactivate their advisory councils. The latter consisted of well-known professionals, academics, municipal lawyers, and government executives who were prepared to assist the area officers in organizing the yearly area program, as well as make contact with people who might become active in the organization. These committees had become dormant during the previous few years but were essential to the health of the area structure. The renewed attention to the areas paid off, and, for a few years, the areas held their educational meetings and elected their officers. Unfortunately, the 1983 demise of the State Planning Division caused yet another change in the organization's agenda, and the areas began to deteriorate yet again.

The second focus of the new leadership was the examination of the ties between the Federation and Rutgers University, especially its Extension Services. This reassessment was caused by the drop in course attendance. In the fall of 1980, only two of the nine scheduled courses had actually taken place; the rest had to be cancelled due to insufficient enrollment. At the same time, planning courses offered by other institutions were flourishing. McKiernan, first in the role of an executive secretary and then as the chairwoman of the education committee, led the reform movement.

The education committee soon discovered that the introductory courses offered by Rutgers University were given at inconvenient times and places for the majority of the new planning board members, and their cost was higher than the cost of the courses offered by other institutions. Also, while a Rutgers University certificate might have been significant in the past, its value had greatly diminished. The committee explored these problems with Rutgers University but found the university reluctant to make meaningful changes.

The committee searched for ways of making the courses more inviting, such as scheduling them on Saturdays instead of in the evenings, but the results were not spectacular. Meanwhile, a mandatory education bill was making its way through the legislature. The Federation had opposed such legislation in the past, but the education committee attempted to formulate its own proposed content of a mandatory education bill. Its proposal consisted of a uniform syllabus prepared by a broadly based committee to be administered by the counties and to be financed jointly by the state and the municipalities. Existing board members and municipal officials would be exempted from having to take the course. The board voted to support the concept of mandated education (Owen cast the only nay) but rejected the committee's specific proposals, partially because it failed to give any role to Rutgers University. Still, the readiness of the directors to support mandatory education for lay planners marked an important shift by the leadership. Clearly, the new leadership was prepared to give the state and the county a stronger voice in the field of planning. According to Gilbert, this was a major policy shift since the Federation was considered to be to the "right" of the League during the previous decades.

The education committee, aware of the strong loyalty many of the directors felt toward the state university, went back to the negotiating table and worked out a new deal with Rutgers University. The university and the Federation would share the responsibility for the courses. The university would supply the instructors and the materials and the Federation, in cooperation with the counties, would supply the location and handle the necessary paperwork for a series of introductory and advanced courses. In addition, the Federation would be prepared to offer a three-session introductory course to any interested county or municipality.

Once these bread-and-butter issues were resolved, the publication of the *Planner* was renewed, and the Federation membership was growing again. The Federation surmised that it was finally in a position to influence state policy. President Gilbert wrote:

> I suggest that the time has come for those of us in the Federation to stand up, look around and ask the broader questions about Land Use Planning in New Jersey. After all, we're a state with a population twice that of Norway; we're larger than Sweden in population; larger than many countries around the world. So our response to the widely acknowledged need for sensible planning for the future should take on, as a minimum, major dimensions. And yet, we all know that we have major planning problems in this state. The local and state responses have for the most part been feeble, non-existent, or swamped in controversy.
>
> I think that this Federation, which has a membership of over 400 of New Jersey's planning and zoning boards, can make a useful contribution to resolving this situation. In fact, we've already made some progress in this regard, having formulated a position on a more workable local-county-state planning relationship and having put that position forward in Trenton.[15]

Gilbert's last words were referring to the work done by the ad hoc committee appointed by him during the previous year. The committee was chaired by Chavooshian and consisted of McKiernan, Ginman, Pozycki, Maslow, Isadore Candeub, and Gilbert. The purpose of the committee was to acquaint the transition team of Governor-elect Thomas H. Kean with the planning needs of the state. It made the following recommendations:

1. That the land use function of Governor Byrne's Office of Policy and Planing be terminated.

2. That the executive branch commit itself to the development and implementation of a statewide master plan.

3. The establishment of a governor's commission of experienced people whose charge shall be:

a. To determine the parameters of a statewide master plan.
b. To devise a procedure for adoption of said plan.
c. To develop a framework for the implementation of the plan.[16]

A letter including these recommendations was sent to the governor-elect and his transition team. This was followed by a meeting between Gary Stein, the newly appointed director of the Office of Policy and Planning, and members of the committee. Stein indicated his interest in the Federation's ideas and asked the committee to develop them further. The committee went hurriedly back to the drawing board.

The leadership's sense of urgency was motivated by two immediate concerns: (1) a knowledge that the pendulum had swung from an emphasis on conservation to an emphasis on growth, and planning had in the past been equated with the former, and (2) an awareness that the Division of State and Regional Planning had lost its traditional raison d'être when the federal government terminated the 701 program in 1981. Ginman, the former director of the division, explained: "In the past we could always go to the state and tell them that we have this federal money coming in on this side but in order to get it, we have to justify that by matching it with a certain amount of state services which together make up a program, and that was always a certain defense for making sure the agency survived. When the money evaporated . . . there was no real monetary support at that time for the planning division."[17]

The ad hoc committee, which believed that there should have been such strong support, aptly presented state planning as an efficient method of achieving rapid state development. Although the committee was certainly aware of the existence of the State Development Guide Plan, as its author, Ginman was one of its members (and possibly even aware of the guide plan's future role in the upcoming *Mt. Laurel II* decision), it decided to avoid the controversy of plan making in favor of a general emphasis on the rational development and use of the state's infrastructure. Thus, the committee's proposed Governor's Statement on New Jersey Land Development Policy started by acknowledging that "the State of

New Jersey requires the benefit of new real estate development in order to strengthen our tax base and our job capacity." However, in order to make such growth as cost-effective as possible, the state should follow the following policies:

1. New development shall be targeted for expeditious consideration when it would be substantially served by existing infrastructure with unused or excess capacity.

2. Redevelopment shall be encouraged when it would help to support needed maintenance or reconstruction of existing infrastructure.

3. New development which would not be served by existing infrastructure shall be encouraged only in proportion to the development's ability to support the cost of new infrastructure.[18]

While awaiting the government's response to these recommendations, Gilbert began a series of meetings with other interested organizations in an effort to form a united front in support of state planning. By the fall of 1982, it became apparent that the Division of Planning was under serious threat, and the Federation joined the League, the home builders, and the land-use section of the New Jersey Bar Association in requesting a meeting with the governor to discuss state support for planning. Yet another series of meetings with Stein ensued. However, the committee members soon discovered that despite his official title, not only wasn't the director particularly interested or involved in planning but also that he considered the establishment of a strong state planning body as "politically premature."

On January 20, 1983, the State Supreme Court handed down its controversial *Mt. Laurel II* decision. No one could any longer accuse the court of fuzziness. The Gordian knot was finally cut. Legislative and executive timidity led to judicial boldness. The court's action was neither sudden nor arbitrary. By 1983, the state's low-income and middle-income housing shortage was not only far from being alleviated but all pleas for voluntary municipal action had clearly fallen on deaf ears. A careful study of the municipal zoning practices between *Mt. Laurel I* and *II* showed that municipal zoning became even more restrictive during that period.[19] A combination of new environmental regulations and the complete overhaul of local master plans and zoning regulations in compliance with the 1975 MLUL probably contributed as much to the tightening of zoning ordinances as municipal defensiveness.

At the heart of the matter remained the citizenry's wholesale rejection of the concept of "balanced community." As the Musto Report maintained, the move from the cities to the suburbs was a move from a heterogeneous society to a homogeneous one, and any attempt to reverse that trend was met with fierce opposition. While it remained doubtful whether the court would succeed in forcing suburbanites to live in a more balanced community, it was already clear that by giving the SDGP a significant role in its ruling, the court forced New Jersey's government to take state planning seriously.

The SDGP was not the first state plan. The first plan was published in 1951 and, in 1966, there were the Horizon and the Ten Million plans; but the state government never adopted any of these plans, not even the SDGP, despite the fact that the federal Department of Housing and Urban Development approved the latter as New Jersey's land-use element in 1978. In 1979, the cabinet committee on development policy and projects directed the Division of Planning to update the plan, but, when the revised draft was published, the cabinet committee failed after a long debate to adopt it and contented itself with the recommendation that the governor adopt the plan. It is a small wonder that the SDGP fared no better with local governments, and, despite dozens of public forums (including many Federation-sponsored ones) in which state planners explained the plan and tried to receive local input as to its content, few municipal officials had bothered to give it their serious attention. However, when the State Supreme Court, in reviewing the cases before it that led to the *Mt. Laurel II* decision, twice asked the attorney general whether the state was serious enough about the SDGP to make it a suitable basis for determining which municipalities should have housing obligations and which shouldn't, the attorney general in cooperation with the Division of Planning answered in the affirmative and gave the court the impression that it was an ongoing serious effort by the administration. The final irony was that within a month of the *Mt. Laurel II* decision, the commissioner of the DCA concluded that the easiest way to cut his department budget was by dismantling the Division of State and Regional Planning. Ginman recalled: "When the Division expired the question came up what about the Guide Plan, and everyone said, well, until it's changed we'll be guided by this at least for Mt. Laurel purposes. The inference is that the Plan then takes on a life of its own even if its creator was no longer there."[20]

The demise of the division had a profound effect on the Federation. The organization had always maintained close ties with the state planners and actively supported most of their endeavors. Division planners routinely participated in the organization's activities, and, despite attempts by some directors in the wake of growing state intervention in local planning and zoning to distance the Federation from the division, the ties remained strong. Furthermore, beyond the obvious frustration of the directors who had been endeavoring to strengthen state planning only to watch the little that was there evaporate, there were practical ramifications to the demise of the division. For years, the division supplied the areas with secretaries who helped the local officers with their chores; now they were gone, and areas that had just been reorganized and rejuvenated came under pressure yet again. Beer, the executive director who had difficulty handling her existing workload, did her best, but activity in the areas kept dwindling, and, by 1985, only the central and northern areas were functioning adequately.

The fate of the yearly planning conference, which was cosponsored by the Federation and the division but which was actually handled by the latter, also became uncertain. At first, it was suggested that the state conference be combined with the Federation's annual meeting, but the office was too busy with its membership drive and both were cancelled in 1984. Luckily, Chavooshian insisted that the organization of the conference involved very little work and that he was prepared to head a committee composed of former State Planning Division members who had organized annual state planning conferences for the past thirty years to do it. Thus, in March 1985, the Federation successfully held its first completely independent statewide conference; it attracted 190 participants and became one of the growing number of services that the division used to provide to municipalities but that were being transferred slowly to the Federation.

Basic publications like the MLUL and the Guide to Planning and Zoning, which used to be published by the division and were a sine qua non for municipalities, were now published by the Federation. Similarly, the division always had young planners or lawyers who were prepared to study and offer solutions to a locality's unique problem. Beer had to take the place of these employees, too.

Luckily, some help was on the way. The Fund for New Jersey was looking for ways to educate localities about the complex *Mt. Laurel II* decision; the Federation appeared a natural candidate for the task. After all, its directors had spent decades illuminating executive, legislative, and judicial directives related to planning. Thus, in 1984, the Federation received a grant of $25,000 from the fund. "The focus of the grant is to help the Federation expand the educational services and to generate income in support of these services by expanding corporate and municipal membership programs."[21]

The new leadership scored yet another coup. It was Evan Spalt, the longest-serving board member, who was the first to commend McKiernan and Schmitt "for achieving something talked about for many a year, the securing of a substantial grant for the organization to begin a forward move."[22]

As is almost always the case, the promise of riches brings more joy than the riches themselves. The money turned out to be useful and most welcome, but the hopes of Spalt and the director of the Fund for New Jersey "that a new chapter in the history of your organization will begin" did not materialize.[23] Some badly needed office equipment was purchased, a full-time clerical worker was employed, and that was about it. The receipt of the money specifically to cover publication expenses facilitated the renewal of the FPIRs and the *Planner*, though a return to the good old days when Hyde published six *Planners* and four FPIRs along with some special reports a year had to await yet another major policy change in the organization.

In August 1984, new Federation president McKiernan held a meeting with her vice president, Schmitt, and her executive secretary, Beer, in order to develop a set of priorities for the Federation. They reached the following decisions:

> High priority items included: income and membership, distribu-
> tion of information (Planner, FPIR, Special Reports), continua-
> tion of Day and a Half of Planning, contribution to publication
> (MLUL), development of training programs for members
> including area meetings and area relations. . . . Medium priority
> was reacting to legislation and low priority were State Wide
> Planning Conference and influencing legislation.[24]

Ironically, the Federation's success in carrying out these priorities was almost in reverse order to their stated importance, with "influencing legislation" scoring the highest number of points. Important as the high-priority items were, they did not offer either the excitement nor the sense of accomplishment that the passage of a hard-fought planning legislation did. Maslow, Gilbert, and even Beer preferred the heady atmosphere of Trenton to the drudgery of the Plainfield office. Again, it was McKiernan and Schmitt who were prepared to take a long hard look at the facts and come up with a novel solution. If it was impossible for the Federation's executives to forego the temptations of Trenton in favor of the efforts required for the efficient management of a service organization, then it was necessary to place the day-to-day running of the Federation in the hands of professional managers specifically contracted for the job. The two recommended that the Federation close its offices and retain the Association Management Corporation to execute the management functions of the Federation.

This revolutionary proposal, and the radical change it implied, caused a major rift within the membership of the Federation's board of directors. The opponents were worried that the move would result in loss of organizational identity and personal touch. The proponents argued that such a move would solve the organization's managerial problems and also force the directors to participate more fully in shaping organizational policy. After all, as important as the executive director was in representing the organization in the halls of power, the real glory had always belonged to a few dedicated individuals who worked for goals they deemed important. They used their ties to the organization in order to give credence to their efforts. The debate was long, and at times acrimoneous. In the end, the leadership was given the go-ahead to give the new system a try. The new management began its operation in the spring of 1986, and Jim Grassi was appointed by the Association Management Corporation to act as the Federation's executive.

It is interesting to note that contemporaneous with this organizational upheaval, the Federation continued to be heavily involved with the development of path-breaking legislation. A decade after the passage of the MLUL, the organization was in a position to help instigate, formulate, and pass the legislation necessary for the revitalization of state planning in New Jersey. Spearheading the Federation's efforts on behalf of state planning was Gilbert, who was thrilled to discover that his call for a strong state planning body, which fell on deaf ears in 1981, was receiving a positive hearing in 1983.

Two events acted as catalysts to the change of heart undergone by New Jersey's state and local officials. The first one was the elimination of the State Planning Division within the DCA. McFadden remarked that the demise of the division was possibly the best thing that could have happened to state planning in New Jersey as it forced the state and local leadership to reevaluate its past record thoroughly and acknowledge the need for a new serious commitment to state planning. After all, with the abolition of the division, "the localities were left with no place to go when they had questions or needs, and the State itself has no coordinating mechanism for the various types of planning that were going on within the Departments of the State."[25]

The second event was the New Jersey Supreme Court ruling referred to as the *Mt. Laurel II* decision. In their ruling, the judges not only gave the SDGP a significant role but also set the end of 1984 as the deadline for updating it. The deadline was not met, but the urgency created by the ruling did not hurt the efforts of the proponents of a State Planning Commission. Gilbert explained: "The Mount Laurel decision has awakened a lot of people, local people—home rule people—to the need for cooperation, to some degree, with their neighbors and with the state, particularly because if there is no updated guide plan within the next couple of years, then the current wild scene with the three regional judges will be even wilder."[26] Thus, as it progressively became more evident to home-rule advocates that the only choice facing them was judicially mandated planning or legislatively mandated planning, they had to acknowledge that they had a better chance to influence the latter (that was the directors' argument for the last decade!).

Consequently, when Gilbert had the opportunity to discuss the need for state planning with Governor Kean during a meeting of the North Jersey Planning Association, he found the governor most cooperative. Governor Kean suggested that Gilbert contact his legal counsel, Cary Edwards, to see if they could come up with an appropriate bill. Before following up on the governor's suggestion, Gilbert got in touch with Jack Trafford, the executive director of the League, whose organization did not lack clout in the state legislature. Trafford agreed with Gilbert that the time had come for the establishment of a viable state planning unit and proceeded to convene a group of planning advocates that met with the governor's counsel, Edwards. After ascertaining that the group represented a genuine grass-roots willingness to provide the bill with the political support necessary for its passage, Edwards proceeded to offer his own support along with that of a member of his legal staff, Amy Piro.

The original group, which consisted of representatives of the League, the Federation, the County Planners' Association, the Consulting Planners' group, NJAPA, and the Land Use Section of the New Jersey Bar Association, was reinforced by representatives of a number of Departments of State—the Department of Community Affairs (DCA), the Department of Environmental Protection (DEP), and the Department of Transportation (DOT); the Regional Plan Association (RPA); and the Mercer–Somerset–Middlesex (MSM) Regional Study Council. Together, they formed the ad hoc committee. Pozycki of the Land Use Section of the New Jersey chapter of the American Bar Association was the committee chairman, and Eugene J. Schneider, the executive director of the Musto Commission, was its vice chairman and the convener of its meetings. The Federation was represented by Gilbert, McFadden, McKiernan, and Beer. After eight weeks of meetings and deliberations, a report was produced on which an accompanying bill, S-1494, establishing the State Planning Commission, was based.

Then something happened. Governor Kean decided to repeat Governor William Cahill's strategy and held the planning bill desired by the municipalities hostage to a housing bill he had to have. The governor requested that the ad hoc committee reconvene and draft a bill that would alleviate the pressure imposed by *Mt. Laurel II* on the lower courts. The committee accepted the challenge and reconvened in 1984 with basically the same membership, only the representatives of the DOT and the DEP were replaced by Ken Meiser of the Department of Public Advocate and Peter Buchsbaum. The committee developed the Fair Housing Act, which was signed into law on July 2, 1985. Clearly, the reason Governor Kean succeeded, where his predecessors failed, was the strong support he received from the state's courageous judiciary. It appears that the medicine prescribed by the judges was so strong that most communities were prepared to switch to another doctor in the hope of finding his medicine more palatable.

The Fair Housing Act created the Council on Affordable Housing and gave municipalities the right to transfer their cases from the jurisdiction of the court to that of the council. The working methods of this council bear a strong resemblance to the working methods of the Pinelands Commission. In both cases, the state-appointed body sets guidelines and then certifies locally developed plans that meet its guidelines. The Council's certification of low-cost and moderate-cost housing provides the municipality six years' repose; in any litigation during the six-year period in which the certified plan is contested, the burden of proof is switched to the complainant.

The reaction to the Housing Act was mixed. Some opposed the act as giving legal sanction to unwarranted judicial activism; others were sure that the council would not be as tough on municipalities as the judges would have been (they were especially dismayed by the provision demanded by Governor Kean to permit the construction of Mt. Laurel housing in urban centers as undermining the basic intent of the original ruling); and, finally, there were those who concluded:

> When the political branches of government balk at enforcing a constitutional obligation, it is the judiciary's role to fill the gap. That isn't so much judicial activism as judicial duty. As Governor Kean and New Jersey Legislature finally realized, the way

to curb that kind of judicial intervention is to make it unnecessary in the first place.[27]

Six months after the passage of the Fair Housing Act, *The Federation Planner* dedicated an entire issue to the passage of yet another piece of landmark legislation. The *Planner* declared:

> On January 2, 1986 Governor Kean signed into law S-1464, *An Act To Create A State Planning Commission.* This bill was the result of a combined effort by many members of the planning community to return comprehensive planning to the state level. However, in order for it to get that far took the tenacious efforts of a New Jersey Federation member, our immediate past president James G. Gilbert, to pull that community together and have them speak with one voice.[28]

The elation of the organization's leadership was justified. Their vision of a meaningful regional solution to the Garden State's development problems was about to become a reality. The Fair Housing Act and the State Planning Act had the same parentage as previous planning legislation. But times had changed. In the seventies, a similar group was advised to distance itself from the DCA and drop all references to state planning. This time, the ad hoc committee not only worked closely with the state executives, but it was also given the task of writing the Fair Housing Act. The committee was successful in accomplishing both tasks, and even tied the two acts together by insisting that the Council on Affordable Housing duly consider the State Development and Redevelopment Plan in its housing allocations.

Preparation of this necessary updating of the SDGP was to be the central function of the State Planning Commission, along with the production of a long-term infrastructure needs assessment and the review of proposed capital project legislation. The commission was also charged with developing planning coordination between the various levels of government and providing local planning assistance.

The commission was placed in the Treasury Department, in part to protect it from future budget cuts and in part because the "Treasury is the Department that, because of the budget, impinges upon every other department, and, really, land use planning cascades over to any number of departments down here in Trenton."[29]

To secure state-county-municipal cooperation, the commission's seventeen members included seven representatives of the state government (five of them cabinet members), four county and municipal representatives, and six members of the public at large. The local, county, and public members were to be appointed by the governor, with the Senate's advice and consent.

The era of exclusive home rule in New Jersey was clearly over, and it appears that the federal government, which was one of the main reasons for the establishment of the rule in the fifties, was yet again one of the main reasons for its demise in the eighties. Schneider, the current manager of long-range planning in the New Jersey Office of Management and Budget, concluded:

> State and local government in New Jersey are increasingly interdependent. While most land use and development decisions take place at the local level, they are subject to the State's regulatory powers and must frequently rely on the State's fiscal resources. The prospective reduction (or elimination) of federal funding which supports many state and local programs is certain to strengthen the state-local interrelation. Current emerging problems and opportunities must, therefore, be addressed cooperatively and require strong effective planning at all levels.[30]

The Federation had numerous representatives at the official signing: Chavooshian, Jager, and Pozycki, the chairman of the ad hoc committee. Unfortunately, Gilbert, the man who was one of the major forces behind uniting the planning community, prodding the governor to action, and tirelessly campaigning for the bill, could not be present. Still, he did get his reward when Governor Kean appointed him the first chairman of the State Planning Commission.

John Sloane, one of the founders of the Federation, was the chairman of the original State Planning Board, and now as the Federation is preparing to celebrate its golden anniversary, it seems fitting that one of its directors would yet again lead the State Planning Commission. Events have come full circle; the old State Planning Board was instrumental in establishing the Federation, and now it was the Federation that took the leadership in establishing the State Planning Commission.

Notes

1. Patricia F. Fingerhood, "Mount Laurel Three Years Later," *New Jersey Magazine* (March 1978):23.
2. Bud Schwartz, "We know we have what you need," *The Federation Planner* (October 1975):1.
3. Federation's Minutes, June 23, 1977, p. 3.
4. "Report on S-3139," *The Federation Planner* (June 1977);2.
5. "Incidental Intelligence," *The Federation Planner* (June 1979):5.
6. Carl G. Lindbloom, AIP, "The New Jersey Pinelands Region Future Development Plan," *Jersey Plans* (Autumn 1964).
7. Draft Comprehensive Management Plan, Pinelands Planning and Management Commission, 1979, p. i.
8. Daniel J. O'Hern, "Home Rule and the Environment," *New Jersey Municipalities* (January 1979):28.
9. Interview with B. Budd Chavooshian, June 28,1986.
10. *Ibid.*
11. Federation's Minutes, May 17, 1979, p. 5.
12. *Ibid.*
13. Federation's Minutes, November 1, 1979, p. 1.
14. Federation's Minutes, January 16, 1980, p. 3.
15. James G. Gilbert, "A Message from the President," *The Federation Planner* (June 1982):3.
16. Federation's Minutes, November 25, 1981, p. 3.
17. Interview with Dick Ginman, May 21, 1986.
18. Federation's Minutes, March 22, 1982, p. 2.
19. Russell S. Harrison, "Zoning Laws and Wealth Segregation in South Jersey: Trends Before Mount Laurel II," Policy Research Series, no. 23, Rutgers/Camden Forum for Policy Research and Public Service (October 1984).
20. Ginman, *op. cit.*
21. "Good News," *The Federation Planner* (April 1984):6.
22. Federation's Minutes, March 1, 1984, p. 4.
23. "Good News," *op. cit.*
24. Federation's Minutes, September 25, 1984, p. 4.

25. James G. Gilbert in testimony given during the public hearing before the Subcommittee of the Senate State Government, Federal and Interstate Relations and Veterans' Affairs Committee on Senate Bill 1464, April 5, 1984.

26. *Ibid.*

27. "Judicial Duty in New Jersey," *New York Times,* February 24, 1986.

28. *The Federation Planner* (Special 1986):1.

29. Gilbert in testimony, *op. cit.*

30. Eugene J. Schneider, "New Jersey Moves into Second Fifty Years of State Planning," *The Federation Planner* (Special 1986):5.

8

Facing the Future

McKim Norton, the past executive director of the Regional Plan
Association (RPA), astutely remarked on a study written about his
organization: "It was a good work, but he [the author] did not give
us credit for having survived for so long."[1] Norton was right; per-
manency is generally translated into power and influence. The
Federation not only survived, but its membership now encompasses
more than five hundred planning boards and boards of adjustment.
Furthermore, it is the only organization of its kind in the nation to
be wholly governed by its lay membership.

The Federation was created "to promote public interest in planning and a coordination of planning boards in New Jersey." It was
one of a number of state, regional, and national organizations established for that purpose. Fifty years later, as planning went through a
process of specialization and institutionalization, the enthusiastic
amateur tended to give way to the carefully trained professional.

While the Federation has successfully resisted any suggestions that
it follow this trend, it has doggedly maintained its identity as a lay
organization by granting voting rights only to current local planning
board members. Interested professionals may and do become active
members, associate directors, and counsels to the organization.
Furthermore, professionals play a crucial role in all Federation functions as educators, advisers, lecturers, and writers. Still, the locus of
power remains firmly in the hands of the lay planners.

185

The value of the amateur nature of the organization transcends such obvious benefits as the development of comradeship within the planning community or the opportunities its members have to share and learn from each other's problems. Important as such benefits are, they are secondary to the lay organization's ability and readiness to play an active role in the political arena. Professionals are basically technocrats hired to help execute policy, and, therefore, as Jim Gilbert maintained, they are neither interested nor able "to take the political heat."[2] Taking such heat is vital to the organization's effectiveness as a promoter of better planning and as a protector of the role of the citizen in the planning process.

During the past fifty years, the Federation has acquired legitimacy as the official representative of the interests of local planning boards, as an organization that has to be consulted prior to any important planning-related initiative, and whose representatives should be placed on all state or regional bodies concerned with land-use issues. Even voluntary single-issue coalitions, like Alliance for Action, tend to ask the Federation for its support, valuing the reputation and proven effectiveness of its leadership.

The quality of the Federation's leadership was at the heart of its accomplishments. The organization's success in attracting and retaining the loyalty of leading figures in the state's planning community added immeasurably to the Federation's clout, as these individuals would frequently be placed in key positions, not necessarily due to their connection with the Federation but as a result of their own reputation. Indirectly, the Federation's representation in various decision-making bodies was frequently increased.

Organizational power and influence were also enhanced by careful nurturing of strong ties with other state and private bodies. Throughout these fifty years, the Federation has enjoyed a kinship with the State Planning Agency, as stated earlier, and with New Jersey State League of Municipalities (the League). Jointly, much has been accomplished and is still being accomplished to strengthen planning in New Jersey. In the established tradition of the corporate state, the Federation formed and participated in various coalitions and developed a reputation of expertise in the field of municipal planning. The story of the municipal land-use drafting committee is an excellent case in point. This committee was formed in 1974 under the auspices of the League in order to formulate long-needed legislation; it was chaired by Harry Maslow (the Federation representative) and included numerous other Federation members representing other organizations. It succeeded in getting through the legislature the updating of the state's Municipal Land Use Law (MLUL), which had eluded the state executive for at least a decade. Even more instructive is the fact that the organizations responsible for the MLUL remained loyal to their agreement to oppose any change in the bill for a period of one year (despite the unhappiness of some of their members). The drafting committee then reconvened in order to devise the amendments necessitated by the field testing of law. Since then, the committee continues to function as a sort of clearinghouse for all suggested modifications of the MLUL. It has excellent legislative contacts, and, according to its chairman, "anyone who has problems with the MLUL comes to us and we look into it."[3] Attempts by "uncooperative parties" to bypass the drafting committee have been summarily rebuffed after careful consideration by the entire committee. The coziness of this arrangement is further enhanced by the way new members are added to the committee. The new members tend to be either the sons and daughters or the law partners of the existing members and thus can be trusted not to rock the boat too strongly.

Gratifying and beneficial as the Federation's political and legislative activities may have been, education and the dissemination of information remain its primary functions. Each year, hundreds of citizens are appointed to local planning boards. Many have little or no knowledge of the complex task they are asked to perform. They need basic training in the tenets of planning and planning legislation. Similarly, the experienced local board members require a constant stream of information to ensure their ability to keep up with the profession's ever-changing assumptions and practices. Without such an ongoing educational effort, the citizen-planner would be forced to abdicate his role to the professional. Such an abdication would strike at the heart of the participatory democracy to which the Federation is so committed. Brian McFadden, a former president of the Federation, explained:

If we don't allow local planning boards a role in determining what happens, we'll be losing a portion of our governmental system, a whole segment of it, which in my view is wrong. Someone else is making the decision for me. Elections are not enough. You must participate. You must get down on your hands and knees if it's going to work. And it is your responsibility to learn and understand as much as you can about what you are doing. It is the Federation's responsibility to bring back to these members as often as we can as much information as we can. Central planning might be more efficient, but it's certainly not the way Washington and Jefferson viewed that. I don't want us, I don't want anyone ending up accepting what comes. One should question everything.[4]

One can also not fail to recognize the echoes of the speeches made so many years ago by such Federation pioneers as Harry Hosking, Benjamin Taub, or John Sloane.

Clearly, the organization appears successful beyond its founding fathers' wildest dreams. Still, all is not well, and the Federation cannot afford to rest on its laurels. Some of its difficulties are of the type that periodically attach themselves to all institutions, such as the tension between various generations of directors, the need to update and modernize the way the organization renders its services, the need to redefine goals and priorities commensurate with the new realities, and the need to restructure the Federation's organization in a way to better accomplish these goals. During the last few years, the Federation has taken major and sometime painful steps to deal with these important problems. Still, it has yet to address two of its major deficiencies, one organizational and the other ideological.

In 1986, the Federation broke with tradition and elected both a president (Al Schmitt) and a vice president (Judith Schleicher) from the same northern area. While the sexual balance that accurately represents the growing clout of women within the organization is commendable, the northern concentration of the new leadership should be deeply worrying to all the Federation's well-wishers. Even more troubling is the lack of awareness of the seriousness of this problem exhibited by the board of directors. Sidney Graybar, a long-time director, did challenge the nominations on the ground that a member from the southern area should have been nominated, but

Proclamation

WHEREAS, the New Jersey Federation of Planning Officials was established 50 years ago in 1938 to promote better planning in New Jersey; and

WHEREAS, the Federation has been a principal supporter of legislation in the area of planning and zoning and has promoted far-reaching amendments to the 1928 Zoning Enabling Act, adoption of the Municipal Planning Act of 1953, enactment of and major amendments to the Municipal Land Use Law of 1975 and passage of the State Planning Act of 1986; and

WHEREAS, over the past 50 years, members of the Federation have given generously of their time and talents to bring land use planning in New Jersey to the highest degree of perfection in the country, serving on local agencies, county planning boards, and the State Planning Commission; and

WHEREAS, the New Jersey Federation of Planning Officials has been the leader in providing educational programs for board members and others engaged in administration of land use regulations, both in cooperation with Rutgers, the State University, and by itself to enable laymen involved in the regulation process to better understand their functions and increase their effectiveness in protecting the public interest; and

WHEREAS, it is desired to accord due recognition to the key role of the Federation in promoting good planning and land use regulations in the State of New Jersey;

NOW, THEREFORE, I, THOMAS H. KEAN, Governor of the State of New Jersey, do hereby proclaim

APRIL 24 - 30, 1988

as

PLANNING WEEK

in New Jersey.

GIVEN, under my hand and the Great Seal of the State of New Jersey, this fifteenth day of April in the year of Our Lord one thousand nine hundred and eighty-eight and of the Independence of the United States, the two hundred and twelfth.

Th H Kean

GOVERNOR

BY G OR:

189

his objections were quickly dismissed despite of the fact that the Federation's constitution stipulates that the president and the vice president should represent different areas, if at all possible. Evan Spalt made light of the problem by noting that "no other area produced a director of the caliber of a Judith Schleicher."[5] He may be right, but that does not solve the difficulty. Obviously, there must be scores of able community leaders in other parts of the state, so why had the Federation failed to attract them?

 Throughout its history, there was one area that surpassed all others in its level of activity and the vitality of its leadership. The northern area carried the banner during the thirties and forties, the central area during the fifties and sixties, and the northern area reclaimed the leadership during the late seventies and eighties. Still, the directors always knew that for the Federation to be perceived as a statewide organization, it must expand its base of operation. Therefore, during the fifties and sixties, the leadership made a concentrated effort to penetrate the southern and northwestern areas of the state. Unfortunately, sometime during the seventies, this issue was allowed to be placed on the back burner and forgotten. Distance and lack of time have been blamed for the slack participation of directors from some parts of the state in the organization's leadership activities. Although pertinent factors, they are certainly not the only ones. Jim Nasuti, the chairman of the Delaware-Atlantic area, angrily remarked: "We drive two hours to a board meeting and all they want to talk about are the problems of the north. They will not spend more than five minutes on our problems."[6] McFadden, a former president of the organization who only recently renewed his activism within the Federation, voiced his exasperation: "There had not been a Southern area meeting for two years. Who am I? I am only one person. You throw a rock and you hit somebody who is prepared to organize a meeting. They simply did not care!"[7] These are strong indictments, and if the Federation leadership wishes to maintain its strong position as the representative of the entire state's local planning boards, it would be wise to pay serious attention to them.

The ideological problem centers around the lack of urban participation in the organization. The issue strikes at the heart of the philosophy of planning. The main aim of planning (and, as such, it is the epitome of corporate liberalism) was to maintain the health of the democratic capitalist system by curbing the freedom of the individual for the sake of securing social harmony. Therefore, the Newark riots of the late sixties ultimately signaled the failure of the protectors of the system, including planners, to fulfill their central task. It is only necessary to revisit the state's larger cities to realize that the powder keg is still there, and even a cursory acquaintance with the affairs of the Federation reveals that its relationship with the urban components of the state leaves much to be desired.

Some of the directors, like Gilbert and Spalt, had voiced their concern over the suburban tilt of the organization as late as 1984. In a way reminiscent of the early years of the Federation, they lamented at the sheer waste involved in the neglect of an existing city infrastructure and its replacement by a costly new one in ecologically sensitive and diminishing undeveloped areas of the state. Budd Chavooshian maintained that the Federation does not have major cities on its roster because the latter do not feel a commonality of interest with the organization. A committee, chaired by Spalt, was appointed to study the special problems of the state's urban centers and make specific recommendations regarding the possible role the Federation could play in their solution. The committee quietly shriveled and died after just a few meetings, its members distracted by the pursuit of some major legislation and organizational restructuring. Recently, the Federation has redirected its attention to the development of a truly regional planning structure throughout the state. The Woodrow Wilson School, the League, and various members of the legislature are all looking into the problem. Perhaps they will come up with a structure that redefines the relationship between the cities and their surrounding areas in a way that would benefit the former. Time has really come for the planning community as a whole, and the Federation in particular, to remember its philosophical parents, the proponents of "city beautiful."

As the New Jersey Federation of Planning Officials completes its first half-century of activity, it can certainly look back with pride. It has made a major contribution to planning in the Garden State and tried hard to ensure that the state strikes a right balance between development and conservation, centralization and local autonomy, and private financial security and social cohesion. When I started this study, the organization's longest-serving director, Spalt, remarked:

"You will find that the basic problems have always been the same."[8] He was right; but the Federation has always been able to contribute to their solution. Now, as a new generation of planners comes to the fore, one can only hope that these leaders will build upon the solid foundation already laid by their distinguished predecessors.

Notes

1. Interview with McKim Norton, June 28, 1986.
2. Interview with Jim Gilbert, February 24, 1988.
3. Interview with Harry Maslow, May 15, 1986.
4. Interview with Brian McFadden, May 14, 1986.
5. Interview with Evan Spalt, July 10, 1986.
6. Interview with Richard Nasuti, May 27, 1986.
7. McFadden, *op. cit.*
8. Spalt, *op. cit.*

APPENDIX 1

Planning Activities

a day and a half of planning

sponsored by the new jersey federation of planning officials, for
the new jersey state league of municipalities

NOV.

16 thursday

17 friday

57th annual convention - 1972 - new jersey state league of municipalities
november 14 - 17, 1972, chalfonte-haddon hall, atlantic city

a $6.00 convention registration fee is required, payable at league registration desks

---

a day and a half of planning

A DAY AND A HALF OF PLANNING PROGRAM

• 10:00 THURSDAY MORNING, November 16, 1972
Carolina Room - Lounge Floor - Chalfonte

SPECIAL SESSION ON PLANNING

PRESIDENT'S WELCOME:

Earle P. Finkbiner, Chairman
Lumberton Board of Adjustment

MODERATOR:
Abraham A. Janz, Federation Past President
Member, Pequannock Planning Board

"TOWARD THE FUTURE OF URBAN PLACES"

GUEST SPEAKERS:
Dr. Mason W. Gross, President Emeritus, Rutgers University
President, Harry Frank Guggenheim Foundation
Imamu Amiri Baraka, Author
Chairman, Committee for Unified Newark
Alvin E. Gershen, AIP, Professional Planner and
Housing Consultant, Trenton
Discussion from the Floor

• 12:00 THURSDAY NOON, November 16, 1972
Sylvan Room - Ground Floor - Chalfonte

FEDERATION MEMBERS' LUNCHEON

CHAIRMAN:
Earle P. Finkbiner, President
Chairman, Lumberton Board of Adjustment

GUEST SPEAKER:
William F. Gillette, Past President
Member, Ocean County Planning Board

Reservations may be purchased from the Executive Vice President. New Jersey Federation of Planning Officials. Reservation sales will close at 10:00 on Thursday, November 16. Reservations are $6.50 for the Luncheon.

A Special Program on Parks and Recreation Planning

Co-sponsored by the FEDERATION
and the N.J. RECREATION AND PARK ASSOCIATION

2:00 WEDNESDAY AFTERNOON, November 15, 1972
Ballroom - Ramada Inn (Behind Haddon Hall, Carolina Ave.)

Parks and Recreation
SPECIFIC TECHNIQUES ON PLANNING

MODERATOR:
Mrs. Doris Dickey
Livingston Recreation Advisory Council

PANELIST:

"COMPREHENSIVE LAND USE PLANS"

E. Eugene Oross, P.P, AIP
President, E. Eugene Oross Associate, New Brunswick

"SITE SPECIFICS"

Kenneth H. Creveling, Jr. AIP
Director of Planning, Edwards & Kelsey, Inc., Newark

"SITE ADMINISTRATION"

Russell W. Myers, Executive Director
Morris County Park Commission, Morristown

"FACILITY AND SITE MAINTENANCE"

Graham M. Skea, Orange County
Parks, Recreation and Conservation Board, Montgomery, N.Y.

72ND ANNUAL CONFERENCE
STATE LEAGUE OF MUNICIPALITIES
1987

A Day and a Half of Planning

JOINT SESSION: The New State Planning Process
Building a Shared Vision of New Jersey's Future

JOINT SESSION: Municipalities and Planning

JOINT SESSION ON ZONING: Legal Problems in Planning and Zoning

PLANNING AND ZONING PERIOD

Panel Discussion

Panel A: *Environmental Control in the Planning Process*
Panel B: *The Working of a Zoning Board of Adjustment*
Panel C: *The Planning Board*
Panel D: *Administrative Procedures*
Panel E: *Traffic—What Do We Do When We Can't Get There From Here?*
Panel F: *Progress and Historic Preservation, Perfect Together*
Panel G: *Establishing Design Standards*
Panel H: *Do We Want Any More Jobs?*

Note: The New Jersey Federation of Planning Officials selects program topics, arranges for speakers and panelists who serve pro bono. As joint sponsors, The New Jersey State League of Municipalities provides meeting room facilities and session listing in the program at no cost to the Federation other than through registration fees charged all conference attendees.

APPENDIX 2

Publication Activities

R-39

T H E   N E W   J E R S E Y   P L A N N E R

Published Under the Joint Sponsorship of the New Jersey
Federation of Official Planning Boards and the
New Jersey State Planning Board

Issued Every Now and Then   Dr. Maurice F. Neufeld, Editor

Vol. 1, No. 1   186 W. State St., Trenton, N.J.   February, 1939

February 23, 1939

To New Jersey County and Municipal
Planning Boards and Planning Board Members:

Gentlemen:

With this issue, there comes to you a new publication, dedicated by its sponsors to assist those who are
interested in planning the future of our State and its many
parts. Dr. Maurice F. Neufeld, Acting Secretary of the New
Jersey State Planning Board, has kindly consented to act as
Editor.

The Interim Executive Committee has taken this forward step at this time because it believes that to get action,
action must be taken, and the Committee wishes to turn over to
the permanent officers of the Federation at the annual meeting
in April, a live, going organization - a real factor in the
planning movement in New Jersey.

The New Jersey Planner is yours. Its success depends on your cooperation. You are urged to read each issue
carefully and to circulate the copies among others who are
interested in planning. You are urged to contribute short
articles, planning news, items of interest and to take an
active part in making the venture a success.

The New Jersey Planner is the organ of the New Jersey
Federation of Official Planning Boards. Follow it carefully
and keep in touch with Federation activities at all times.

Lastly, What is your idea? What can be done to further
planning interests? Will you write in and offer your suggestions?

Sincerely yours,

Harry Hosking, Chairman
Livingston, N.J.   Interim Executive Committee

*Note: This bulletin, inaugurated in the first year of the Federation, covers timely topics solicited from or
volunteered by professional and legal experts. Coming events are announced and there are occasional messages from
the president. Eleven copies are mailed to each member of the planning board and zoning board of adjustment, thus
providing alternate as well as regular members of these boards with their individual copies. One copy is mailed to all
other members. Current publication schedule is four to six issues per year. Acceptance of paid advertising was
authorized on an experimental basis late in 1987.

The Federation Planner

FEBRUARY 1988

NEW JERSEY FEDERATION OF PLANNING OFFICIALS

"Dedicated to Better Planning in New Jersey"

From the Courts

Jerome G. Rose *

Should a Developer Be Able to Rely on a Building Permit When the Validity of the Underlying Zoning Ordinance Is Challenged?

It is not uncommon for a developer to apply for a zoning amendment to authorize the use of his land in accordance with his proposed plan. If the governing body amends the zoning ordinance to permit the proposed land use, the developer will get a building permit based on the amended law and will proceed with his development. The developer may then make substantial investments in reliance on that building permit. At that point, he is considered to have a "vested right" and is protected against any later change in the zoning law that would "deauthorize" the land use on which the building permit was based.

In a recent case, *Godfrey v. Zoning Board of Adjustment,* [1] the North Carolina Supreme Court was confronted with an interesting variation of this problem. The validity of the zoning amendment on which the building permit was based was challenged in court as "spot zoning." When the action was instituted, the developer was faced with a serious dilemma: If he were to hold off all further construction, he would thereby renounce whatever vested rights he had previously acquired at a time at which he had no way of knowing whether the lawsuit would be prosecuted to judgment and what the court's decision would be. On the other hand, if he were to continue the construction, he would run the risk of a judicial determination that the building permit was invalid because it was based on an invalid zoning ordinance.

The developer decided to proceed with his development and, in fact, had completed all construction seven months before the trial court's decision that the zoning amendment was invalid "spot zoning." The court of appeals affirmed that decision.

The developer then applied to the zoning board of adjustment for permission to continue operation of the facility under an ordinance provision authorizing zoning board relief in "non-

conformity situations." The zoning board granted this application. The zoning board's decision was challenged as "arbitrary and capricious." The trial court upheld the decision of the zoning board and the court of appeals affirmed. On appeal, the North Carolina Supreme Court responded to three issues raised by these facts: (1) Was the zoning amendment invalid "spot zoning"? (2) Did the developer obtain a "vested right"? (3) Was the developer's facility encompassed by the "nonconforming situation" provision of the zoning ordinance?

WHEN IS A ZONING AMENDMENT INVALID AS "SPOT ZONING"?

The issue of spot zoning raises fundamental questions of separation of powers and the power of successive legislative bodies to enact laws not consistent with those adopted by previous elected officials. Unless proscribed by the state constitution or by a statute, each succeeding municipal governing body has as much lawmaking authority as the preceding governing body. For example, a governing body in office has the power to repeal

(Please turn to Page 2)

New NJFPO exec named

SPRINGFIELD---Steve Changaris has been named executive director of the New Jersey Federation of Planning Officials as of Jan. 1, 1988.

Changaris has more than ten years of professional and association management experience including serving as executive director of the New Jersey Chiropractic Society, the American Association for Music Therapy, and the National Council of Acoustical Consultants.

He has managed a variety of budgets, legislative affairs, and lobbying, association events, and public relations.

Changaris holds an undergraduate degree from Pennsylvania State University and a master's degree from Drew University. He resides with his wife, Anne and daughter, Emily, in New Brunswick.

Federation Planning Information Reports

The following listing of reports (short title F.P.I.R.) is representative of the range of subjects and the caliber of authorship made available to planning and zoning boards—as well as to all classes of dues paying members.

F.P.I.R.s are mailed postpaid upon publication; additional copies are made available until exhausted.

I-1 *SUBDIVISION CONTROL IN NEW JERSEY*
Harvey S. Moskowitz   January   1966

I-2 *AN ASSIGNMENT JUDGE'S VIEW ON PLANNING &*
ZONING
Honorable Joseph Halpern   March   1966

PLANNING & ZONING—THE POSITIVE TOOLS OF
GOVERNMENT
Honorable Frederick W. Hall

I-3 *COMMUNITY GUIDELINES FOR INDUSTRIAL*
DEVELOPMENT
Herbert H. Smith   May   1966

I-4 *THE MUNICIPAL MASTER PLAN—AND HOW TO SELL*
IT
E. Eugene Oross   September   1966

I-5 *THE MUNICIPAL BOARD OF ADJUSTMENT—ITS*
POWER AND PROCEDURES
Harold Feinberg, Esq.   November   1966

II-1 Title and Copy Unavailable

II-2 Title and Copy Unavailable

II-3 Title and Copy Unavailable

II-4 Title and Copy Unavailable

II-5 Title and Copy Unavailable

III-1   APARTMENTS—GENERAL FACTORS IN PLANNING
       Alvin E. Gershen   January   1968

III-2   AN APPELLATE COURT JUDGE LOOKS AT PLANNING
& ZONING
       Honorable Milton B. Conford   March   1968

III-3   DOWNTOWN—A FUNCTIONAL ANALYSIS
       Laurence A. Alexander   May   1968

III-4   Title and Copy Unavailable

III-5   THE CONTEMPORARY URBAN CRISIS & THE FUTURE
OF LOCAL PLANNING IN NEW JERSEY AND AN
APPENDIX EMPLOYMENT AND TRANSPORTATION
ASPECT OF THE GHETTO PROBLEM
       Dr. Lawrence D. Mann   November 1968

IV-1   COMMUNITY PLANNING & SOIL SURVEYS
       Peter B. Dorram   January   1969

      SOIL SURVEYS AND COMMUNITY PLANNING (THE
      OTHER SIDE OF THE COIN)
       Eugene C. Hanchett

IV-2   STATE RESPONSIBILITIES IN PLANNING
       Hon. Richard J. Hughes, Governor—New Jersey
       Hon. John V. Lindsay, Mayor—City of New York
       Sidney L. Willis, Planning Director—Dept. of
           Community Affairs   March   1969

IV-3   UNDERGROUND WIRING
       Candeub, Fleissig & Associates
       Isadore Candeub, A.I.P.—Director of Planning
       Robert L. Friedman, Planner in Charge of Study   May   1969

IV-4   PLANNED UNIT DEVELOPMENT—A NEW TOOL FOR
ACHIEVING A MORE DESIRABLE ENVIRONMENT
       Roger Scattergood, Esq.   September 1969

V-1   Title and Copy Unavailable

V-2   COMMUNITY APPEARANCE—WHY AND HOW TO
CARE FOR OUR HOME TOWN
       Charles K. Agle, F.A.I.A., A.I.P.   March   1970

V-3 *FLOOD LOSS REDUCTION—THROUGH PLANNING &*
REGULATING FLOOD PLAIN DEVELOPMENT
Peter B. Dorram, A.I.P. May 1970

V-4 Title and Copy Unavailable

VI-1 *PREMATURE SUBDIVISION—WITH A N.J. CASE STUDY*
Stephen Sussna, Ph.D., A.I.P.
Jack Kirchoff, A.I.P. Spring 1971

VI-2 Title and Copy Unavailable

VI-3 Title and Copy Unavailable

VI-4 Title and Copy Unavailable

VII-1 *PLANNED UNIT DEVELOPMENT—AN ANALYSIS OF*
ITS PROGRESS IN NEW JERSEY
George Sternlieb, Ph.D.
Robert W. Burchell, Ph.D. Spring 1972

VII-2 Title and Copy Unavailable

VII-3 *SOME PLAIN TALK ABOUT SERVICE STATIONS*
R. Lee Hobaugh, A.I.P.
Leo J. Carling, III, A.I.P. Autumn 1972

VII-4 *ON THE STATE OF FARMING AND AN URBAN*
AGRICULTURE IN NEW JERSEY
Wallace A. Mitcheltree Winter 1972

VIII-1 Title and Copy Unavailable

VIII-2 *THE COMMUNITY SHOPPING CENTER—A NEW*
DOWNTOWN FOR SUBURBIA
Dean K. Boorman, A.I.P. Summer 1973

VIII-3 *FURTHER LEGAL ASPECTS OF NEW JERSEY*
Daniel S. Bernstein, Esq. Autumn 1973

VIII-4 *TRANSFER OF DEVELOPMENT RIGHTS—A NEW*
CONCEPT IN LAND USE MANAGEMENT
B. Budd Chavooshian and Thomas Norman,
Esq. Winter 1973

IX-1 Title and Copy Unavailable

IX-2 *THE ENERGY CRISIS AND COMMUNITY PLANNING*
      Charles K. Agle, F.A.I.A., A.I.P.   Summer   1974

IX-3 *PERMANENT FARMLANDS IN NEW JERSEY*
      William L. Park, Ph.D.   Fall   1974

IX-4 *WATER VS. LAND USE—A NEW CONCEPT IN ZONING*
      AND LAND USE MANAGEMENT WHERE GEOLOGIC
      DATA HELP DETERMINE DENSITIES
      Peter B. Dorram, A.I.P.   Winter   1974

X-1   *THE ENVIRONMENTAL IMPACT STATEMENT—THE*
      NEWEST HOUSEHOLD PHRASE IN STATE AND LOCAL
      PLANNING
      Robert W. Burchell, Ph.D.
      David Listokin   Spring   1975

X-2   *COMMENTARY ON LEGAL ASPECTS OF N.J.*
      ZONING—OFF SITE IMPROVEMENT
      Daniel S. Bernstein, Esq.
      Nathan M. Edelstein   Summer   1975

X-3   *A DISCUSSION OF TIMED DEVELOPMENT*
      John Madden   Autumn   1975

X-4   *IMPROVING MUNICIPAL HOUSING WITH COMMUNITY*
      DEVELOPMENT FUNDS
      Thomas L. Ogren   Winter   1975

XI-1 *TRANSFER OF DEVELOPMENT CREDITS—TDC, A*
      NEW FORM OF CLUSTER ZONING
      William Queale, Jr., A.I.P., P.P.   Spring   1976

XI-2 *THE HOUSING ASSISTANCE PLAN—HUD'S NEW*
      ENTICEMENT TO IMPLEMENT HOUSING FOR LOW &
      MODERATE INCOME PEOPLE   Summer   1976

XI-3 *A MUNICIPAL LAND USE PROCEDURES*
      ORDINANCE—FOR THE NEW JERSEY LAND USE LAW
      (Chapter 291, Laws of New Jersey 1975)
      William M. Cox, Esq.   Autumn   1976

XI-4 *PREPARING A MASTER PLAN—AN APPROACH TO THE*
      PROCESS PURSUANT TO THE MUNICIPAL LAND USE

LAW, CHAPTER 291, LAWS OF N.J. 1975
Malcolm Kasler, A.I.P., P.P.
Harry A. Maslow, A.I.A./A.I.P. Winter 1976

XII-1 *A JUDICIAL ANALYSIS OF N.J. NEW MUNICIPAL LAND USE LAW*
Hon. Milton A. Feller—Superior Court Judge of
Union County Spring 1977

XII-2 *THE DEFINITIONS IN THE MUNICIPAL LAND USE LAW CHAPTER 291, LAWS OF NEW JERSEY 1975*
Barry M. Hoffman, Esq. Summer 1977

XII-3 Title and Copy Unavailable

XII-4 Title and Copy Unavailable

XIII-1 *MUNICIPAL FINANCIAL PLANNING—TECHNIQUES TO EVALUATE THE PUBLIC SERVICE—COST OF LAND DEVELOPMENT* Autumn 1978

XIII-2 Title and Copy Unavailable

XIII-3 Title and Copy Unavailable

XIII-4 Title and Copy Unavailable

XIV-1 *GROWTH MANAGEMENT PROBLEMS WITHIN THE MUNICIPAL PLANNING PROCESS*
R. Lee Hobaugh, A.I.C.P., P.P. Summer 1979

XIV-2 *NOTES ON FUTURE RESIDENTIAL HOUSING*
Charles K. Agle, F.A.I.A., A.I.C.P. Autumn 1979

XIV-3 *ADAPTIVE REUSE PLANNING—A REALISTIC APPROACH TO URBAN RENEWAL AND NEIGHBORHOOD PRESERVATION FOR THE 1980'S*
Robert W. Burchell, Ph.D.
David Listokin, Ph.D. Winter 1979

XIV-4 Title and Copy Unavailable

XV-1 *MUNICIPAL CAPITAL IMPROVEMENTS PROGRAMMING IN NJ*
Andrew C. Paszkowski, P.P., A.I.C.P. Spring 1980

XV-2   Title and Copy Unavailable

XV-3   Title and Copy Unavailable

XV-4   Title and Copy Unavailable

XVI-1   *MOUNT LAUREL II, PROFILE OF GROWTH AREA*
TOWNS
    Malcolm Kasler, A.I.C.P., P.P.   Spring 1983

XVI-2   *WHY JUDGES REVERSE ZONING DECISIONS*
    Judge Richard S. Cohen   Fall   1983

XVI-3   Title and Copy Unavailable

XVI-4   Title and Copy Unavailable

XVII-1   *MOUNT LAUREL II—THE CHALLENGE AND*
DELIVERY OF LOW COST HOUSING
    Robert W. Burchell
    W. Patrick Beaton
    David Listokin   Summer 1984

XVII-2   *1984 AMENDMENTS TO THE MUNICIPAL LAND USE*
LAW—AN EXPLANATION OF THE CHANGES BY
MEMBERS OF THE MUNICIPAL LAND USE LAW
DRAFTING COMMITTEE   Summer 1984

XVII-3   *A MUNICIPALITY LOOKS AT AFFORDABLE HOUSING*
    Stuart Bressler
    Jerome Shaw   Fall   1984

XVII-4   Title and Copy Unavailable

SPECIAL REPORT
    FAIR SHARE METHODOLOGIES—IMPROVED
    APPROACHES TO NEED CALCULATION AND
    DISTRIBUTION
      Mary Winder, A.I.C.P., P.P.
      Francis J. Banisch III, A.I.C.P., P.P. October 1984

XVIII-1   *WHO PLANS: A LOOK AT WHO SITS ON N.J.*
PLANNING BOARDS
    Harvey S. Moskowitz, Ph.D., P.A. Spring 1985

XVIII-2 THE PLANNED RESIDENTIAL NEIGHBORHOOD
Charles K. Agle, A.I.A./A.I.C.P. Spring 1985

SPECIAL REPORT
A DESCRIPTION OF THE FAIR HOUSING ACT
James R. Jager, Esq. September 1985

XVIII-3 REEXAMINATION OF THE MASTER PLAN: THE REQUIREMENTS AND HOW TO DO IT PROFESSIONALLY
E. Eugene Oross, President
E. Eugene Oross Associates Fall 1985

XVIII-4 TRANSFER OF DEVELOPMENT RIGHTS: TWO CASE HISTORIES
Dr. Peter J. Pizor Winter 1985

XIX-1 RECYCLING IN NEW JERSEY
(1) AN ELEMENT IN THE STATE'S SOLID WASTE MANAGEMENT PLAN
Mary T. Shell, Administrator—Office of Recycling—NJ DEP and Dept. of Energy
(2) MANDATORY RECYCLING ORDINANCES— SHOULD YOUR TOWN HAVE ONE?
Sandy Batty—Director, Recycling Project Association of N.J. Environmental Comm. Spring 1986

XIX-2 A DESCRIPTION OF CHANGES IN THE MUNICIPAL LAND USE LAW SINCE MARCH 1984
James R. Jager, Esq. Summer 1986

XIX-3 NEW JERSEY COUNCIL ON AFFORDABLE HOUSING PROCEDURAL REGULATIONS Fall 1986

XIX-4 INTRODUCTION TO THE ACCESSORY HOUSING OPTION
Cecelia Urban, Esq. Winter 1986

XX-1 BASIC RECORDS MANAGEMENT FOR PLANNING AND ZONING BOARDS
Louis S. Revesz
Miktoria K. Sobel Spring 1987

XX-2   *HISTORIC PRESERVATION LAW: A NEW HYBRID*
         STATUTE WITH NEW LEGAL PROBLEMS
                  Jerome G. Rose   Summer   1987

XX-3   *SUMMARY OF PUBLIC OPINION ROLL—NJ STATE*
         PLANNING COMMISSION—OFFICE OF STATE
         PLANNING
                  James G. Gilbert, Chairman
                  John W. Epling, Director   Summer   1987

XX-4   *STATE MASTER PLAN*
                  Gordon Bishop   Fall   1987

XXI-1 *CONSTITUTIONAL GUARANTEE OF HOME RULE IN*
         ZONING
                  Address by Milton A. Feller, Superior Court
                           Judge   Winter   1988

APPENDIX 3

Income and Expense Reports
1939 and 1987

Income and Expense Report[*]
New Jersey Federation of Official Planning Boards
1939

	Balance carried forward, as per amount submitted by Mr. Villanueva, $69.11			$ 69.11

Receipts

July	20	— Nutley dues	$ 5.00	
August	8	— Passaic dues	20.00	
August	17	— Bernardsville dues	5.00	
August	21	— Maplewood dues	15.00	
August	22	— Summit dues	15.00	
August	24	— Livingston dues	5.00	65.00
				$ 134.11

Disbursements

July	18	— A.V. Gross—stamps	1.50	
August	10	— Savings Investment Tr. Co.—overdrawal of former account	1.00	
September	12	A.V. Gross—stamps	2.00	4.50
				$ 129.61

[*] As shown in the minutes of the Directors meeting, held at the Newark City Hall, Annex, on September 14, 1939.

Income and Expense Report
New Jersey Federation of Planning Officials
1987

Income

Dues	$ 60,863.00
Publications & Donations	26,256.97
Other Income	14,732.57
Total Income & Revenue	**$ 101,852.54**

Expenses

Association Management Corporation	$ 52,333.00
President's Expense	.00
Travel	266.02
Printing & Supplies	6,972.51
Telephone	774.58
Postage	4,345.91
Audit	3,532.30
Insurance & Bond	256.50
Membership Campaign	.00
Dues & Subscriptions	40.00
Committee	659.92
Publications	16,503.35
Meetings	5,680.34
Courses	60.00
Area Expenses	6,092.96
Miscellaneous	4,233.07
Total Expenses	**$ 101,750.46**
Net Income or Loss	**$ 102.08**

APPENDIX 4

Conference Activities

T H E   N E W   J E R S E Y   P L A N N E R

Published Under the Joint Sponsorship of the New Jersey
Federation of Official Planning Boards and the
New Jersey State Planning Board

C O N F E R E N C E   I S S U E

Issued Every Now and Then   Dr. Maurice F. Neufeld, Editor

Vol. 1, No. 2   186 W. State St., Trenton, N.J.   April, 1939

F I R S T   A N N U A L   C O N F E R E N C E

NEW JERSEY FEDERATION OF OFFICIAL PLANNING BOARDS

In Cooperation with the New Jersey State Planning Board

Continuing the Annual Conference Formerly Sponsored

by the New Jersey State Planning Board

Saturday, April 22, 1939

at the

Robert Treat Hotel, Newark, N. J.

PROGRAM

9:00 A. M. .... Registration - No fee

9:30 A. M. .... First annual business meeting -
Planning of activities for the
coming year.

11:00 A. M. .... Discussion of county and State
planning problems.

12:30 P. M. .... Luncheon

2:00 P. M. .... Planning Problems Forum - Discussion of municipal planning prob-
lems by those present.

5:00 P. M. .... Election of officers for the
coming year.

6:30 P. M. .... Dinner - Speakers: E. Donald
Sterner, State Highway Commis-
sioner, and J. W. Faust, National Recreational Association.

LET'S MAKE THE CONFERENCE A REAL SUCCESS

A BOOST FOR THE FEDERATION IS A BOOST FOR PLANNING

MOUNT LAUREL II
25th • Silver Anniversary Conference • 25th
FRIDAY, APRIL 22, 1983 • CAPITOL PLAZA HOTEL • TRENTON, NEW JERSEY

8:30- 9:30   REGISTRATION • Continental Breakfast • NEW JERSEY STATE MUSEUM AUDITORIUM

9:45-10:15   OPENING OF THE 25th ANNUAL STATE PLANNING CONFERENCE
Introductions: Conference Chairman
Key to the City: Arthur J. Holland, Mayor of Trenton
Resolution of the Council: Carmen J. Armenti, President of Trenton City Council
Welcome: James G. Gilbert: President, N.J. Federation of Planning Officials
Statement of Purpose: Helyn N. Beer, Executive Director of the Federation

10:15-11:45   PLENARY SESSION: NEW JERSEY STATE MUSEUM AUDITORIUM
Mount Laurel II. The New Decision

Overview - Jerome G. Rose
Professor of Urban Planning, Rutgers University
One of two court appointed planning experts in the
Washington Township case - Mt. Laurel I

Panelists
Carl Bisgaier, Esq.
Bisgaier & Pancotto, Esqs., Cherry Hill, Formerly with
Public Advocate's Office

Stuart M. Hutt, Esq., Hutt, Berkow,
Hollander & Jankowski, Esqs. Woodbridge
General Counsel, New Jersey Home Builders Assoc.

Thomas Norman, Esq., Medford, Author, N.J. Chapter
A.P.A. "Amicus Curiae" for Mount Laurel II

NOON   LUNCHEON CAPITAL PLAZA HOTEL CRYSTAL ROOM, TOP FLOOR
Featured Speaker: Leo Molinaro, President, American City Corporation
Honored Guest: Honorable Frederick W. Hall (Ret.) N.J. Supreme Court (Invited)
BILL OF FARE

1:30- 3:00   CONCURRENT SESSIONS AND WORKSHOPS • CAPITOL PLAZA HOTEL • ROOMS TO BE POSTED

Proposed Municipal Land Use Law Amendments
Moderator - Harry A. Maslow, AIA/AICP
Maslow-Miller-Holzman & Associates,
Berkeley Heights

Glen Kienz, Esq. - Ewing Township

Fred G. Stickel, III, Esq.
Stickel & Koenig - Cedar Grove

Harry S. Pozycki, Jr., Esq.
Frizell & Pozycki - Metuchen

State Regional
Environmental Planning and Municipal Land Use
Moderator - B. Budd Chavooshian, Cook College
• John R. Weingart, Acting Director,
Division of Coastal Resources, DEP
• Chester Mattson, Director,
Environmental Programs and Planning,
Hackensack
Meadowlands Development Commission
• Terrence Moore, Executive Director,
Pinelands Commission
• James Amon, Executive Director,
Delaware and Raritan Canal Commission

D.O.T. Operations and Municipal Land Use
Moderator - Melvin R. Lehr
Assistant Commissioner, Transportation Services
New Jersey Department of Transportation
• Highway Access Permits — The Process and the Purpose
Robert McCai   Charles R. Carmalt
Supervisor of Permits, NJDOT   Bureau of Statewide
                       Planning, NJDOT
• Corridor and Subregional Planning
Alfred H. Herf, Acting Director
Transportation Planning and Research, NJDOT
• Municipal Planning for Transit, Jeffrey M. Zupan, Director
Division of Developmental Planning, NJ TRANSIT

3:00- 4:30

Mt. Laurel - Effect on the Local Municipality
Moderator - William Queale, Jr., Planning Consultant
Queale & Lynch, Inc., Morrisville, Pa.

Harvey Moskowitz, Planning Consultant
Harvey S. Moskowitz A Assoc., Livingston

Carl Hintz, Planner - East Brunswick

Daniel S. Bernstein, Esq.
Bernstein, Hoffman, and Clark - Scotch Plains

William M. Cox, Esq.
Dolan & Dolan - Newton

State Development Guide Plan - Past and Future?
Moderator - Donald H. Stansfield, Chief-Statewide Planning

Donald Linky,
New Jersey Business and Industry Association

Roger S. Hoeh,
Section Supervisor-Statewide Planning

Samuel Hamill,
Executive Director-MSM Study Council

Sean M. Riley,
Planning Consultant

The Future of Regional Planning in New Jersey
Moderator - B. Budd Chavooshian, Cook College
• Great Swamp Watershed - Anne Morris,
Chairman, Great Swamp Watershed Assoc.
• Hudson River Waterfront - Helen Manogue,
Co-chair, Waterfront Coalition of Hudson and
Bergen and Chair,
Hoboken Environment Committee.
• Raritan River and Bayshore - Douglas Opalski,
Director, Middlesex County Planning Board.
• Northern Watershed - Robert Holmes, Executive
Director, Newark Watershed Conservation
and Development Corporation.

5:00   DAY'S END HOSPITALITY SUITE

APPENDIX 5

Constitution
1948-1981

FEDERATION OF OFFICIAL PLANNING BOARDS
CONSTITUTION
1948

ARTICLE I —NAME: The name of this organization shall be the New Jersey Federation of Official Planning Boards.

ARTICLE II —OBJECT: The object of the Federation shall be to promote public interest in municipal and regional planning and to foster the co-operation of the planning boards throughout New Jersey in furthering the aims of planning.

ARTICLE III —MEMBERSHIP: All planning boards of New Jersey are eligible for membership. All officials and civic minded organizations and citizens sympathizing with the objects of the Federation shall also be eligible for membership.

ARTICLE IV —GOVERNMENT: The government of the Federation shall be vested in a board composed of a President, Vice President, Secretary and Treasurer, together with nine Directors. One Director shall be from the State Department of Economic Development. A quorum shall consist of five such members present. The President shall preside at all meetings of the Federation and the Board.

ARTICLE V —MEETINGS: The annual meeting of the Federation shall be held during the month of May. At this meeting the Officers and the Directors for the ensuing year shall be elected. The chairman of all committees shall submit their yearly reports at the annual meeting. The day, hour, and place of the annual meeting are to be determined by the Officers and Directors, and notice of the meeting shall be mailed to all members fifteen days prior to the meeting. The Officers and Directors shall meet monthly, except during July and August or as may be provided by the by-laws.

ARTICLE VI —AMENDMENTS: This Constitution may be amended by a majority of all members present at any annual meeting, or at any special meeting called for that purpose, providing at least thirty days notice is given prior to the date of the meeting, and the notice shall contain a draft of the proposed amendment.

BY-LAWS

ARTICLE I   —MEMBERSHIP: Membership in the Federation shall be composed of the following classes:
Class A   —Official Planning Boards.
Class B   —Official or civic-minded organizations.
Class C   —Individuals.
Elections to membership shall be by a majority vote at a meeting of the Officers and Directors.

ARTICLE II   —DUES: The annual dues from a planning board, other official board, or a civic-minded organization shall be based on the population of its community:
Up   to 50,000   population   \$15.—
50,000   to 100,000   population   10.—
100,000   and over   25.—
Individual membership dues shall be \$5.— annually. Annual dues shall be based on a fiscal year starting January 1.

ARTICLE III   —QUALIFICATIONS OF VOTERS: Each officer and director shall have one vote. The officially designated representation of a Class A member shall be entitled to vote. Class B and Class C members shall not be entitled to any vote.

The privilege to vote shall be withdrawn from any member which is three months in arrears in dues.

ARTICLE IV   —ELECTIONS: The Officers and Directors shall be elected for a term of one year, or until their successors are elected and qualified by acceptance and assumption of office. Two months prior to the annual meeting the President shall appoint a nominating committee of three persons to prepare a list of nominations for the coming year. The nominating committee shall make public its report one month previous to the annual meeting. At the annual meeting additional nominations may be made from the floor.

Any vacancies that may occur by registration or otherwise of Officers and Directors shall be filled by the Officers or Directors for the unexpired term.

ARTICLE V   —MEETINGS: The Board shall hold regular monthly meetings except during July and August. A special meeting of the Board may be called by the President or three of the members of the Board on 24-hours' notice, stating the purpose of the meeting.

A special meeting of the Federation may be called by the President or by the majority of the Federation.

ARTICLE VI —AMENDMENTS: These by-laws may be amended by a majority of all members present at any annual meeting, or at any special meeting called for that purpose, providing at least thirty days notice is given prior to the date of the meeting, and the notice shall contain a draft of the proposed amendment.

NEW JERSEY FEDERATION OF PLANNING OFFICIALS
CONSTITUTION AND BY-LAWS INDEX
1981

ARTICLE I   NAME

ARTICLE II   PURPOSE

ARTICLE III   MEMBERSHIP

ARTICLE IV   OFFICERS

        Section 1.   Officers/Election
        Section 2.   Limitation of Terms
        Section 3.   President
        Section 4.   Vice-President
        Section 5.   Executive Vice-President
        Section 6.   Treasurer
        Section 7.   General Counsel

ARTICLE V   BOARD OF DIRECTORS

        Section 1.   Membership of Board of Directors
        Section 2.   General Governance
        Section 3.   Appointments by Board
        Section 4.   Secretariat
        Section 5.   Power and Authority
        Section 6.   Executive Committee Authority
        Section 7.   Quorum
        Section 8.   Removal from Office

ARTICLE VI   MEETINGS

        Section 1.   State Federation Meetings
            a.   Annual Meeting
            b.   Other Meetings
            c.   Notice
        Section 2.   Board of Directors
            a.   Time of Board Meetings
            b.   Responsibility for Notice

CONSTITUTION

ARTICLE VII   AREAS

    Section 1.   Authorization, Location, Description, Governance
    Section 2.   New Areas
    Section 3.   Area Officers
    Section 4.   Area Meetings
    Section 5.   Minutes
        a.   Recording of
        b.   Financial Records

ARTICLE VIII   MEMBERSHIP AND DUES

    Section 1.   Membership
    Section 2.   Dues

ARTICLE IX   QUALIFICATION OF VOTERS

ARTICLE X   STATE ELECTIONS

    Section 1.   Nominating Committee Appointment
    Section 2.   Nominating Committee Duties
    Section 3.   Election Process, Ballotting

ARTICLE XI   LIFE MEMBERSHIPS

ARTICLE XII   COMMITTEES

    Section 1.   Legislative Committee
    Section 2.   Standing Committees
    Section 3.   Other Committees

ARTICLE XIII   FEDERATION POLICY

ARTICLE XIV   AMENDMENTS

ARTICLE XV   ADOPTION OF SUPPLEMENTARY REGULATIONS

APPENDIX 6

Presidents
1939-1988

Harry Hosking	1939	– 1941	Livingston
Marcel Villanueva	1941	– 1942	Orange
Benjamin M. Taub	1942	– 1945	Passaic
John E. Sloane	1945	– 1947	West Orange
Samuel Rabkin	1947	– 1949	Union
John R. Burnett	1949	– 1952	Newark
Mariano J. Rinaldi	1952	– 1954	Newark
William A. Sutherland	1954	– 1956	Bound Brook
Henry R. Williams	1956	– 1958	Pequannock Township
Leo J. Carling	1958	– 1960	Eatontown
Thomas A. Hyde	1960	– 1962	Mountainside
William F. Gillette	1962	– 1964	Point Pleasant Beach
Harry A. Maslow	1964	– 1966	Berkeley Heights
Donald E. Kanouse	1966	– 1967	Pequannock Township
Samuel P. Owen	1967	– 1969	Metuchen
Jules W. Marron	1969	– 1971	Newton
Abraham A. Janz	1971	– 1972	Pompton Plains
James B. Ashwell	1972*		Metuchen
Earle P. Finkbinder	1972	– 1974	Lumberton
Edna A. Horn	1974	– 1975*	Delaware Township
Bud Schwartz	1975	– 1976	Franklin Lakes
Henry J. Tomkinson	1976	– 1977	Sayerville
Elwood Bray	1977	– 1979	Phillipsburg
John M. Reuter	1979	– 1981	Eatontown
James G. Gilbert	1981	– 1983	Englewood
K. Brian McFadden	1983	– 1984	Millville
Patricia A. McKiernan	1984	– 1986	Belle Mead
Alois E. Schmitt	1986	– 1988	Belleville
Judith Schleicher	1988	–	Denville

* Died in office

APPENDIX 7

Federation Membership
1939-1987

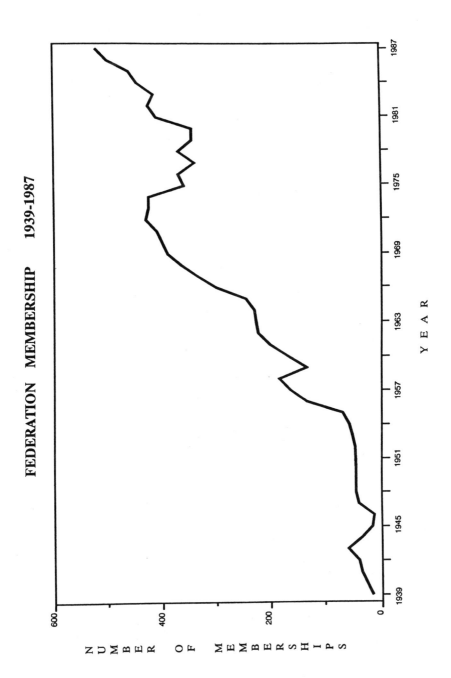

FEDERATION MEMBERSHIP 1939-1987

Index

Ackerman, Frederick L., 32
Adjustment boards, 96
Advisory Planning Board (Newark), 32
Airport location, 51, 52
Alexander, Harry, 55
Alliance for Action, 186
Altshuler, Alan, 124
American Institute of Planners (AIP),
    102–103
American Planning Association, 4
American Society of Planning Officials
    (ASPO), 11, 103
  New Jersey chapter, 22, 23
  1962 Convention, 92–95
Antiplanning bills, 67, 71
Arbitration board, 72
ASPO. *See* American Society of Planning
    Officials
Association Management Corporation,
    177, 178
Atkinson, Henry, 49

Beer, Helyn, 165, 175, 177
Bernstein, Harry E., 65, 69, 92, 99,
    108, 127, 128, 142, 164
Bill of Rights, 44
Bill S–803, 136, 139
Bill S–1464, 181
Bill S–1494, 179–180
Bill S–3139, 159
Billboards, 106
Biro, Ernest P., 8, 10, 11, 22, 55

Bishop, A. Thornton, 48
Black, Russell VanNest, 11, 12, 19, 24,
    30, 31, 33, 36, 44, 64
Blakeman, T. Ledyard, 51, 53, 55
Blucher, Walter, 120
Bradley, Marie, 165, 166
Buchsbaum, Peter, 180
Bullitt, John C., 132–133
Bureau of Urban Research (Princeton
    University), 37
Burlingham, Robert, 53
Burnett, John, 55, 64–65
Burton, Charles O., 87
Buttenheim, Harold, 55
Byrne, Brendan T., 145

Cahill, William, 139
Carling, Leo J., 75, 83, 93, 95
Carpenter, William, 24, 40, 42
Case, Clifford P., 97, 110
Casino gambling, 162
Chavooshian, B. Budd, 5, 85, 92, 135,
    156, 161, 162, 175, 191
Chicago fire, 2
City planners, 2, 17
City planning
  history of, 1
  interest in, 37, 49
  post-World War II, 49–51
  public view of, 17–18
City planning movement, 13–14

233

City of Rahway vs. Raritan Homes, Inc.,
    66
Coastal Area Facility Review Act
    (CAFRA), 142, 157
Cocchia, Frances, 77
Constitution, Federation, 55, 58–62,
    76–77, 127, 219–223
Constitution, New Jersey, 17, 52
Corporate liberalism, 3
Council on Affordable Housing, 180,
    181
County Planners Association, 100, 137
County Planning Act, 100, 137
Cox, Bill, 162
Craig, David, 121
Crane, Jacob, 19
Currier, Stuart D., 39, 42, 43

Davidoff, Paul, 125
Day and a Half of Planning, 195–196
Defense housing, 38
Defense industry in suburbs, 33
Defense planning during World War II,
    30–32
Delfause, Roland J., 128
Department of Community Affairs
    (DCA), 109–110, 127, 134, 155,
    178
Department of Economic Development,
    42, 50
Department of Environmental Protec-
    tion, 154, 157
Division of Planning and Engineering,
    42
Drainage systems, 1
Driscoll, Alfred E., 52, 67

Edge, Walter E., 44
Education programs, 66, 73, 101, 130,
    132, 133, 165, 169–170
Edwards, Cary, 179
Edwards, Robert, 67, 74
Elderly people, 105–106
Ellenberg, David, 163
Environmental legislation, 142–143
Epidemics, 1
Erdman, Charles R., 40, 43
Executive Order, 35, 159

Fair Housing Act, 180–181

Farmland Assessment Amendment, 107
Farny, George, 11, 21, 28–29
Faure, Andrew, 45
Faust, J. M., 15
Federal Demonstration Cities Act, 125
Federal Housing Act of 1954, 74, 75
Federal 701 program, 84, 85, 139, 160,
    172
Federal Urban Renewal Administration,
    75
Federation. *See* New Jersey Federation
    of Official Planning Boards
The Federation Planner, 53, 54, 91, 104,
    129–130, 165–166, 170, 176, 200
Federation Planning Information Reports
    (FPIR), 130, 165–166, 176, 201–
    208
Finkbiner, Earle, 143
Fitch, Lyle, 121–122
Flood Plains Bill, 142
Forsgate Conference, 104
Furman, David D., 141

Garbe, William, 91
Garden State Parkway, 64
Gershen, Alvin, 145
Gilbert, James G., 128, 163, 166, 169,
    170, 171, 177–179, 181, 186, 191
Gillette, William, 92, 109, 123, 129
Ginman, Richard, 4, 160, 164, 172, 175
Grassi, Jim, 178
Graybar, Sidney, 157, 188, 190
Great Depression, 27
Green Acres Program, 107
Greenberg, Martin L., 159
Greier, George, 105
Griffin, Florence, 129
Gross, Mason, 82, 120–121
Guide to Planning and Zoning, 176

Hackensack Meadowlands Development
    Commission (HMDC), 133, 161.
    See also Meadowlands
Hall, Frederick W., 130, 138
Halpern, Joseph, 130
Hampson, Edna A., 37, 39–40
Hardy, C. Colburn, 39
Hawley, Ellis W., 3
Health hazards, 1
Highway construction, 50

Hillsborough Township, 109
Historical preservation, 106–107
Hoboken Planning Board, 75
Holland, John, 121, 124
Home Builders' Association, 135
Home Guards, 28
Home rule, 55, 62, 110
  and influence of planners, 124
  problems for, 130, 133
Home-rule bill, 69
Horizon plan, 174
Horn, Edna, 99, 129, 143–144
Hosking, Harry E., 8, 11, 12, 14–17,
  20–22, 29, 33–34, 40, 46, 89, 96,
  97
Housing
  bills, 139–142, 159–160, 180–181.
  See also individual bills
  defense, 38
  executive order 35 and, 159
  introduction of small suburban, 33
  low-income, 124–125, 139–142
  regulation of, 133
  shortage of low- and middle-priced,
  75–76
Housing Forum, 155
Housing and Urban Development Act,
  101
Hughes, Richard J., 97–98, 123
Hume, Edmond T., 139
Hyde, Thomas A., 91–93, 95, 107,
  126, 129–132, 142, 154–156,
  163–164, 169

Ickes, Harold L., 3
Imler, Robert, 162
Immigration, 1–2
Indus Valley, 1
Industrial park, 52
Industry
  cooperation with Federation, 104
  decentralization of, 50
  planning as means of attracting, 51
Institute of Municipal Attorneys, 67,
  135, 137
Island Beach, 64

Jacobson, Eduard, 11
Janz, Abraham, 148–149
Jersey Plans, 97

Joint Defense Committee, 33–35
Joint Resolution 13, 73

Kanouse, Donald, 111–112, 127, 129
Kaplan, Harold, 75
Kean, Thomas H., 171, 179, 180
Kelly, John, 11
Kennedy, John F., 152
Koch, Virginia, 163

League. *See* New Jersey State League of
  Municipalities
Lighting fixtures, 1
Lindbloom, Carl G., 160
Lionshead v. Wayne Township, 65
Look-alike ordinances, 106
Los Angeles, 3

McDowell, William, 48
McFadden, Brian, 163, 178, 187–188,
  190
McKiernan, Patricia, 164–165, 169,
  176–177
McKiernan, Robert, 40
McLean, Joseph, 75
Marron, Jules W., 139
Marshall Plan, 45
Maslow, Harry A., 6, 92, 127, 128,
  130, 132, 135, 144, 147, 156–157,
  177, 187
Meadowlands, 85, 133–134, 161
Meiser, Ken, 180
Messick, Charles P., 40
Meyner, Robert B., 74
Military strategic planning, 30
Miller, Marshall, 40
MLUL. *See* Municipal Land Use Law
Mobile homes, 120
Molt, Albert N., 40
Moore, A. Harry, 20, 29
Moore, John Brewer, 70, 106–107
Mortgages, 49–50
Moskowitz, Harvey, 6, 108, 130
Mount Laurel I decision, 144–145,
  153–154
Mount Laurel II decision, 172, 173,
  175, 176, 178–180
Mulcahy, Robert E., 160
Mumford, Louis, 74–75
Municipal Land Use Law (MLUL), 141,
  146, 147, 153, 156, 176, 187

Municipal planning, 75. *See also* City planning; Planning
Municipal Planning Act, 65
Municipalities
  financial situation of developing, 62–64
  planning requirements for, 69, 83–84
  right of self-determination, 125
Musto Report, 122–123, 133, 179

Nasuti, Jim, 190
National Association of Home Builders, 70
National planning, 41. *See also* City planning; Planning
National Resources Planning Board, 3, 36, 41
New Deal era, 14
New Jersey
  economic growth in, 83
  population of, 37, 105
  reliance on property tax by, 121–122
New Jersey American Planning Association (NJAPA), 166
New Jersey Association of Housing and Redevelopment Authorities, 132
New Jersey Federation of Official Planning Boards. *See* New Jersey Federation of Planning Officials
New Jersey Federation of Official Planning Boards conferences
  activities of, 215–216
  publication of proceedings, 19–20
  schedule of, 18
New Jersey Federation of Planning Officials
  between 1965–1975, 123–149
  constitution, 55, 58–62, 76–77, 127, 219–223
  creation of, 3, 8
  directors of, 5–6, 227
  during late 1970s and 1980s, 154–183
  expansion during 1960s of, 126–127
  first conference and annual meeting of, 10–11
  founders of, 11
  functions of, 129–130
  future of, 185–192
  income and expense reports of, 211–212

on legislative issues, 24, 134–149
local activities of, 20
membership, 24, 84–85, 96, 126, 147–148, 154–156, 231
newspaper coverage of, 20
organizational chart of, 9
planning activities of, 195–196
post-World War II rejuvenation of, 48–77
publications of, 199–208. *See also* *Federation Planner;* Federation Planning Information Reports; *New Jersey Planner*
and relationship with other organizations, 3–5, 13, 16–17, 24, 186
role between 1955–1965 of, 84–112
support for, 13–16
on taxation, 123–124
New Jersey Land Use Advisory Commission, 50
New Jersey Municipalities, 10, 13, 20, 97
New Jersey Planner, 10, 19, 23, 41, 43, 45, 199
New Jersey Plans, 53
New Jersey State Constitution, 17, 52
New Jersey State League of Municipalities, 4, 10, 63, 191
  annual conference, 41
  legislative committee, 143, 144
  relationship with Federation, 13, 16–17, 186
  support of S-3139 by, 159
New Jersey State Planning Board. *See* State Planning Board
New Jersey Supreme Court, 138, 174–175, 178
New Jersey Turnpike, 64
New Jersey Welfare Conference, 132
New York, 2–3
Newark
  planning board in, 32
  redevelopment program, 75
  riots in, 131, 191
Newark Area Transportation Study, 85
Newark Defense Council, 34
Newark Evening News, 20
Newark Star Ledger, 20
Newark WPA Planning Project, 32
Newspaper coverage of Federation, 20
Nonlook-alike ordinances, 106
Norman, Tom, 140

Norton, C. McKim, 55, 56, 67, 72, 122, 185

Oakwood at Madison v. Madison Township, 141
O'Hern, Daniel J., 161
Osborne, Harold, 11, 22
Owen, Sam, 92, 100–101, 127, 128, 137, 138, 140, 144, 159–160, 170

Parks, 1
Parkway Bill, 43
Passaic Herald News, 20
Paterson Morning Call, 20
Pekarsky, Alex, 163
PenJerDel, 90, 104
Physical Planning, 125
Pinelands, 85, 180
Pinelands National Reserve Act, 142, 160, 161
Piro, Amy, 179
Planned Unit Development (PUD) legislation, 135–136, 147
Planners, state, 74
Planning. *See also* City Planning
  centralization of, 125–126
  courses in, 66, 73, 130, 132
  physical, 125
  post-war, 42, 49–51
  profession of, 102
  social, 125, 132–133
Planning bill of 1953, 67, 69, 71, 134
Planning boards
  funding for, 15–16
  legal limits of, 84
  members of, 17
  post-World War II, 31–32
Platting of land, 18
Police force, 1
Pollution
  regulations, 133
  State Supreme Court on, 138
Pond, Henry, 21, 45
Population of New Jersey, 37, 105
Powell, Douglas, 103
Property rights, 84
Property taxes, 83, 121–122
Proposition 13, 153
Public works, 42–43
Public Works Reserve, 36
PUD bill, 135–136, 147

Rabkin, Samuel, 23–24, 42, 48, 49
Ranney, David, 124–125
Redevelopment Agencies Act, 75
Reeves, Glenn, 11
Regional approach, 110–111
Regional Plan Association (RPA), 2, 4
  relationship with Federation, 13, 90, 104
Reid, Charles A., 138–139
Reuter, John M., 163
Riker, Russell, 69
Rinaldi, Mariano, 55, 69
Roadside Council, 37
Roe, Robert, 110–111, 134
Roman Catholic Diocese of Newark v. Borough of Ho-Ho-Kus, 138
Romney, George, 139
Roosevelt, Franklin D., 3, 36
Round Valley Reservoir site, 64
RPA. *See* Regional Plan Association
Rubidge, Frederick T., 8, 10, 29
Ruckelshaus, William, 142
Rural Community Planning Conference, 126
Rutgers Bureau of Conservation and Environmental Health, 105
Rutgers University, 4, 104, 133
  courses, 66, 73, 101, 130, 132, 165, 169–170
  extension services, 169

Schleicher, Judith, 188, 190
Schmitt, Al, 176, 177, 188
Schneider, Eugene J., 179, 182
Schwartz, Bud, 154–156, 162, 164
SDGP. *See* State Development Guide Plan
Self-determination of municipality, 125
701 program, 84, 85, 139, 160, 172
Sloane, John, 11, 21, 22, 28–29, 33, 34, 46, 55, 182
Small house program, 33–34
Smith, Herbert H., 64, 66, 67, 89, 93–94, 111, 130
Social planning, 125, 132–133
Social workers, 132
Southern Burlington County vs. Mount Laurel, 144–145, 153–154
Spalt, Evan, 52, 90, 108, 176, 190–192
"Spread City," 107–108

State Board of Professional Planners, 102
State Commission on Post-War Economic Welfare, 44
State Defense Council, 29, 39
State Defense League, 39
State Department of Economic Development, 42
State Development Guide Plan (SDGP), 160, 172, 174, 178, 181
State planners, 74
State Planning Act, 181
State Planning Board, 3, 37
  financial assistance for *New Jersey Planner* by, 19
  financial difficulties of, 41–42
  relationship between Federation and, 3–4, 13, 53
State Planning Bureau, 85–86
State Planning Commission, 181–183
State Planning and Development Commission, 140
State Planning Task Force, 143
Stein, Gary, 172, 173
Stevens Institute, 75
Stickel, Fred G., III, 5, 67, 69, 78, 137–138, 144
Strong, George, 40
Subdivision control, 65–67, 72
Suburbs
  as independent commercial and industrial centers, 123
  1930 to 1940 population shift to, 33
Supreme Court. *See* New Jersey Supreme Court; U.S. Supreme Court
Sutherland, William A., 72, 73, 79, 88–89
Swain, C. Roy, 34

Taub, Benjamin M., 8, 10–12, 16, 19, 28–29, 32, 36, 40–42, 44, 46
Taxes
  property, 83, 121–122
  state, 123
  zoning to reduce, 18
Taxpayers' Association, 39
Taylor, James S., 33
Technical planning assistance, 73, 74
Ten Million plan, 174
Title 40, 101

Trafford, Jack, 179
Trailer camps, 83
Transportation Department, 109
Transportation Study Commission, 109
Tri-State Transportation Commission, 109

Uniform Building Code, 157
United States Public Health Service, 105
U.S. Supreme Court, 2
Urban renewal
  courses in, 132
  defense industry needs and, 33–34

Vanderbeek, Horace A., 91, 95
Vanderlipp, William T., 43
Vaughn-Eames, Henry, 89, 99
Villanueva, Marcel, 11, 12, 14, 21, 22, 27–28, 30, 34, 36, 38, 40

Water, 1
Water Supply Bill, 107
"Welcome to North-South Dumpford," 115–119
Wetlands bill, 134, 142
Wharton tract, 64
Wilkens, Edward B., 55, 57, 67, 86, 88
Williams, Henry, 89, 95, 108
Williams, Leslie, 50, 62
Williams, Norman, Jr., 125
Williams, Sidney, 140
Woodrow Wilson School, 191
World War I, 14
World War II, 27–28
Worthington tract, 64

Ylvisaker, Paul N., 135, 136

Zoning
  courts on, 138, 141
  for industry, 51–52
  need for, 18
  post-World War II, 45, 64
Zoning Enabling Act of 1924, 2, 16–17
Zoning ordinances
  federal assistance formulation of, 84
  history of, 2
  increase in, 69
  and Municipal Land Use Law, 146
  state constitution and, 17

307.12 KLINGHOFFER, Judith
KLI

6-14-2003